THE
OBSERVER
ON SOCCER

THE OBSERVER

ON SOCCER

An Anthology
of the Best Soccer Writing

Edited and Compiled
by
Tony Pawson

UNWIN

HYMAN

London   Sydney   Wellington

First published in Great Britain by the Trade Division
of Unwin Hyman Limited in 1989

UNWIN HYMAN LIMITED
15–17 Broadwick Street
London W 1 V 1 FP

Allen & Unwin Australia Pty Ltd
8 Napier Street, North Sydney, N S W 2060, Australia

Allen & Unwin New Zealand Pty Ltd with the Port Nicholson Press
Compusales Building, 75 Ghuznee Street, Wellington, New Zealand

British Library Cataloguing in Publication Data
The Observer on soccer: an anthology of the best
soccer writing.
1. Association football
I. Pawson, Tony, *1921–*
796.334

ISBN 0–04–440533–2

Typeset in 10 on 12 point Garamond by Wyvern Typesetting Ltd, Bristol
Printed in Great Britain at the University Press, Cambridge

Contents

Chapter 3   The World and International Scene

Chapter 4 Football's Characters

Chapter 5 The Supporting Cast

Chapter 6   Occasional Pieces and Unusual Aspects

List of Illustrations

Foreword

by Hugh McIlvanney

Anyone who takes pleasure from writing reports of football matches, or is consistently proud of the results he achieves, should be removed quietly to a suitable clinical environment where his alienation from reality can receive the treatment it requires. Attempting to render an hour-and-a-half of often hectic, usually complicated action (involving a minimum of 22 players) within 500 or even 1,000 hastily written words is an exercise so plainly doomed to compromise and frustration that only the seriously deluded can ever be satisfied with their efforts to cope. The sports writer who has succeeded, against the odds, in holding on to most of his marbles will regard match reporting as one of the most demanding, least gratifying chores on his schedule.

Obviously there are plenty of occasions when the extraordinary joy of watching great football brings out the fan in the most jaded reporter and makes him happy to acknowledge that professional aggravations are a small price to pay for the privilege of seeing Pelé or Best, Cruyff or Moore or Maradona in the magical flesh. Even then, however, he is likely to envy anybody who can go straight from a seat in the stands to the nearest bar, there to compound and prolong the enjoyment of the game by unloading the flood of instant profundities with which all spectators are duty-bound to be brimming at such moments. Somehow certitude and eloquence come less readily when filtered through a biro or a Tandy than when let loose directly from a tongue assisted by grape or grain.

A few demented egos always excepted, the denizens of the press box freely admit that there is more than a hint of struggle associated with filing on deadline in the knowledge that all attempts at description, interpretation and analysis will be preserved in cold print – to be scrutinised and dissected at leisure by readers whose own perhaps sketchy impressions of what occurred have been hardened and clarified by a bombardment of television replays. If you think reading the stuff can be an ordeal, you should try writing it. But don't ask for my job at *The Observer* just yet. As a means of paying the rent, it beats carrying the hod.

It is also preferable to chuntering on about the game four or five times a week for a daily paper, especially the kind of tabloid that cares less about how well a winger puts the ball over than how often he gets his leg over. Even when the enthusiasms of such publications are not at their sleaziest,

xiii

there is so much more concern with what is said off the field than what is done on it that reporting by ear rather than eye has become their norm. Sprinkled among their employees are men whose efficiency would scarcely be diminished if they went blind. Any powers of judgment these aural recorders ever possessed have been atrophied beyond hope of recovery by habitual reliance on the quote, however banal.

Of course, it is equally true that some of the most perceptive football reporters in the country are popular paper men, just as some of the most turgid and unenlightening copy can be read on the sports pages of the heavies, daily and Sunday. The difference is that those of us appearing in what are seen as the quality papers have less of an excuse if we turn out dross, since nobody coerced us into lowering our sights. Certainly all the writers represented in this anthology have had a clear awareness of how fortunate they have been to work for *The Observer* and for one or several of the many outstanding Sports Editors who have served it.

Operating weekly is in itself a significant advantage, protecting us as it does from the assault on perspective represented by the deluge of fixtures that swamps the English domestic season. At the great festivals of the game, like the European Championships or the World Cup, the Sunday writer is even more conspicuously blessed in being able to avoid insular preoccupation with the campaigns of the teams from these islands and concern himself with the challenges of others who may have more right to consider themselves the supreme powers of football.

Some of my most fascinating experiences of the sport have come from involvement with the Brazilians, the Dutch and West Germans in particular, from having time and opportunity to spend many illuminating hours inside their camps as a prelude to watching them perform wonders on the field. Talking to Helmut Schoen about management or to Beckenbauer, Cruyff, Neeskens, Pelé or Tostão about playing was not a matter of collecting quotes. Inevitably (whether through an interpreter or without the need of one) quotes came in vivid abundance. But, to anyone not obliged to scurry off to a 'phone at the first hint of usable material, men of such calibre could invariably convey far more – sometimes an affecting glimpse of the wellsprings of their own love affair with football, perhaps a sense of the strengths beyond skill that had made them masters, certainly always a reaffirmation of the belief that millions of us are justified in regarding this diversion with a ball as a beautiful adjunct to our lives.

That freedom to try for more than a superficial appreciation of heroic figures has brightened our working round at home, too. If discrepancies in age prevent some of us from being on anything closer than courteous professional terms with the current generation of footballers, that is reasonable enough. When it was more natural for me to have warm friendships with players, I had the luck to get along with quite a few who combined towering talent with interesting natures. Indeed that last phrase would qualify as an understatement when applied to such as Denis Law, Paddy Crerand, George Best, John Giles, Charlie Cooke, Jim Baxter, Jack Charlton, Bobby Moore and a clutch of others. They were so interesting at times that you needed a strong constitution to survive their company. One thing I never found them doing was asking me to arrange an interview (and a fee) through an agent. Even today, when many of the most obscure footballers seem to feel naked unless they have appointed a half-baked hustler to put a price on their less than riveting utterances, those of us who toil in *The Observer*'s corner of the vineyard are immune to the nonsense.

The only agent I have had to deal with has been the impeccably genuine Jon Holmes and there was no question of money involved, rather the exercise of his good offices to facilitate productive and enjoyable meetings with two or three of his distinguished clients. Whatever publication employs you, much scruffiness will be encountered in the covering of football in this country (for a start, there are First Division press boxes so inadequate that they would not be tolerated for a moment by local paper reporters in the US, though our complaints are bound to appear frivolous when set alongside the primitive and dangerous conditions inflicted on so many thousands of spectators). However, being spared the worst consequences of the modern plague of jumped-up agents is just one of numerous consolations available to non-tabloid scribblers.

In fact, doing matches and features for *The Observer* is such an agreeable way of chronicling the glory game that the only means by which any of us so favoured can justify our luck is by offering something acceptable to the readers. If what you find in the following pages does not suggest that the chance has been taken, that is not Tony Pawson's fault. As an anthologist, Tony has played about as well as he did on that Boxing Day of 1952 when, as a Charlton winger, he gave Alf Ramsey a memorably hard time. A lot of the by-lines he has gathered here belong to people with whom I have had some of the best times of my working life. I think you, too, will find that the pleasures of football are considerably deepened by having them around.

Preface

For me as a footballer and lover of the game diving into this part of *The Observer* archives has been a fascinating experience. So much of the writing stirs memories of great games and great players. In contrast to cricket, football has little reputation for humour so it was a pleasure also to be reminded of a number of light-hearted articles about a game which often takes itself much too seriously.

Football's almost universal attraction is based on the simplicity of its rules, its tactics and its techniques. There are millions of words in which 'experts' try to make it sound unbelievably complex, yet the best of managers and teams have always followed the dictum 'make it simple'. So we can all understand the game and share its excitements and appreciate its skills much better than in a genuinely complex sport like cricket. That is reflected in the remarkable range of writers making intelligent contribution. While you might expect Elizabeth Taylor or Barry Norman to dissect plays or films here they are with probing analyses of George Best and Bertie Mee. Clement Freud and Kenneth Harris are more associated with politics, but just as penetrating on soccer. A literary figure like Philip Toynbee can write as elegantly on his conversion to the game, although only in *The Observer* are you likely to get a football sporting print beginning, 'Arthur Koestler was only too right . . .'

The selection in the book aims to reflect that great diversity of writers and styles rather than concentrate solely on great events, or great authorities of the day from J. A. H. Catton, to John Arlott to Ronald Atkin and Hugh McIlvanney. Hugh, for instance, has written so long for *The Observer* and for so long been regarded as the outstanding sports journalist of his time that it would be only too easy to fill a couple of books with 'the best of McIlvanney'.

My intention is to reflect also the changed attitudes and atmosphere of the game. Robertson-Glasgow switched for once from his concentration on cricket and rugby to turn his sharp eye on the 1948 Cup Final. The scene was so fresh to him that happily he has preserved for us the rituals of the day with 'Mr Cager resplendent in white flannels' conducting the community singing and 3s 6d tickets changing hands at a bit closer to today's inflated prices. A few years later a couple of sentences from Philip Toynbee finger the dramatic change in crowd behaviour from my playing days to the present . . . a change I still find unbelievable and unexplained. Commenting on his conversion to soccer in the fifties he pointed to Twickenham's one advantage as more raucous crowd support: 'I was appalled by the dignified silence in which the Chelsea match was watched. Too many Old Wykehamists, perhaps.' Not even Ken Bates would claim that the crowd at Stamford Bridge now watch in dignified silence and his is a lone voice in claiming that Chelsea's supporters still follow my old school motto of 'Manners Makyth Man'.

Happily the archives reflect only one significant change in *The Observer*'s reporting of football. There is massive coverage now compared to relative neglect in the immediate post-war years when gates and interest were at their highest. *The Observer* gave no mention at all, for instance, to the 1950 World Cup, the first in which England took part, and only a few paragraphs to the whole of the entertaining 1954 World Championship. The weekly Sporting Prints concentrated on Robertson-Glasgow's cricket in and out of season or on rugby, golf, racing or fishing, or even pigeon-shooting or billiards. But for several years there was never a sporting print related solely to soccer.

So selection was relatively easy until the sixties when more and more space began to be given to the glory game. Happily there is no reflection in *Observer* writing over the years of that other general change, to ever shriller reporting with extremes of praise or criticism – usually criticism – the fashionable trend. That was recently summed up for me when the next seat in the press-box was filled by a journalist, unknown to me, who explained he was deputising for the regular correspondent. 'He's off ill with food poisoning . . . probably through swallowing his own words,' was an explanation which made sense to me. Critical comment there often is in *The Observer*, but aiming to be fair and constructive. If a pot-shot is taken at the pianist it is because he is not perceived as doing his best and no great wound can result. Elsewhere, dedicated characters, trying their hardest, like Bobby Robson, are too often hunted to destruction by those who appear to make a sport of the chase and to enjoy the kill.

My thanks have to go to my nine sports editors all of whom have let me express myself as I wished without dictating style or content. No doubt they have only tolerated me through thirty-seven years of regular writing as I have never missed a deadline or often got the facts wrong – and because there was enough fine writing from others to support my more prosaic contributions. For me it has been an education and a pleasure to have colleagues of the calibre of Alan Ross, John Arlott, Hugh McIlvanney or Julie Welch, who has written so entertainingly and perceptively about a game which captured her childhood imagination. It was typical of good editorial judgement that she should be invited to write regularly when many perceived it as odd that a woman should be asked to report so 'manly' a sport.

From my own viewpoint I owe a special debt to my first sports editor, Michael Davie. He was one of the first to accept that cricketers and footballers of ability were not just flannelled fools or muddied oafs when it came to writing about their own game and that they were capable of expressing themselves without a 'ghost' as medium. It was that attitude which encouraged Danny Blanchflower to do his early writing for *The Observer* after being voted player of the year and with captaincy of Ireland in the 1958 World Cup in prospect. He saw that as the one way to establish that the words appearing in his name were indeed his own, before moving on to more lucrative contracts with the 'populars' where the natural assumption is that every top sportsman's articles are written for him. Footballers generally also owe a debt to *The Observer* and to Chris Brasher, in particular, for helping them in practical ways to battle for reasonable contracts and pay. So included is the effect of *The Observer* commissioning and publishing a Q C's opinion with instant reaction from League and F A.

Making this selection has been an enjoyable and nostalgic exercise for me and I hope it stirs memories or excites interest for you as well. Having written for so long inevitably I have had to include some of my own writing. Inevitably too as player or writer it has been impossible to avoid the urge to add a comment or two to preface some of the contributions. These comments I have personalised rather than keep adding 'Editor's Notes'.

Tony Pawson

CHAPTER 1

The Two Faces of Football

They call it the Glory Game, but for some the 'Gory Game' is an apter title. Observer writers have covered its compulsive attraction, but looked also at its occasional repulsive aspects. Hugh McIlvanney charted some of the greatest British triumphs while Eamonn McCabe witnessed England's day of shame in the carnage at the Heysel Stadium. Others described the numbing pain of defeat, or the reasons for changing loyalties.

But first Julie Welch reflects on her own film 'Those Glory, Glory, Days' which centred on her early love affair with the glamorous Tottenham team. She then looks at the two faces of her favourite football player, a Jekyll and Hyde character hard on the field, soft off it.

Spurs Through my Double Vision

Heaven knows how many times I saved Danny Blanchflower from drowning, and when I wasn't hauling him out of spuming and torrential rapids there was always Cliff Jones to be dragged from a burning building or Dave Mackay to be snatched at the last minute from the path of an oncoming train. In those days of my pullulating pre-teen imagination, Tottenham was such an extraordinarily perilous environment that it was a wonder that anyone risked emerging from their homes to venture down the High Street, so liable were they to be confronted with terrifying conflagrations, engulfed by rivers in full flood, flattened by out-of-control locomotives, from which I would be busy, at huge danger to my 12-year-old self, preserving the lives of the Tottenham Hotspur football team and asking nothing in return except, if possible, a couple of tickets to the 1961 Cup Final.

Film budgets being what they are, it was, thank goodness, beyond the means of Goldcrest Television to commit the wildest of my childhood fantasies to celluloid. Even so, 'Those Glory, Glory Days' logs some of the more ridiculous creations that lounged about my head and are still recalled to mind with a sense of acute embarrassment. Did I really attend lessons in body only, mind feverishly preoccupied with Scenario A, in which Bill Nicholson implored me, as the only person in the world with the necessary tactical genius, to halt Spurs' disastrous run of defeats and take them from the brink of relegation to the League championship? Was that me, talking dementedly in an empty bedroom, because in my imagination the entire Spurs team was sitting there, rapt with admiration for my perception of the game?

I dare say that this private self-aggrandisement is common. What was less so, was the choice of footballers as objects of these imaginary deeds of heroism by a plump and rather pompous middle class girl who lived in stockbroker belt, went to public school, and might have been assumed to nurture more predictable affections, say for Margot Fonteyn and Pat Smythe.

It is never easy, though, to explain away passion. Danny the pseudonymous heroine of those 'Glory, Glory Days', develops her obsession with Spurs as a kind of emotional displacement activity to compensate for her parents' failing marriage. This certainly was not true of me, and Danny's egregious father and mother are quite unlike my own dear ma and pa. Unlike Danny, too, I can't claim to have been exposed to the heady delights of the game of Matthews and Finney in early childhood, when, at least according to the Jesuits, you are supposed to be at your most receptive to indoctrination. At eight, I was a confirmed horse racing nut. I'd reached at least 11 before I went to a football match, and its impact was so small that I can't now recall which two teams decided the results.

Maybe there's some accident of personality that makes you a football buff rather than a train-spotter or a Morris dancer. Maybe my friends and I – there were three other Spurs besotted girls in Form 4B – were simply at an age when we were looking for romantic heroes, decided that Cliff Richard was wet and happened on a football team instead. Of course that double-winning Spurs team of 1960–61 – Brown, Baker, Henry, Blanchflower, Norman, Mackay, Jones, White, Smith, Allen and Dyson – was an abundant source of heroic material.

Could it happen now – I mean if we were 12 years old now and looking for people to worship, would we expend our amorous intensity on a present-day football team? Twenty-two years on from the season in which Spurs won the double and captured at least one heart – this one – for life, I have my doubts. Players are less singular, less unique now, managers are

2

too chummy and human, and modern media coverage exposes the ordinaryness, often the banality, that was always there but possible to overlook in the days before the post-match interview (just take us through the goal, Gary). But maybe I'm wrong. It could be that four schoolgirls are standing outside the White Hart Lane gates now worshipping at the shrine. It would be really nice to think that one of them has changed her name to Ossie.

13 November 1983   *Julie Welch*

Norman Hunter was Julie's favourite player, whom she described as a hard man with a soft centre. Norman admitted to her that he was a changed person on the field, carried away by the passions of football and the drive to win.

'I'm two different people on and off. I don't know why it should be. You've got to win, you see; that's what keeps you going. You've *got* to. You can't say, well, we won that last year, we'll take it easy this.

'I'm fairly quick tempered, but it's up and down and gone. No grudges. Just for two seconds I really go. The silliest thing I ever did was to go after that fellow Rivera in the Cup Winner's Cup at Salonika.

'He kicked me and I went after him. If he'd been closer, I'd have hit him, but he'd walked away. By the time I'd trudged all that distance, my temper had gone down again and I didn't want to do anything. I just laid my hands on him and I got sent off.

'It was a bit emotional, walking down the tunnel. We'd lost to Sunderland, we were trying to win something back, we'd played so well and then I had to get sent off. It was a long tunnel. I'd only got halfway when the final whistle went. We deserved to hammer them, and it was all over and I was in that tunnel, and we'd lost.

'When I lose I've got to talk about it. Some keep it inside them. I go home and relive it with the wife. She just nods and says yes or no.

'Sometimes I'm close to tears. I'm emotional you see. Football makes me emotional. Not many people can explain what it's like when you play all season and you get to Wembley or somewhere, and at the end you and the lads walk down the tunnel while the other lot are doing the lap of honour.'

Julie Welch

What is soccer's appeal to the spectator? In 1954 Philip Toynbee wrote of his own conversion to watching soccer.

Loyalty Check

Arthur Koestler was only too right when he wrote that renegades are treated with contempt, even by the sides to which they renege. A year ago I declared in this column my transference of loyalty from Rugby to Association football, suggesting at the same time that the former would be improved by the introduction of a round ball.

My motives for this provocative action were simple in the extreme. For one thing, it had at last dawned on me that soccer, contrary to current theory, is the social superior of its nineteenth-century offspring. Members of the Pegasus team come out of a higher drawer than members of Blackheath. More gentlemanly gentlemen send their sons to Winchester, Charterhouse, Eton and Westminster than those who make do with Uppingham, Sedbergh, Dulwich and Bedford. Secondly, soccer has the advantage of being the sport of the majority. I thought that by joining the ranks of its supporters I would not only be improving my social status but also guaranteeing that in any future war – rival headquarters would be Twickenham and Wembley – I would be on the stronger side.

Intelligent calculations, it would surely be supposed – but I had forgotten Koestler's bitter warning. A hundred savage letters reached me from the green pork-pie hats, while the bowlers and cloth caps kept a disdainful silence. I had lost old friends and made no new ones. And yet there is no going back. All I can do now is to go on wooing the soccer fans by becoming ever more virulent in my attacks on rugger.

Twickenham, then: the University match. Almost the whole of the second half was spent in a prolonged scrum in the right-hand section of the Oxford twenty-five. If the ball ever appeared it was promptly bungled by one or other of the three-quarter lines, or else kicked tamely into touch. An exceptionally bad game? But it was no worse than the games in 1952 and 1953.

Stamford Bridge and Red Banner. An exceptionally bad game according to the Press, whose natural tendency, one should add, is to make every game of anything into a very good or a very bad one. Beautiful and precise football by the Hungarians, marred only, so far as I could see, by a robust and tireless Chelsea defence. The *thrill*, in any case, was so continuous that I came away in a state of exhausted relief that the better side (let's face it) had not managed to win. At Twickenham neither side ever looked as if they were capable of scoring a try: at Stamford Bridge both sides were constantly threatening the other's goal. The suddenness with which the ball can be transferred from one penalty area to the other is a constant surprise to a spectator who is inured to the slogging and tortoise-like movements of present-day Rugby. And the skill of a Hidegkuti or a Blunstone is, of course, incomparably greater than the skill of even the most nimble stand-off half.

I also enjoy the histrionics of soccer – the arms flung wide in simulated disgust at a decision, the exaggerated tumbles, the moving reconciliations between opposing players who have opposed each other too vigorously. I even enjoyed it when the Hungarians persistently kicked the ball into the crowd to express their disagreement with the award of a penalty (unsuccessful) against them.

There is only one advantage to Twickenham. They shout a great deal louder. I was appalled by the dignified silence in which the Chelsea match was watched. Too many Old Wykehamists, perhaps.

19 December 1954   *Philip Toynbee*

For many the glory game is about fulfilling dreams and the nation rejoiced when England at last fulfilled theirs and won the World Cup. The volume of noise should have satisfied Philip Toynbee as the victory brought another V-Day celebration twenty-one years on from the war's end. Hugh McIlvanney recorded the Final triumph.

Hurst Hat-trick Clinches It For England

England 4 West Germany 2
Hurst, 3, Peters Haller, Weber
(after extra time) Att. 93,000

THE GREATEST moment in the history of English football came at 5.15 this afternoon when Geoff Hurst shot the magnificent goal that made certain of the World Cup. It was Hurst's third goal, England's fourth, and, coming as it did in the final seconds of extra time, it shattered the last remnants of German resistance.

Germany had equalised with almost the last kick in the regular 90 minutes, and they had just gone within inches of repeating the blow in extra time when Seeler lunged in on a headed pass by Held. But Moore took the ball coolly out of defence and lifted it upfield to Hurst 10 yards inside the German half. The referee was already looking at his watch and three England supporters had prematurely invaded the pitch as Hurst collected the ball on his chest.

At first he seemed inclined to dawdle-out time. Then abruptly he sprinted through in the inside-left position with a German defender pressing him. As Tilkowski prepared to move out, Hurst swung his left foot and drove the ball breathtakingly into the top of the net.

The scene that followed was unforgettable. Stiles and Cohen collapsed in a tearful embrace on the ground, young Ball turned wild cartwheels, and Bobby Charlton dropped to his knees, felled by emotion.

Almost immediately it was over, and the honour that had escaped England for so long had been won. Soon the players, who had forgotten the crippling weariness of a few minutes before, were hugging and laughing, and crying with manager Alf Ramsey and the reserves, who must go through the rest of their lives with bitter-sweet memories of how it looked from the touch-line.

'Ramsey, Ramsey,' the crowd roared, and in his moment of vindication it was a tribute that no one could grudge him. Eventually, Moore led his men up to the Royal Box to receive the gold Jules Rimet trophy from the Queen, and the slow, ecstatic lap of honour began. 'Ee-aye-addio, we've won the Cup,' sang the crowd, as Moore threw it in a golden arc above his head and caught it again.

England had, indeed, won the Cup, producing more determined aggression and flair than they had shown at any earlier stage of the competition. In such a triumph there could be no failures, but if one had to name outstanding heroes they were Hurst, Ball, Moore and the brothers Charlton.

Hurst, who just a month ago appeared to have only the remotest chance of figuring in the World Cup, had emerged as the destructive star of a feverishly exciting game, becoming the first man to score a hat-trick in the final. Ball, who looked like a boy, had done the work of two men. Moore, showing again that he is stimulated by the demands of the great occasion, played with an imaginative self-confidence that made it unnecessary for anyone to ask who was the England captain.

Beside him, Jack Charlton was a giant of a player. And through the whole performance there ran the inspiration of Bobby Charlton. In the first half, when the foundations of England's victory were being laid, it was his relentless but unhurried foraging, his ability to impose his experience and his class on the team's play, that counted most.

Every one of the others responded superbly and if some were sometimes short of inspiration, none ever lacked courage, or total commitment.

Of course, the Germans were on the field, too, and they let England know about it, often enough. They may regret now that they set Beckenbauer to mark Charlton, for the young half-back had little opportunity to exploit his attacking genius until it was too late. Held and Haller, with tremendous early assistance from Seeler, did plenty of damage, but ultimately it was Tilkowski and his defenders who were left to try to save Germany.

They tried mightily but in the end England's spirit broke them. Germany had already won the World Cup, England had not, so they had a right to accept defeat with pride. They did, and the crowd cheered almost as much for their lap of honour as for England's.

Wembley was charged with an atmosphere it had never known before. Long before the teams appeared the great crowd was chanting and singing. It might have been Anfield (England did wear red) and there can be no greater tribute.

When the band of the Royal Marines, who had played a tune for each of the 16 competing nations, came to play the National Anthem it was sung as it may never be sung again. Deutschland Uber Alles boomed out in its wake and the battle was on.

The Germans began rather nervously, standing off from the tackle and letting the England forwards move smoothly up to the edge of the penalty area. Charlton and Peters were able to work the ball along the left at their leisure and there was anxiety in the German defence before the cross was cleared.

Charlton wandered purposefully all over the field, bringing composure and smoothness wherever he went, was again making comparisons with di Stefano seem relevant.

One of Hunt's few imaginative passes set Stiles clear on the right and his high cross beat Tilkowski before Hottges headed it away. The ball was returned smartly by Bobby Charlton and Tilkowski had so much difficulty punching it away from Hurst that he knocked himself out.

The goalkeeper was prostrate, the whistle had gone and the German defenders had stopped challenging by the time Moore put the ball in the net. The crowd cheered in the hope that next time it would be the real thing.

Jack Charlton, carrying the ball forward on his forehead with a skill that would have done credit to his brother, moved swiftly out of defence and his finely judged diagonal pass let Peters in for a quick powerful shot from the edge of the penalty area. Tilkowski, diving desperately to his left, punched the ball round the post. Hurst met Ball's corner on the volley but sent it much too high.

At that point Weber chose to give one of the agonised performances that have been one of the German hallmarks in the competition, but Mr Dienst quickly let him know that he was fooling nobody.

Peters emphasised the eagerness of the England attack by surging in from the right to shoot the ball only 2 ft wide from 25 yards.

Then, stunningly, in the tenth minute England found themselves a goal behind. And it was a goal that anyone who had watched their magnificent defensive play earlier in the tournament could scarcely believe. Held glided a high cross from the left wing and Wilson jumping for the ball in comfortable isolation incredibly headed it precisely down to the feet of Haller, standing a dozen yards out and directly in front of Banks , Haller had time to steady and pivot to turn his right-foot shot on the ground past Banks' right side.

It took England only six minutes to reassure the crowd. Overath had been warned for a severe foul on Ball and now he committed another one on Moore, tripping the England captain as he turned away with the ball. Moore himself took the free kick and from 40 yards out near the left touch-line he flighted the ball beautifully towards the far post. Hurst, timing his run superbly to slip through the defence much as he had done against the Argentine, struck a perfect header low inside Tilkowski's right-hand post.

Moore held one arm aloft in the familiar gladiator salute while Hurst was smothered with congratulations. It was another reminder of the huge contribution West Ham have made to England's success in this World Cup.

Bobby Charlton reasserted himself with a sharp run across the face of the goal from the right and a left-foot shot. It troubled Tilkowski but he gathered it at his second attempt. The Germans retaliated through Haller, who was just beaten by Banks in a race for a through pass but the most sustained aggression was still coming from England. Moore, playing with wonderful control and assurance, was driving up among the forwards, joining intelligently in the moves initiated by Bobby Charlton.

Unfortunately, however, Charlton could not be in two places at once. Time and again the attacks he conceived from deep positions cried out to be climaxed with his killing power.

After Ball had been rebuked for showing dissent he took part in one of England's more effective attacks. Cohen crossed the ball long from the right and Hurst rose magnificently to deflect in another header which Tilkowski could only scramble away from his right hand post. Ball turned the ball back into the goal mouth and the Germans' desperation was unmistakable as Overath came hurtling in to scythe the ball away for a corner.

Not all the uneasy moments were around Tilkowski, however. First Ball and then Cohen toyed riskily with Held near the byline. Jack Charlton, maintaining the remarkable standard of his World Cup performances, had to intervene with a prodigious sweeping tackle on the ground to get them out of trouble. It cost him a corner and the corner almost cost England a goal. The ball went to Overath and from 20 yards he drove it in fiercely at chest height. Banks beat it out and when Emmeroch hammered it back from an acute angle the goalkeeper caught it surely.

When a Wilson header into goal was headed down by Hurst Hunt appeared certain to score. But when the Liverpool man forced in his left foot volley Tilkowski was in the way. Soon afterwards a subtle pass from Charlton bewildered the German defence but Peters could not quite reach the ball for the shot.

The hectic fluctuating pattern of the first half was stressed again before the interval when Overath hit a bludgeoning shot from 20 yards and Banks turned the ball brilliantly over his crossbar.

Bobby Charlton, moving through on Moore's pass early in the second half, fell after being tackled by Schulz but the claims for a penalty were understandably half-hearted. Cohen was making regular runs on the right wing but his centres were easily cut out.

Mr Dienst was at his most officious but he was entitled to reprimand Stiles after the wing-half had bounced the ball in disgust at a harsh decision. Hunt was crowded out in the last stride as he met a cross from the left, but after 5 minutes he had a hand in England's second goal.

He pushed a pass to Ball and when the winger shot Tilkowski pushed the ball on to the outside of his net. Following the corner Hurst's shot from the left was deflected across goal by Schulz, and Peters, strangely neglected by the German defenders, came in swiftly to take the ball on the half volley and drive it into the net from four or five yards.

A free kick given against Stiles was guided accurately above the English defenders by Emmerich, and Weber should have done more than head weakly past. In the last seconds of the 90 minutes the English supporters were silenced by an equalising goal.

Charlton was doubtfully penalised after jumping to a header and from the free-kick Emmerich drove the ball through the English wall. As it cannoned across the face of the goal it appeared to hit Schnellinger on the arm but the referee saw nothing illegal and Weber at the far post was able to score powerfully.

From the kick-off in extra time England swept the Germans back into their penalty area. Ball had a wonderful shot from 20 yards edged over the crossbar by Tilkowski. Then Charlton hit a low drive that Tilkowski pushed against his left-hand upright.

The Germans looked weary but their swift breaks out of defence were still dangerous. Emmerich moved in on Banks but when he passed Held was slow to control the ball and Stiles cleared. Then Held compensated for this by dribbling clear of the entire English defence and turning the ball back invitingly across goal. But there was nobody following up.

When England took the lead again in the tenth minute of extra time they did it controversially. Ball made an opening for himself on the right and when the ball went in to Hurst the inside forward resolutely worked for a clear view of the goal. His rising right-foot shot on the turn from 10 yards was pushed against the underside of the crossbar by Tilkowski and when it bounced the England players appealed as one man for a goal. The referee spoke to the Russian linesman on the side away from the main stand and turned to award a goal. The delayed-action cheers shook the stadium.

Then we were up yelling and stamping, and slapping one another as Hurst shot that last staggering goal. The sky had been overcast all afternoon, but now the clouds split and the sun glared down on the stadium. Maybe those fellows were right when they said God was an Englishman.

England – Banks: Cohen, J Charlton, Moore, Wilson: Stiles, R Charlton, Ball: Hurst, Hunt, Peters
Germany – Tilkowski: Höttes, Schulz, Weber, Schnellinger: Haller, Beckenbauer: Seeler, Held, Overath, Emmerich.

Referee – D Dienst (Switzerland)

31 July 1966   *Hugh McIlvanney*

Hugh McIlvanney also had cause for rejoicing when Celtic became the first British club to win the European Cup in 1967.

What a Performance!

Today Lisbon is almost, but not quite, back in Portuguese hands at the end of the most hysterically exuberant occupation any city has ever known.

Pockets of Celtic supporters are holding out in unlikely corners, noisily defending their own carnival atmosphere against the returning tide of normality, determined to preserve the moment, to make the party go on and on.

They emerge with a sudden flood of Glasgow accents from taxis or cafés, or let their voices carry with it an irresistible aggregate of decibels across hotel lounges. Always, even among the refugees who turn up at the British Embassy bereft of everything but the rumpled clothes they stand in, the talk is of that magical hour-and-a-half under the hot sun on Thursday in the breathtaking, tree-fringed amphitheatre of the national stadium.

At the airport, the impression is of a Dunkirk with happiness. The discomforts of mass evacuation are tolerable when your team have just won the greatest victory yet achieved by a British football club, and completed a clean sweep of the trophies available to them that has never been equalled anywhere in the world.

They even cheered Helenio Herrera and his shattered Inter when the Italians left for Milan yesterday evening. 'Inter, Inter, Inter.' The chant resounded convincingly through the departure lounge, but no one was misled. In that mood, overflowing with conquerors' magnanimity they might have given Scot Symon a round of applause.

Typically, within a minute the same happily dishevelled groups were singing: 'Eee Aye Addio, Herrara's on the Buroo.' The suggestion that the most highly paid manager in Europe is likely to be queueing at the Labour Exchange is rather wild but the comment emphasised that even the least analytical fan had seen through the hectic excitement of a unique performance to the essential meaning of the event.

Mundo Desportivo of Lisbon put it another way: 'It was inevitable. Sooner or later the Inter of Herrera, the Inter of *catenaccio*, of negative football, of marginal victories, had to pay for their refusal to play entertaining football.' The Portuguese rejoiced over the magnificent style in which Celtic had taken retribution on behalf of the entire game.

A few of us condemned Herrera unequivocally two years ago after Inter had won the European Cup at their own San Siro Stadium by defending with neurotic caution to protect a luckily gained one-goal lead against a Benfica side with only nine fit men. But he continued to receive around £30,000 a year for stifling the flair, imagination, boldness and spontaneity that make football what it is. And he was still held in awe by people who felt that the statistics of his record justified the sterility of his methods.

Now, however, nearly everyone appreciates the dangers of his influence. The twelfth European Cup final showed how shabbily his philosophy compares with the dynamically positive thinking of Jock Stein. Before the match Stein told me: 'Inter will play it defensively. That's their way and it's their business. But we feel we have a duty to play the game our way, and our way is to attack.

'Win or lose, we want to make the game worth remembering. Just to be involved in an occasion like this is a tremendous honour and we think it puts an obligation on us. We can be as hard and professional as anybody, but I mean it when I say that we don't just want to win this cup. We want to win it playing good football, to make neutrals glad we've done it, glad to remember how we did it.'

The effects of such thinking, and of Stein's genius for giving it practical expression, were there for all the football world to see on Thursday. Of course, he has wonderful players, a team without a serious weakness and with tremendous strengths in vital positions. But when one had eulogised the exhilarating speed and the bewildering variety of skills that destroyed Inter – the unshakable assurance of Clark, the murderously swift overlapping of the full-backs, the creative energy of Auld in midfield, the endlessly astonishing virtuosity of Johnstone, the intelligent and ceaseless running of Chalmers – even with all this, ultimately the element that impressed most profoundly was the massive heart of this Celtic side.

Nothing symbolised it more vividly than the incredible display of Gemmell. He was almost on his knees with fatigue before scoring that thunderous equaliser in the 63rd minute but somehow his courage forced him to go on dredging up the strength to continue with the exhausting runs along the left-wing that did more than any other single factor to demoralise Inter.

Gemmell has the same aggressive pride, the same contempt for any thought of defeat, that emanates from Auld. Before the game Auld cut short a discussion about the possible ill-effects of the heat and the firm ground with a blunt declaration that they would lick the Italians in any conditions.

When he had been rescued from the delirious crowd and was walking back to the dressing-rooms after Celtic had overcome all the bad breaks to vindicate his confidence, Auld – naked to the waist except for an Inter shirt knotted round his neck like a scarf – suddenly stopped in his tracks and shouted to Ronnie Simpson, who was walking ahead: 'Hey, Ronnie Simpson! What are we? What are we, son ?' He stood there sweating, showing his white teeth between parched lips, flecked with saliva. Then he answered his own question with a belligerent roar. 'We're the greatest. That's what we are. The greatest.' Simpson came running back and they embraced for a full minute.

In the dressing-room, as the other players unashamedly sang their supporters' songs in the showers and drank champagne from the huge Cup ('Have you had a bevy out of this?'), Auld leaned forward to Sean Fallon, the trainer, and asked with mock seriousness: 'Would you say I was the best? Was I your best man?'

'They've all got Stein's heart', said a Glasgow colleague. 'There's a bit of the big man in all of them.'

Certainly the preparation for this final and the winning of it were impregnated with Stein's personality. Whether warning the players against exposing themselves to the sun ('I don't even want you near the windows in your rooms. If there's as much as a freckle on any man's arm he's for home') or joking with reporters beside the hotel swimming-pool in Estoril, his was the all-pervading influence.

Despite the extreme tension he must have felt, he never lost the bantering humour that keeps the morale of his expeditions unfailingly high. The impact of the Celtic invasion on the local Catholic churches was a rewarding theme for him. 'They're getting some gates since we came. The nine o'clock and ten o'clock Masses were all-ticket. They've had to get extra plates. How do they divide the takings here? Is it fifty-fifty or in favour of the home club?'

It was hard work appearing so relaxed and the effort eventually took its toll of Stein when he made a dive for the dressingrooms a minute before the end of the game, unable to stand any more. When we reached him there, he kept muttering: 'What a performance. What a performance.' It was left to Bill Shankly, the Scottish manager of Liverpool (and the only English club manager present), to supply the summing-up quote. 'John,' Shankly said with the solemnity of a man to whom football is a religion, 'you're immortal.'

An elderly Portuguese official cornered Stein and delivered ecstatic praise of Celtic's adventurous approach. 'This attacking play, this is the real meaning of football. This is the true game.' Stein slapped him on the shoulder. 'Go on, I could listen to you all night.' Then, turning to the rest of us, 'Fancy anybody saying that about a Scottish team.'

There is good reason to hope that people will say such things about Scottish and English clubs with increasing frequency in the near future.

13

Now that the Continental monopoly of the European Cup has been broken, British football is poised for a period of domination.

Glasgow Rangers can strike the next blow when they meet Bayern Munich in the final of the European Cup for Cup Winners at Nurnberg next Wednesday. Scot Symon has rebuilt his Rangers team with patient thoroughness this season, and their thrilling draw with Celtic at Ibrox three weeks ago confirmed how far they have come. Spurred by their great rivals' achievement, they will not be easily denied.

Continental clubs can expect no respite next season when the powerful challenge from Scotland will be backed by the presence of Manchester United and Tottenham Hotspur in the two major competitions. It seems unlikely that anything short of the personal intervention of de Gaulle can prevent us from being in among the European prizes again.

18 May 1967   *Hugh McIlvanney*

Manchester United's 1968 final at Wembley stirred even deeper emotions after the club's endeavours and misfortunes in the competition. Hugh McIlvanney echoed the feelings of so many who found the waiting intolerable:

Waiting for United

Perhaps the trick is to retreat to a cottage in Wester Ross with a case of whisky or half a pound of aspirins. That way we could anaesthetise ourselves next Wednesday and wait for the result of the European Cup final to filter through, hoping that its emotional effects would be softened by the delay.

However, there is no escape. We will have to sit there at Wembley and watch United wrestle with the most significant assignment in their history, just one thrust away from the realisation of their obsessive ambition, one slip away from failure and a bleak residue of gloom. . . .

Judging United purely on a technical assessment of their recent form the danger of defeat might appear considerable. Now that Law is a hospital case, United's list of outstanding footballers, of names that would be meaningful anywhere, would fall short of that offered by Benfica.

In answer to Best, Charlton, Crerand and Stiles one must say Eusebio, Coluna, Torres, Augusto, Simoes and possibly Graca. . . .

Heart may be United's greatest asset at Wembley and their courage should give them time to settle to their own splendid natural game.

26 May 1968   *Hugh McIlvanney*

After a rough and scoreless first half Bobby Charlton had the crowd in ecstasy with one of his rare headed goals. In the final twenty minutes, however, Benfica came back strongly to equalise. Indeed but for a remarkable save by Stepney from Eusebio they would have won. In extra time two goals by Brian Kidd and one by George Best saw Manchester home amid wild celebration. McIlvanney caught up with Bobby Charlton as he prepared a day later for an international.

Charlton Reflects

He was sitting in the lounge of the Esso Motor Hotel wearing football boots and shorts. His socks were at his ankles, his eyelids were heavy and the narrow strangely affecting face beneath the isolated strands of yellow hair was more deeply lined than usual. For a moment it seemed he might have come straight from Wembley without changing or sleeping. It took the blue track suit top and the England insignia to remind us that he was beginning a new cycle, that for him great victories merely lead to more battles. He must pick up the laurel wreath on the run. . . .

It became clear afterwards that Charlton, Stiles and Stepney are not only being sustained by euphoria, but insulated by it. The reality of Wednesday night is taking time to seep into their minds.

'It's just dawning on me now,' admitted Charlton, his eyes looking beyond me to the memory of those two incredible hours at Wembley. Inevitably his thoughts dwell on the last 15 or 20 minutes of regular time when United almost as one man slowed to a stagger and Benfica began to reach confidently for a prize which should have been swept irrevocably away long before.

'We were really gone. None of us could run. It was a terrible helpless

15

feeling. My legs were killing me, both of them. It wasn't like ordinary cramp. They just sort of seized up and there wasn't a real stoppage in that last quarter so you didn't have a chance to get down and give them a shake to loosen them. It was murder.' He slapped his calf muscles as he spoke studying them critically as if they might yield some reason for their perfidy.

'When they scored it looked on for them, considering the state we were in, but we held on somehow and when full time came they lost their advantage. It was starting all over again and we had a breather, a chance to get ourselves going again. We were flopped out there like dead men, but we were ready to go when we had to. Matt said, "Just keep going; you can still beat these." We were more like ourselves again when extra time began, we got a quick break and they could do nothing with us. . . .'

Extra time was the supreme test of spirit and United, sharing the advantage of massive home support which had assisted England through the same ordeal in the World Cup, responded magnificently, Benfica, understandably, caved in.

Charlton, Stiles, Best and Stepney were the great players on whom a great victory was built. But they acknowledged their debt to the others. 'What about Brian Kidd? He was like Roger Hunt, working for everybody. And John Aston with those runs? What a game he had. Paralysed that poor fellow Adolfo.' And Crerand whose intelligence and perception meant so much and the inimitable George Best, who made up for his earlier indiscretions with his brilliant goal, and Dunne, and Foulkes – indeed all of them and most vitally perhaps Matt Busby who expressed everything that had to be expressed when he said 'That's it. We've done it.'

3 June 1968   *Hugh McIlvanney*

The glory game heightens the dejection of defeat as Hugh McIlvanney witnessed in the 1966 World Cup. For many visiting teams there was also the shock of coming up against Nobby Stiles.

Just Quiet Suppressed Sobbing

At this point of the World Cup success is still an ideal to be pursued, and the only reality is failure. It is much too early for the laurel wreath, but in Rome and Rio they already have good use for the stocks.

The ejection of Italy by North Korea, undoubtedly the most ridiculous result in the tournament since the United States beat England in 1950, is black comedy. But the fact that Brazil, the most convincing champions the World Cup has known, could not reach the quarter-finals this time evokes a sadness that affects even the most callous survivors.

The Brazilians were doing their best to hide in London yesterday. They have gone into retreat to prepare for a homecoming that will combine the charms of a funeral and a lynching. They make bitter jokes about the reception that awaits them, but in fact their private sadness is too great to let them worry about public abuse. On the morning after the defeat by Portugal which put them out of the competition they gathered for a post mortem in their hotel at Lymm in Cheshire.

'I've never known anything so solemn or so moving,' the manager of the hotel said afterwards. 'Nothing hysterical. Just this quiet, suppressed sobbing. And the tears running down their faces. It was terrible. I had a lump in my throat, I tell you. It's been a great experience having them here but it's all ended so sadly.' He sounded as if he almost regretted becoming too involved. Next time, one felt, any football team that stayed at his place would be just customers.

Among the Brazilians themselves, of course, not everyone is content to mourn. There are many who are ready to condemn. 'Four years' work, a million pounds spent, and what did we get? Two free kicks.' The journalist who said that probably had special reason for resentment. There were about 250 newspapermen and broadcasters from Brazil in the Liverpool area and there were few of them who did not have contracts to write books on how Brazil won her third World Cup. What happened at Goodison Park last week must have put the country's publishing industry in a precarious situation.

At such a time suicidal impulses are to be expected and the talk of mass resignations among the officials is understandable, but some of the other reactions are more disturbing. Even Doctor Hilton Gosling, who has always managed to be both intellectual and level-headed, spoke earnestly of a need to revolutionise Brazil's approach to the game. They would, he said, have to cope with the new harder, faster football played by other countries. 'The time for walking football is past,' he said.

There is something dangerously masochistic in this sort of self-denigration. Brazil failed not because their style was outdated, but because they no longer had the men to execute it with the devastating flair that crushed all opposition in 1958 and again, with rather less authority, in 1962. References to walking football are misleading. They walked when they

17

could afford to walk, a principle too long ignored by English players who, for generations, had a pathological addiction to haste and insisted on playing at a speed that outstripped their technique.

When the great Brazilian team chose to apply pace, it was perhaps the most killing ever seen in the game. When Garrincha made a break along the wing and Vava came surging in to meet the centre the image of walking football could not have been more remote. This is the real point, of course. Garrincha is a walking footballer now because he has no option. He is too old and in the party that came to England he was as much an anachronism as Vava would have been.

I said before the competition began that the Brazilian selectors appeared to be insuring themselves against violent recriminations by choosing legendary heroes whose greatness was palpably behind them. Then there seemed little justification for bringing Garrincha and Djalma Santos. Now there seems even less. The Brazilian challenge was undermined by timidity and dubious judgment. Why, for example, should they bring the 16-year-old prodigy Edu to this country if they were not prepared to risk him when faced with a crisis?

No doubt their defensive weaknesses are fundamental and would have made it almost impossible for them to maintain their domination of the World Cup but even with diminished resources they could have made a better show. The injuries that spread through their party like an epidemic had a crucial influence and they are entitled to feel rancour about the way Pele, who was never bursting with fitness at any stage of the competition, was ruthlessly cut down by Portugal. Had Mr George McCabe been less of a diplomat and more of a referee at Goodison on Tuesday, Morais of Portugal would have been ordered off.

Nevertheless, the nervous uncertainty of the Brazilian officials, which finally led to the muted panic that sent them out against Portugal with nine changes from the side that lost to Hungary, may have brought disaster where there should have been honourable defeat. 'The team changes were made a year too late,' said a Brazilian reporter. 'No football team lasts eight years.'

Certainly there was something depressingly shabby about the way the champions were dismissed. It was like watching Sugar Ray Robinson being pushed around by an opponent he would have destroyed in his prime.

Most of the pugilistic analogies last week concerned Nobby Stiles, whose physical contribution was the most memorable if not the most pleasant feature of England's paralysingly drab victory over France. The Peruvian referee, Mr Yamasaki, accidentally felled Stiles early in the game, but the Manchester United wing-half retained enough combative zeal to persuade the official to take his name.

Since then there have been attempts to convince us that Stiles is being victimised, a point of view that must cause cynical hilarity among those who have played against him. Off the field he is a friendly, likeable little man but on it he commits fouls with a regularity that makes the warning from FIFA about his conduct neither surprising nor regrettable. At times it seems that Stiles can scarcely challenge for the ball without breaking the rules, and it is astonishing that so many of the players who have found him flailing in from behind have been able to control their responses.

It has been seriously suggested that Stiles, who has defective eyesight and wears contact lenses when he plays, commits some of the fouls simply because he misjudges distances and collides with opponents unintentionally. This is not a ludicrous explanation, for Christopher Brasher admits that when he used contact lenses for steeplechasing he had difficulty in measuring distances, but there is no doubt that with Stiles it is mainly a matter of attitude.

His kind of competitive spirit is an essential part of all successful teams, but clearly there must be limits. Alf Ramsey and many of the England players are enthusiastic in their praise of the relentless aggression in Stiles's game, but it is questionable if that admiration would come so readily if they were opposed to him.

'Nobby goes in like a bloody whirlwind,' one England forward said in a tone which indicated that he did not know whether to admire or condemn. In Belgrade last year Sekularac, the great and notoriously violent Yugoslav inside-forward, watched Stiles make a couple of tackles, then turned to the Press seats and said: 'Once, yes. Twice, no.' He made a breaking gesture with his hands. It would be remarkable if Stiles went through this World Cup without provoking a similar reaction from another player.

24 July 1966   *Hugh McIlvanney*

Ronald Atkin watched a 1980 attempt to come to terms with defeat. After a season of success it all turned sour for Arsenal as they lost two Finals within a week.

Sweat and Tears

Arsenal had just lost their second Cup Final in five days and if the players contrived to carry smiles with them on to the team-bus, the grief of their supporters was pitiful to behold.

On one side of the vehicle a fair-haired youth, stunned by the deadly combination of bad news and Belgian beer, subsided on to the tarmac in majestic slow motion as his girl companion tugged at his yellow scarf in a vain bid to keep him upright. On the other side of the bus a lad vented a combination of grief, indignation and disbelief on his mother's shoulder. 'We were the better team,' he bawled through the tears.

Back at the hotel a crowd of supporters assembled in the lobby cheered and applauded, and now it was the turn of a footballer or two to wipe a watering eye or blow the nose before they got down to putting some liquid nourishment under their belts and a lot of unpleasant memories out of their heads.

To lose the F A Cup Final at Wembley, and with it a guaranteed spot in Europe next season, was upsetting enough, to be beaten by Valencia in the Cup Winners Final amounted to a boot in the groin and the manner of that defeat could not have been more sickening.

At 10.40 on a chilly Brussels night Arsenal's season, already stretching back through 68 matches, came to a tragic and farcical climax with a penalty kick competition, the late-night equivalent of pistols at dawn.

Of the six men from each side who took the kicks, the three left-foot specialists Kempes, Brady and Rix – were the only ones who missed and if it was Pereira's plunging save of Rix's shot which plucked the Cup from Arsenal's grasp, Brady's failure was no less crucial, though the Spanish goalkeeper clearly moved before each of Arsenal's penalties and was fortunate not to be punished by an otherwise vigilant Czechoslovakian referee.

It must all have been an uncomfortable reminder to one spectator, Ulli Hoeness, now the Bayern Munich manager, of the last time a big match was settled by this particular throw of the dice. Then the stakes were even higher, the European Championship of 1976 no less, and Hoeness's spot-kick blunder cost West Germany the title against Czechoslovakia.

The reaction was predictable, particularly from the English side. The match should have gone to another replay, it should have been decided on corners, on fouls, on shots at goal, on a spin of the coin even.

It took Terry Neill, suppressing his deep distress behind a barricade of reasoned calm, to point out one or two verities. 'Those were the rules and we totally accept them,' said the Arsenal manager. 'There must be rules for anything, for life itself, and you have to live by them.'

Neill's understandable bitterness surfaced only briefly when he explained the absence of Valencia's manager Alfredo di Stefano thus: 'He is not here because he fainted, he couldn't believe the result. He has gone to church to say 500 Hail Marys and he ought to keep on going to church every day if he can have that sort of luck.'

Di Stefano, who puffed his way through more cigarettes during the evening than that other outstanding booster for the tobacco industry Cesar Luis Menotti, of Argentina, agreed with Neill. 'In football luck must come into it and we were lucky. But the record book will show the words "Valencia champions" and in that respect the result was more important than the game.'

Di Stefano also offered the opinion that the final should have gone to a replay, and though this could be interpreted as no more than consoling comment from the victor's rostrum, few would argue that there was far too much at stake for the Cup to be arbitrarily parcelled out in this fashion.

Rather like the annual mid-winter furore over under-soil heating for Britain's frozen pitches, the discussion and recrimination will probably subside until it happens again, which is a pity.

Despite Rix's assertion that if it had been a boxing match the referee would have halted the contest and awarded the verdict to Arsenal, an uninvolved observer could have found little to separate the finalists.

Pereira's spectacular denial of goal attempts by Brady and Sunderland, and Carrete's header off the line from Stapleton were equalised by Jennings's skills in turning away an early shot by Kempes and blocking Bonhof when the German was allowed to make unchallenged progress through the same right flank of Arsenal's defence which had permitted the build-up to West Ham's winner at Wembley.

If O'Leary strengthened opinions that he is Britain's best centre-half by his energetic obliteration of a strangely lethargic Kempes, Valencia's central defenders, Arias and the teenager Tendillo, were equally impressive in denying Stapleton and Sunderland time or space.

The industry of Talbot, the only one to have played in all 68 of those Arsenal games this season, and the running and distribution of Rix and Brady (who surely impressed his prospective purchaser Hoeness) were matched by the deft work of Solsona, Saura and Pablo.

The team's attitude towards the final was also similar. Defeat had to be avoided rather than victory sought and it was their reluctance, or perhaps inability, to go in spirited pursuit of a positive result that muted feelings about Arsenal's lack of fortune.

They are a team geared to grind out victories rather than plunder them (they last scored more than one goal in a game as far back as Easter Monday) and though they had clearly been heavily affected by the pro-longed trench warfare with Liverpool, Arsenal could have benefited by pushing more men forward, particularly against the hysterical and incautious right back Carrete.

But Arsenal have given much sweat this season to wind up with disappointingly little and one's feelings had to be of pity as they wandered disconsolately to their supporters' end of the Heysel Stadium to accept the cheers of consolation.

They could certainly have done without the final indignity of the music chosen to accompany Valencia's lap of triumph. It was 'The Battle Hymn of the Republic', or as it is better known on the terraces 'Glory, Glory, Hallelujah', the song which belongs to Arsenal's North London rivals Tottenham.

18 May 1980   *Ronald Atkin*

Everton in 1985 at least had a handsome win in the Cup Winners Cup before losing that same week in the FA Cup Final . . . and to ten men. Ronald Atkin's comments highlight two strange aspects of those two finals. The Merseysiders supporting Everton made a good impression in Holland only weeks before Liverpool's supporters were involved in the Heysel disaster in Belgium . . . and Kevin Moran became the first player to be sent off in over a hundred years of FA Cup Finals.

Everton's Cups

There is a saying in Holland that the people of Rotterdam, a workmanlike bunch, buy their shirts with the sleeves already rolled up.

That's why the citizens took Everton and the club's multitudes of supporters to their hearts last Wednesday. They loved the way the Merseyside club demolished Rapid Vienna in the Cup Winners' Cup.

Yesterday, the people of Rotterdam would surely have draped their shirts around the shoulders of Manchester United's battling 10 men for the manner in which they outran and outplayed the opposition.

Norman Whiteside, one of the leading artisans, said he practises the move which won the Cup a lot. 'I like doing it in training so it was nice to see it come off at Wembley.' He also agreed it was easily the most difficult of the three chances he had had, however. 'Norman loves Wembley,' said United's manager Ron Atkinson. 'We should have realised he was sure to

22

score. As soon as he put that shot in flight I knew there was no way the ball would stay out.'

Dipping heavily into the hyperbole, Atkinson claimed; 'That's the greatest Cup win any side will have at Wembley, bearing everything in mind.' His excess of enthusiasm was, of course, understandable as was his bitterness about Kevin Moran's sending off.

'I didn't think it was deserved at the time and after seeing the television replay I now know the referee made a mistake. I suppose I will get a volley for saying that but if we had got beaten after such a decision I shudder to think what might have happened outside the stadium afterwards. It was not the sort of game that warranted a sending off.'

Moran also considered he was hard done by. 'I have never been sent off in my life before,' he said. 'I go in fair, not dirty and nobody thought I should have been sent off that time either. Peter Reid (who was involved in the foul) came over to me and said he couldn't believe the decision and Howard Kendall the Everton Manager told me the same.'

Perhaps Moran was unlucky. For certain if he was, he made up for all those lucky people who *hadn't* been sent off in over a hundred years of Cup Finals because no sending off was a tradition in this show-piece match. Sir Stanley Rous used to recall his own experience of warning a player in the final that he would be off if he committed another foul and having to deal sternly with the blithe answer that no one *could* be sent off in a Final. After Kevin Moran that myth no longer persists.

19 May 1985   *Ronald Atkin*

The Glory Game was the title of a book by Hunter Davies. In reviewing it Arthur Hopcraft was particularly impressed with the fact that it highlighted the other aspects as well. For him the most poignant passages were those dealing with the abject despair of professional footballers who had lost an important match.

1984 in the Dressing-room

Hunter Davies is a journalist, a novelist, the Beatles' biographer by appointment and a Tottenham Hotspur supporter. Last season he was permitted to live the football fan's dream of ultimate delight: he travelled with his team. The result is a fascinating book, 'The Glory Game'.

For his title he is indebted to a former Tottenham captain, Danny Blanchflower: 'The great fallacy is that the game is first and last about winning. It's nothing of the kind. The game is about glory.' Danny is an idealist, and as such he graced football on the field and left it abruptly when he recognised that his physical powers were waning. But Mr Davies's excellent book is the work of a realist, and it shows us that professional football is about many things other than glory.

There is, for example, the abject despair of these affluent athletes after defeat. Mr Davies describes the scene after Tottenham had lost a League Cup semi-final to Chelsea because one of the full-backs, Cyril Knowles, miskicked in the goalmouth:—

'It was the first time I'd heard the fan going in the dressing room . . . Its low, insistent hum seemed to reverberate round the walls, getting louder and louder, as if trying to drive everyone mad, an Orwell 1984 room, a torture chamber where everyone is face to face with his worst fears . . . Knowles seemed to be crying. His eyes were red and swollen. His arms were shaking. No one could look at anyone else.' There is an account of a train trip to an away match with a mob of skinheads that amuses and disturbs at once. We learn that Ralph Coates, bought by Tottenham from Burnley for £190,000, erupted in mysterious lumps through the sheer nervousness of waiting for the move to be completed.

A journey to a reserves match as the privileged passenger in Bill Nicholson's car gave Mr Davies a wealth of insight into the Tottenham manager's personality. Nicholson's wistful regret at the loss of Blanch-flower, the fulcrum of the Tottenham team that won the League Championship and the FA Cup in 1961, lingers with the reader as it obviously does with this tough, tramelled Yorkshireman.

'Since Danny went,' Nicholson told Mr Davies, 'I've never been able to talk as well to anyone about the team.' And he did not disguise his opinion that both the 1961 team and the one he himself played in a decade before were better than the one he manages now. Middle-aged managers, like middle-aged fans, have to soldier on with the game, even if the present lacks the joy of the past.

29 October 1972   *Arthur Hopcraft*

24

Writing for The Observer *while captaining Ireland in the 1958 World Cup, Danny Blanchflower took a more philosophical view of defeat.*

Chasing the Referee
(or Controlling Your Despair?)

Tylosand, Sweden, June 14
In the highly intensive world of professional football the sun rises and sets with alarming suddenness. This world turns over every 24 hours, but not with the smooth astronomical rhythm that compels our planet. It just gives a quick, impulsive spin, and the character who has been basking in the summit sunshine unexpectedly finds himself clinging desperately to the South Pole with cold, bare fingers.

The difference of performance between winning and losing a game is often a razor's edge; but the difference of feelings that accompany victory and defeat are always poles apart. Playing in the World Cup competition one is more aware of these feelings.

At this level a football match is no mere sporting occasion. The player carries on to the field responsibilities that would weaken the knees of any Cabinet Minister. He is there to represent his country and he knows that nothing short of victory will satisfy all those who share his nationality.

It is some consolation to realise that players of other countries fight the same fates and share the same feelings. I shall not forget the evidence of quiet despair as the Czechoslovakians retreated from the ground after we had defeated them last Sunday. I felt sorry for them. And I will always remember the extreme exhilaration of the Argentinians as they defeated us last Wednesday. Yet in their moment of triumph I believe they felt kindly towards us.

In some quiet way I was pleasantly surprised to read that the Russian goalkeeper had chased the referee after he had awarded a penalty to England last Sunday. It was a little reassuring to think that the much drilled and disciplined Russians could not entirely control their despair.

And a friend of mine brought me a glad little story which suggests that even the uninhibited Brazilians share in the general anxieties. A Brazilian journalist told him, 'The trouble with Brazilian football is that it is too platonic.' My friend was a little bewildered and remembering the colourful and exciting habits of the Brazilians explained that in English the word means something without passion. The Brazilian journalist just raised his eyebrows and remarked: 'Exactly, exactly. Brazilian football is too platonic. The ball is God. The goal does not matter.'

But as this competition quickens towards the finishing tape even the Brazilians will learn that the ball is not God and the goal matters very much. Each game becomes more tense and each goal explodes the highly charged atmosphere changing feelings from joy to despair.

14 June 1958   *Danny Blanchflower*

There is constant talk of 'fear' and 'pressure' on the players. They at least have the relief of action. At the highest level the pressure on managers can be a greater trial as Hugh McIlvanney found in the 1978 World Cup.

Bearing the World's Burden

When this World Cup is over the faces that will live most vividly in the memory will not be young and eager and shining with athleticism, but ageing and agitated and sucked hollow by dread.

They will be the faces not of the footballers but of the managers, those who compete by proxy, who must suffer on the touchline while their dreams and stratagems, their reputations and careers are left at the mercy of other men's talents and other men's courage.

No one who is following the competition, whether on a remote television screen or here in living close-up, can have failed to be amazed and alarmed at the depth of the strain imposed on these managers by what is supposed to be a sporting event. Enzo Bearzot of Italy is so emaciated by anxiety that he makes Sir Alex Douglas-Home look like the winner of a pie-eating contest. Cesar Luis Menotti of Argentina stares out desperately from the bench through a constantly thickening cloud of cigarette smoke. Marcos Calderon of Peru jumps up and down like a boxer's second who has just seen a hand grenade in the opponent's glove.

And, of course, there was Ally McLeod. After Scotland had played two matches he had the appearance of someone stumbling away from a plane crash.

These men give the impression of being slowly disembowelled by the demands made upon them, of being pushed to the edge of their resources and beyond by an insistent, mindless nationalism channelled at them in waves by journalists and broadcasters. That pressure combined as it is with the often squalid implications of the inexhaustible commercialism in football, the squabbles over bonuses and contracts with sports equipment manufacturers, makes most of them feel they are playing Russian roulette with a Gatling gun.

Of the 16 managers who reached the finals in Argentina hardly one has avoided experiencing some wearing drama or other. If it was not the kind of quiet coup by amateur officials that severely diminished the authority of Brazil's Claudio Coutinho it was the undignified shenanigans over makers' boot markings that left Michel Hidalgo of France angrily disillusioned with his gifted squad and impatient to be home, or the extraordinary attempt by some German reporters to harass and even to discredit Helmut Schoen.

The last phenomenon is a forceful reminder that the international team manager who quits while he is ahead of the game is a dramatic exception to the rule. Schoen, at 62, has the most impressive record in the modern game. Having taken West Germany to the World Cup final in 1966, the semi-final in 1970 and victory in the final of 1974 (as well as the European Championship in 1972 and second place in 1976) he long ago announced that he would hand over to Jupp Derwall after the present tournament and was entitled to expect that he would depart full of honours and with troops of friends.

Yet the failure of his attack to find scoring form in the early matches, and the consequent need to rely on his defence for survival, has brought such a sustained assault on Schoen's handling of the team that the president of the West German Football Association, Hermann Neuberger, felt obliged in the week to make a declaration of confidence in the old general and to call for more fairness from his critics. Schoen has a philosophical strength, a belief that his own *langmut*, his patience, will see him through. But he admitted during a long, quiet conversation on Friday that if he had known how hectic this World Cup would be, how thoughtless and excessive the public criticism would become, he would have tried harder than he did for an earlier retirement.

'The World Cups of 1958 and 1962 were garden parties compared with what is involved now, with the pressures that have developed,' he said. 'The increase in pressure seems continuous from one competition to the next. In 1966 it was already terrific, in 1970 it was worse, in 1974 still more terrible and now it is almost completely out of hand. In nearly all countries of the world football is the most popular sport and today the media bring it

27

to the masses and bring the feelings and demands of the masses back to those working in the game. Football has become almost a kind of war.'

Jack Charlton was in our small group around a dining table at Asochinga, the Germans' superb training camp 70 kilometres from Cordoba, and now Schoen, looking more than ever like a benevolent Basset hound, directed a sad thought at the former England centre half. 'It is my great fear,' he said, 'that one day, perhaps soon, the World Cup will no longer be the sporting event that you and I have enjoyed and competed in. It may all become too big, too important, too hard on the people concerned, just impossible to go on with.'

18 June 1978   *Hugh McIlvanney*

With fear a dominant feature of football at the top Peter Dobereiner included soccer in his investigation into whether fear could enhance as well as detract from performance.

Untroubled by Fear

Danny Blanchflower, architect and captain of the Spurs famous double team, was never troubled by fear, even on one memorable occasion when Jimmy Scoular picked him out for special and violent attention, accompanying each onslaught with, 'Take that, you Fenian bastard.' At half-time, as the teams walked from the pitch, Blanchflower remarked to Scoular, 'By the way, Jim, I'm a Protestant.' Scoular embraced him like a brother and switched his violence to other targets in the second half.

Blanchflower's main contribution to the team was intellectual. From start to finish of every match he was preoccupied with analysing the opposition's strength and weaknesses and planning ways to counter them. In distributing the ball he knew which of his men were the runners and wanted the pass ahead of them, and which were the ball-players who wanted it to their feet, but he also had a couple of players who were 'hiders'. They were good as gold once they received the ball, but apprehensive beforehand, putting themselves into eclipse behind defenders.

Blanchflower well understood this fear of getting the ball and knew how

28

it enhanced performance when the ball actually arrived, and he devised a repertoire of flicks, lobs and curled passes to find the 'hiders'.

30 October 1983   *Peter Dobereiner*

There has been no better indication of the emotions soccer can arouse and of the deep feelings which fans have for their heroes than the aftermath of the 1958 Munich air crash. Roy Perrott wrote of the bereavement which touched the whole country.

Old Trafford in Bereavement

The supporters at Old Trafford who have watched the young men of Manchester United develop from Saturday to Saturday, behaving on the terraces like so many anxious parents, are feeling personally bereaved.

It will be hard for them to forget the players who will not be seen again. There was Roger Byrne, the most immaculate of defenders on his day. He expounded his captaincy, so to speak, through his boots and his own play. Supporters will remember the times when, with the United goal under pressure, the dignity, as much as the precision, of one of Byrne's clearances was like a steadying word.

And who could possibly forget Whelan, that artistic inside-right, and his whimsical enjoyment of the game; or his odd way of making a dribble look like a progressive stagger, shuffling the ball through with pantomime feet; or his way of sketching out a grand tactical design with a pass, always entirely forgivable even when it did not come off. He was a Dublin lad. There was genius there.

Then, of course, Tommy Taylor, whose dash gave a heroic aspect to the United forward line on the big days – 'like a true Hotspur' as a late colleague described him at Belgrade. Or young Colman, the right-half, looking like a schoolboy but already delighting us with his wise, carpet-slippered touches . . . and so, too, the mercurial young Pegg, a match-winner on his day, and Mark Jones the centre-half, another player of steadily maturing skill.

There will be fervent hopes at Old Trafford that the injured players will

29

not have to hang up their boots. It would be unthinkable not to see the ebullient Edwards again and his way of approaching a goal like a child at a coconut-shy; or the witty inside-forward play of Viollet, or Blanchflower and the others.

All these, under Busby's most patient, schoolmastering, were just finding their wings as a team – almost certainly as one of the greatest of all times.

Matt Busby's masterly light touch in management gave the team its hallmark; he allowed his young players' talents to grow. So, although a good many of them were scarcely out of their schooldays, it was already a team rich in personalities. Their play in the era of the 'Babes' had a wonderful breath of freedom and imagination about it.

They had reached that happy stage at Old Trafford where the team and the supporters – the men from the sombre industrial suburbs on the terraces, the men from the city in the stands – were welded into a very solid community. Saturday afternoons were becoming family reunions. Inspiration on the great occasions passed both ways across the touchline. You could see this especially in those European Cup games under floodlights. No one who was there could possibly forget the great 10-goal victory against Anderlecht; or the superb battles with Borussia, Bilbao and Real Madrid.

The soaring plainsong of cheers from the terraces made them the most awesome sporting occasions many of us have ever seen. Every lover of the game will hope that those times will come again.

9 February 1958   *Roy Perrott*

Norris McWhirter used to compile a series for The Observer *on the main events of the week. On 5 April 1959 the lead item in his 'Seven Days of Sport' was devoted to football violence by South American players:*

Tearful International

Tear gas played a decisive part in the vital Brazil *v.* Uruguay match in the South American championships in Buenos Aires, Good Friday. Brazil's virtuoso centre-forward, Almir, ignited the already explosive situation when he tried to lay out the Uruguayan goalkeeper, Leiva.

The Uruguayans were soon winning with three Brazilians seriously injured against only moderate head injuries to their left back, Martinez. Aided by police and the liberal use of Chloracetophenone, the referee was able after 25 minutes' fighting to send off two combatants from each side.

The match was resumed with nine walking wounded a side. The Latin temperament having cooled from white to red heat, the Brazilian World Champions played with their accustomed ardour and clairvoyance to win 3–1. The deciding match between Brazil and Argentina is unlikely to be dull.

5 April 1959   *Norris McWhirter*

There is a sick side to soccer as well as a sad one. Too often it is the catalyst for violence and hooliganism. From afar it was possible to take a tragi-comic view of outrageous excesses abroad before the tragedies struck home for Britain too. So Chris Davies was able to take a light-hearted approach to a qualifying match between Honduras and Mexico in the run-up to the 1986 Finals:

Mexico v. Honduras

Mexico face Honduras today at noon knowing that if they fail to beat the hosts of the CONCACAF group in the Honduran capital of Teguci-galpa, they should stay there for a few weeks for their own safety.

Following their disaster in the 1978 World Cup Finals in Argentina, Mexican players were given a torrid time by their fans upon arriving home.

'They were waiting for us at the airport,' remembers their captain Leonardo Cuellar. 'I had police living in my home for 30 days. One or two of the other players were beaten up and had their cars smashed.'

Until you've seen a match in Tegucigalpa your soccer education isn't complete. The atmosphere in the stadium makes the Kop seem like a meeting of the noise-abatement society. It seats 50,000 and for afternoon games the supporters start to queue at 5.0 a.m. for the privilege of sitting in the shade out of the burning sun.

Honduras' earlier match with El Salvador was potentially explosive since when the two met in a World Cup qualifier, it signalled the start of the 100-Day War. Over 2,000 civilians, mainly Hondurans, were killed and El Salvador are now managed by the man who scored the winning goal last time round – Pipo Rodriguez.

However, under strict instructions from above the Honduran press did not mention the 1969 game. In the event the match ended 0–0 and Honduras were assured of qualification. It's a miracle El Salvador even has a football team. The players are so worried by the situation at home they will tell you they wake up thinking every day may be their last.

The best player of El Salvador was killed seven months ago by guerrillas and his body dumped in a dustbin. Three other players have had relatives murdered.

Chris Davies

In his 'Sidelines', David Randall wrote of footballing discords in Colombia which ended in death. Perhaps it was fortunate the 1986 World Cup was finally staged in Mexico.

Bucaramanga v. Athletico Juniors

Whatever carnage occurs next June when the Spanish police encounters the playful element among British football supporters, it will be as nothing compared with what could be achieved at the 1986 World Cup finals in Colombia. Here crowd disturbances are on an almost cosmic scale.

The recent league match between Bucaramanga and Athletico Juniors was a stunning demonstration of the Colombians' capabilities. With the home side losing 1–2 the game was proceeding in the usual atmosphere of acrimony and intemperance, the steady murmur of discontent from the terraces pierced only by the plaintive cries of the inebriate.

This delicate balance was upset when, in a mad moment, the referee overruled a linesman and refused the home team a penalty. Their supporters anxious that the laws of the game be properly applied, broke from their confines with revenge in their hearts. The referee, pausing only to ascertain the general direction of the nearest exit, fled the scene with the resentful mob in pursuit and closing all the time. He only just gained the sanctuary of a police-guarded changing-room in time.

But it was when army reinforcements were summoned that things began to get a little out of hand. The Colombian infantry, being somewhat deprived of actual combat experience, were determined not to squander this opportunity. Ordered to fire into the air, they took careful aim. Two spectators fell dead, one a 16-year-old boy, shot in the back. When hostilities ceased two more fans lay dead from beatings and three of the 40 injured were in hospital in a serious condition.

Meanwhile the South American press would hate anyone to draw any hasty conclusions from the riot. One paper commented, 'Such incidents should however have no bearing on the 1986 World Cup Finals scheduled to be staged in Colombia.' It adds reassuringly, 'South America's fanatical fans rarely work up anything like the same fanaticism for internationals.' They might not, but what about the army?

David Randall

In 1972 Colin Welland could still write humorously of boisterous and seemingly eccentric Leeds supporters having fun and being welcome abroad.

How we Taught the Turks the Meaning of Worship

If Soccer is the new religion I've just met the 12 Apostles. There they sat in Ankara Stadium, Turkish pastries wrapped around their faces, hurling healthy abuse at an inept Romanian referee, chatting 'intimately' from stand to pitch with Don, and Billy and Norman and swinging with reckless defiance on bank after bank of bloodthirsty Turks. 'Super Leeds,' they cried. 'Super Leeds' – their arms thrown wide in salute – and, passionately, they believed every word.

'Super Leeds' were performing a quiet, ultra-professional suffocating job on a local side all torrid and volatile, full of bounce but with no real football brains. As a policy it was predictable, and to be honest, it was boring. It was also completely inconsequential to the roaring enjoyment of an expeditionary force of 12 Leeds fanatics bent on football and a bloody good time.

Two thousand miles they'd come. Moving with the speed of light infantry – and under the cover of a blue-black sky – they hit the unsuspecting Turkish capital before last Tuesday's dawn . . . and soon even this city, well used to the petulance of old Mother Earth, was shuddering to its very foundations.

Mind you, who'd have guessed? We must have looked quite a respectable lot boarding the plane at Heathrow. A couple of local businessmen and wives, a Yorkshire League ref and son, who won the trip in a newspaper competition (people actually fill them in), a muck and brass type company director travelling alone – and (here's the crunch) four Bradford publicans who, with a master window cleaner called Big H, provided the party's real firepower. These last five were ready for anything. Inevitably anything wasn't available – but they sure made the most of what was.

On second thoughts perhaps Turkish Airlines should have realised when during the solemn search for arms Gilbert (who looked like Charlie Williams and had a voice to match) earnestly requested that the Arab passenger in long flowing robes be given another good do – as he looked like their kid – and he wouldn't trust *him* as far as he could throw him. Surely their suspicions should have been roused when, once airborne, Big H stood proudly and introduced himself to the crowded, sweaty cabin as H. Bower window cleaner, no job too large or small – as the rest laced the Turkish coffees with duty free Scotch explaining that that's how its done 'in the Gaelic'.

A wiser, more worldly crew would have radioed ahead crying 'Siege.' But then, despite their reputation, they're a kind-hearted lot, the Turks, and fate is often cruel to the kind.

Ankara, although the capital, is by our standards quite an unsophisticated place. Football there is still a game, not a creed. The men are gentle and cling to one another's arms. The women, though no longer veiled, are essentially demure.

Still, we were there to enjoy ourselves, and we set about doing just that. A guide was summoned to show us the sights. An earnest strip of a lad he was, a student, briefed in local ethnological history, eager to trace for us in detail the development of Turkish ceramic art. Give us our due, we gave him a hearing – enjoyed it – but it took a fleeting glimpse of a shapely ballerina flitting across the open doors of the State ballet rehearsal rooms to really fire our dormant imaginations. In a flash we were in with the chat.

'Dame Margot Fonteyn! Yes! Lovely!' The girls were kind and tolerant and we swept out triumphant to the sun and the mountain air and the spread of our chests.

Ankara was fast becoming our oyster when Leeds flew in and somebody mentioned football and the match. The match! What a fantastic experience that was – not the game, the event. The city, naïvely new to European football, was engagingly enthusiastic. Curious knots of locals clustered about us smiling, clutching our hands. We were proud to be Leedsites, here, miles from anywhere. We patted heads like newly descended gods as exotic sounds and smells crowded our senses.

Suddenly across the compound staggered an unearthly figure. It was hairy, wild-eyed and uttering weird cries, strangely familiar. 'A ticket lads – a ticket?' wailed the creature, his face festooned with mosquito bites. Eight days on the road he'd hitched from Leeds. We pressed him to our bosoms, tended his wounds and gave him a ticket. As he sobbed out his thanks we rebuked him and reminded him that in spite of all he was still British.

And so were we, like it or not. Once inside, Her Majesty's Consul opened his paternal arms and sat us firmly in his private enclosure surrounded by armed troops thoughtfully and insistently provided by the largest standing army in Europe. From what, we asked, were they protecting us? Kindness?

Leeds came, and saw and contained – like benign Victorian grandfathers ... but this was football à l'Orient, immune from 'civilising' influences. It was a game in which goalkeeper and penalty-taker embrace before the shot, linesmen throw bouquets of flowers to the crowd and bonfires and rockets celebrate a goal.

Afterwards we sat like kings surrounded by adoring Turks who whistled Leeds admiringly through their teeth. Superior beings will scoff at those who travel 2,000 miles to see a game of football. But our lives were enriched by this particular journey.

By necessity I had to leave the following day with half the week still to go. I flew home with the team and their speedily sobering chat of Leicester on Saturday and the points. I left behind the new Gilbert, and Big H and the rest lunching at the Embassy ... But later that evening, secure in the belief that language barriers just don't exist they'd be swopping yarns over black, sweet Turkish coffee with our new-found Ankaran friends.

I cannot help feeling that this beautiful city will look back with affection not only on the visit of Leeds United but of their 12 supporters.

17 September 1972   *Colin Welland*

A few years later the excessive enthusiasms had turned to unacceptable behaviour by growing numbers, and Welland himself was writing more seriously on 'How to Disarm the Football Hooligan'. Despite the concern, the investigations, the suggestions, the hooligan menace grew and moved inexorably to final tragedy and national disgrace. Eamonn McCabe, trying to photograph Platini, found himself focusing instead on bodies and destruction as the 1985 European Cup final became the chaos of the Heysel.

The Heysel

I heard a vicious crack as the wall broke. Arms were flailing everywhere, men and women were crying, but the chants in the stadium kept going.

People were going to die. It was soon evident that they were falling and getting crushed. Panic had taken over.

Soon there were bodies everywhere, blue with death. The brick dust covering the bodies gave them the appearance of having been there for a long time. I had come to photograph Platini (the Juventus captain) and had ended up photographing war.

I noticed middle-aged, plump Italian women lying on the floor clutching flags – dead. A man standing on the terrace in the middle of the bodies yelled, 'Carlo, Carlo,' not knowing if his friend had escaped to the field or had been removed dead.

I found myself working beside a French photographer taking pictures of the row of dead bodies outside the stadium. Suddenly a young man attacked him, cracking him on the back of his head.

I appealed to him to stop – he was hysterical, English, a Liverpool fan. I explained we had to do what we were doing but were hating every minute – he told me a Juventus fan had died in his arms.

He was distraught – we hugged each other: two strangers in the middle of all this horror.

As the terraces were cleared of the corpses, I was struck by all the shoes that had fallen off in the tide of panic. Some Liverpool fans, realising the extent of the tragedy, took a collection of money in a cardboard box.

They ran to the other end where the Juventus fans were still chanting 'Juve, Juve' and threw the money in.

A mad scramble followed as the young fans gathered the coins and notes.

But it was the wrong end; the people who lost their shoes and their lives had been at the other end.

2 June 1985   *Eamonn McCabe*

The 1989 FA Cup semi-final at Hillsborough on Saturady 15 April was an even blacker day for English football. Ninety-five fans died as overcrowding at the Liverpool end turned to unforeseen and unbelievable disaster. Millions watched in disbelief as television revealed the mounting toll from an incident the seriousness of which was not at first apparent even to those close by. This extract from Hugh McIlvanney's report described the scene as the tragedy developed below him:

Children Among Victims on Field of Tragedy

Only seven minutes of the match between Liverpool and Nottingham Forest had been played when bodies started tumbling over the high fence of metal bars and strong mesh fronting the shallow enclosure that housed a seething group of Merseyside fans.

All over what had been the Forest penalty area and far out on to the touchline under the main South Stand, small frantic huddles surrounded the worst of the casualties. In at least a dozen places a feverish pumping on chests left no doubt that there would be fatalities.

Some of the rescue workers bent over victims of the crush to try the kiss of life, but before long the steady procession of those being ferried away on makeshift stretchers made from advertising hoardings included a substantial number with their faces covered by articles of clothing.

The alarming sights were almost too numerous to be counted. Down on the touchline, 40 yards from the press box, one young man was undergoing the kind of violent massage that is often the last hope of saving a life. When he appeared to come round, a huge cheer went up and some of his mates around him began to dance in relief. But a policeman supervising the revival team waved at them to stay away. All too rapidly it became clear that their friend was slipping back towards death.

Firemen with oxygen equipment arrived, but for many they had come too late. One man was stripped down to his underpants and socks and shoes as his chest was thumped repeatedly for minute after minute. The signs were that his struggle, too, would be a losing one.

16 April 1989   *Hugh McIlvanney*

For the second time in four years Liverpool had to come to terms with football acting as catalyst to disaster and death as well as to triumph and joy. The following week Hugh McIlvanney looked at the social attitudes which underlay soccer's intense attraction. This time the main cause of tragedy was not hooliganism, but overcrowding on one of those open terraces so many fans still preferred to more comfortable seating.

The Lost Tribes

Many would cringe last week at the bathetic resonance of the Football Association's efforts to justify their decision to go ahead with this year's Cup Final in spite of the awful happenings in Sheffield eight days ago.

The Chief Executive of the F A, Mr Graham Kelly, declared that a Final at Wembley Stadium on 20 May would be a 'fitting memorial to those who gave their lives in the cause of football on Saturday'.

In the cause of football? Even normally sensible individuals can give way to jarringly inappropriate utterances in the aftermath of major calamities and – since words, good or bad, don't count for much in the overall context of suffering and grief – it is natural that spectacularly gross statements should draw no more than a passing wince. Certainly there is no virtue in being hard on Mr Kelly, who finds himself involved in a nightmare after only a couple of months in a new job.

But there is a very real significance in the fact that he felt no uneasiness about saying what he did. Such language came readily to his lips because it is a direct echo of the desperately exaggerated importance which so many in Britain tend to attach to football.

Everybody knows that after the astonishingly rapid popularisation of the professional game in the latter part of the nineteenth century it grew to occupy an absolutely (indeed alarmingly) central place in the cultural experience of millions of working class people.

Inevitably less well understood is the complex way in which football, while continuing to have an extraordinarily pervasive and totemic relevance for a substantial percentage of the population, has found its total following appreciably reduced and attitudes to it considerably altered by processes of social change that have been dramatically accelerated under the Thatcher Government.

Hooliganism is only one extreme manifestation of a haphazard but profound adjustment in the nation's relationship with its favourite sport. And maybe it isn't the most telling one, since there must be a fair measure of truth in the argument that football's main contribution to the hooligan plague comes through the provision of clan banners and obvious battle-grounds for elements whose violence is too serious to be dissipated by the mere removal of such conveniences.

Thuggery had nothing to do with the terrible events at Hillsborough, but the behaviour of football supporters towards one another assuredly did. Grief over all the innocent victims and sympathy with the families left heartbroken cannot be allowed to obscure that reality. Of course, others in the end may be held far more culpable. Large, excited crowds can never be depended upon to behave rationally, even with self-preservation as an incentive. They have to be protected from themselves and at Hillsborough that job would seem to have been badly mishandled.

There was a fatal distortion of priorities that had its origins in the thinking responsible for the iniquitous and ill-designed containment fences which denied escape from the brutal crush at the Leppings Lane end of the ground. Something of the same negative cast of mind could be discerned in the slowness with which the police realised that they were dealing not with disorder but disaster.

Perhaps it is understandable that policemen go to football matches these days with their thoughts concentrated on keeping hostile mobs at bay rather than on supervising the safety of a mass audience. But that predis-position carries the seeds of deadly consequences.

It is especially dangerous because of how it interacts with an unmistak-able change in the mentality of football crowds. The memory of craning on tip-toe as a schoolboy in a crowd of 143,000 at Hampden Park, feeling scared for a while as others of my age and younger were passed from hand to hand down the great slope of the terracing to the perimeter track, but soon being able to relax sufficiently to enjoy a tight struggle between Rangers and Hibernian, makes me shudder now at the awareness of how much potential for catastrophe there was in allowing such numbers to cram together in vast standing, violently swaying congregations.

That more dreadful accidents did not occur in those far-off days (when 135,000 was the regularly reached capacity at Hampden, whereas 73,000 is the old ground's current limit) may have been due to the greater prevalence of a passive herd instinct among spectators.

Probably there was more inclination to yield to authority, whether it was the boss or a policeman on a horse, and maybe generations of being treated like cattle had made fans almost as docile. The treatment has not improved more than marginally, though the responses can be very different.

There is an anachronistic shortage of seating at all but two or three British stadiums, and some of the biggest clubs betray no embarrassment about letting the tenants of their executive boxes look out – with large drinks in their hands – on hard-core supporters who are pressed together in outrageous discomfort, lumbered with a poor view of the action and a fair chance of having their shoes splashed with urine.

To their credit, Liverpool FC have so far declined to follow the trend towards those fancy boxes for corporate clients, but there should be relief that the Kop, for all its romantic connotations, will shortly be replaced with seating.

The ambiguous feelings likely to be stirred by that overdue modernisation of Anfield, and similar updating of other grounds, points to the peculiar mix of values today's football crowds are liable to take to the stadium. In many senses they are pretty much, probably too much, as they always were, but in others they are not at all the same.

They are patently more fragmented and volatile than in the past and the conviction that they are definitely less easily controlled is not undermined by the knowledge that fans who broke through closed gates precipitated the crush that caused 33 deaths at Bolton in 1946.

Perhaps the frightening scene enacted outside a gate at the west end of Hillsborough immediately before the Liverpool–Nottingham Forest kick-off could just as easily have developed 40 years ago, but it is hard to believe that the presence of a few mounted policemen would not have had far more disciplining impact than was achieved last weekend. The police of the earlier era would have expected that to be the case and so would those they were marshalling.

It is 21 years since Arthur Hopcraft produced one of the best books ever written about the game, *The Football Man*, but several of the assertions he made in his introduction are as pertinent today as they were in 1968:

'The point about football in Britain is that it is not just a sport people take to, like cricket or tennis or running long distances. It is inherent in the people. It is built into the urban psyche, as much a common experience to our children as are uncles and school. It is not a phenomenon; it is an everyday matter. There is more eccentricity in deliberately disregarding it than in devoting a life to it. It has more significance in the national character than theatre has.'

Hopcraft would be the first to acknowledge that football is not basic to the fabric of nearly as many lives now as it was then. He would admit, too, that another claim in *The Football Man* – that the game's 'sudden withdrawal from the people would bring deeper disconsolation than to deprive them of television' – is now utterly untenable.

Given the increasing unevenness of the contest between TV and all other leisure activities in this country – and considering the extent to which the standards of skill and entertainment offered by football have plummeted since the days when Hopcraft regularly watched such as Best, Law, Charlton and Crerand perform in the same Manchester United team – what is amazing is how much of its hold on the urban psyche this sport has retained. . . .

At a deeper level it appears that the battering suffered in Thatcher's Britain by our industrial strongholds of the past, like Liverpool, to name the week's most relevant example, has left tens of thousands needing football as much as their forebears ever did. They need it as an escape from the drabness imposed by unemployment and poverty, and they need it for the defiant sense of unity they can find in the crowd, a rough camaraderie that was more of an everyday experience when factories were big and busy.

From the terracing they can, for an hour or two at least, look down on Yuppiedom with unanimous contempt. But at football grounds, as elsewhere, they run the risk of being too ready to accept deprivation and callous treatment as their natural inheritance. They should convince themselves first, and then those who take their money, that the old pleasure of watching football is not contaminated by a few modern comforts.

A great deal requires to be done if a repetition of the Hillsborough carnage is to become unimaginable. But it would be a crucial first step if Britain's vast football public started to press their case on the basis that even addicts have rights.

23 April 1989   *Hugh McIlvanney*

That week too John Sweeney visited Liverpool to report on a city in shock and grief. This extract reflected the mood of the city and the scene at Anfield.

The Cellophane Shrine

When the wind soughs in from the Irish Sea, the thousands upon thousands of cellophane-wrapped wreaths crowding the Kop's goalmouth at Anfield whisper like dead leaves. It is all the more eerie for such a slight, dry, thin sound.

The cellophane shrine at Anfield has become the focal point of Liverpool as it comes to terms with the Hillsborough disaster. It is so miserable you are often caught out wanting to block the whole wretched thing from your mind, but there is no other place in the city where it feels right to be.

To the eye Anfield is a curiously gaily coloured shrine, in its reds and blues and whites more like a Hindu temple or a Buddhist shrine than a Christian place of mourning. When the sun shines, the light bounces off the cellophane like the sea. The paintbox colours are given the lie, however, by the one face in every 10 or 20 shattered with grief; the thick-set, tough-necked Scousers clutching yet another wreath to add to the whispering. It smells like a florist's shop. . . .

Days after the disaster, the cellophane-and-scarf shrine is still drawing in huge numbers of people. Their faces tell their stories. Some weep publicly; others walk high up into the stands and sob quietly. Still others are there to show their sympathy and respect, but also to see for themselves the spectacle of a city's mass grief. The Anfield shrine with its long queue wrapped round the ground provokes comparison with Lenin's tomb; there is the same reverence, the same sense of a religious need fulfilled.

Disasters catch people unawares, unthinking. No doubt the BBC interviewer who asked Liverpool manager Kenny Dalglish 'How do you feel, second time around?' now wishes his mind had come up with something better, but the moment is past.

The tabloids had heaped agony on agony, blown up and extruded 'facts' where they had no need to. The simple narrative of the tragedy was story enough. That, and the daily reality of life in the city the disaster had scythed through.

23 April 1989   *John Sweeney*

Peter Corrigan then pointed to The Saving Grace of Liverpool, whose club and players acted with calm and dignity.

The Saving Grace of Liverpool

For any clear thoughts on the Hillsborough disaster to survive last week's chaos of outrage and denunciation one's eyes had to be firmly focused upon Liverpool Football Club, whose calm bearing was a telling contrast to the irrational reactions of those who ought to have been displaying the leadership and reassurance vital to such a time.

Although at the epicentre of the shock and grief, the club showed not a flicker of panic or anger, nor did they fall to the temptation of spraying blame around like a burst from a machine gun.

God knows they had cause to, given their opposition to that venue, but they let the storm rage around them and concentrated on the practicalities of what could be done for their bereaved and injured, and how they could best serve the game and their followers in future. Only once did they show a shiver of annoyance. When the Football Association hurriedly and crassly announced a new date for the fixture that will forever be an accursed memory, the Liverpool board shamed them for bothering with such details at a time when their entire attention was on their people.

It was just one example of the inadequacies displayed by the football authorities as they sought to come to terms with the tragedy, and again we must wonder if there is enough wisdom in that quarter to manoeuvre our national game out of the calamitous cul-de-sac into which it is wedged.

It was Liverpool's manager Kenny Dalglish, ironically much criticised for his lack of public relations acumen, who set the tone of sincere and respectful concern for those most affected and it was taken up by his players, who appeared at services, hospitals, funerals and among the crowds at Anfield – not regimented as a team but spontaneously, in ones and twos, blending into the background of the mourning.

And, as they threw open the doors of Anfield as a shrine to comfort and unite the grieving, Liverpool found time to indicate unflinchingly what must be done to avoid future catastrophes. Since it involves adding the name of their beloved Kop to the list of casualties, it was a profoundly difficult gesture to have to make.

But it was necessary. It is one thing for the Home Secretary to announce a need for all-seater grounds. That was just a political pronouncement that might or might not get through the necessary legislation. When Liverpool announced the death of the Kop, all-seater stadiums became a certainty.

Many other reforms are possible if football can be made to face up to such brave decisions. Among the game's great handicaps are the chains that bind the clubs, and the millions who follow them, to our footballing past.

43

One legacy from that fearful tragedy is the sudden realisation that the packed terracings from which so many of us fell in love with soccer can no longer be tolerated. We continued to defend them as an essential part of the game's fabric even when they bred the hooliganism that was the underlying cause of most of the elements leading to the events at Hillsborough. But any facet of football capable of creating such horror must be removed.

Given such a good reason to look objectively upon those swaying banks, they seem as relevant to modern football as the queue for the one-and-nines is to the film industry. In any case, if Liverpool can surrender the Kop what argument can other clubs have against following suit?

This development, and the wide brief given to Lord Justice Taylor's inquiry into Hillsborough and the lessons to be learned, creates a completely new atmosphere in which to discuss the future of soccer-watching in this country and would appear to make the government's *blitzkrieg* on identity cards irrelevant, at least temporarily.

I was in favour of a modified version of the scheme because I recognised the need for some control but events have unquestionably overtaken it. However, it represents the only firm measure against violence generally that Mrs Thatcher has proposed and I fear that persuading her to drop it is like getting a bone off a Rottweiler.

It is vital, meanwhile, that hooliganism does not reveal itself and there is some anxiety attached to the ripping out of perimeter fences. There is no doubt that the fencing assisted the tragedy but I believe the inquiry will reveal that the lateral fences, creating that fatal pen, made a much bigger contribution and they were there at the instigation of the police and not to prevent pitch invasion.

Liverpool's first thought was that the fence in front of the Kop should stay. Subsequently, they yielded to public opinion and agreed to remove it, stressing that they were placing a trust in the fans.

There is a body of opinion that the shock of Hillsborough will cool down the hot-headedness that leads to hooliganism. I am wary of such confidence but it is right to test any willingness on behalf of our crowds to exercise some self-control, and no better place exists for that to be witnessed than Anfield.

Allegations of misbehaviour by Liverpool fans in Sheffield were grossly insensitive last week but it cannot be avoided that the passion and volatile enthusiasm of the club's followers has now been a major factor in the game's last two big disasters, however different the circumstances.

It was a point certainly not overlooked by officials and commentators abroad. Many countries observed pre-match silences and the San Siro stadium in Milan gave a moving rendition of the Anfield anthem 'You'll Never Walk Alone' before the European Cup semi-final on Wednesday, but less sympathetic voices were damning the Liverpool fans and calling for the ban on English clubs to be continued indefinitely.

Unfriendly eyes will be watching every disturbance and if the Government genuinely want to aid the game through this tortured time they must co-operate to dissuade supporters from following the England national team on their visits to the continent between now and next year's World Cup. They must also heed the pleas to divert some of the annual £250 million football earns them in tax into assisting it to bring more seats into the stadiums.

More immediately, Liverpool will have to decide what they want to do about the unfinished semi-final against Nottingham Forest. There can surely be no meaning left in this season's competition. It has been suggested that a Liverpool–Everton final at Wembley would be a fitting tribute to the dead – a blank on the FA Cup where the winner's name should be would be more honestly appropriate.

Liverpool would want to win for the sake of their dead. Would Everton want to stop them? Football is nothing if not competitive, and they realise that on Merseyside more than anywhere.

It is better for Liverpool and football to begin immediately to plan the rebuilding of the game and its surroundings. There's much to be considered, many old attitudes to be laid to rest along with the fallen.

But if fate had to select one club to bear the brunt of football's failings and lead this shambles of a game to a better future, it chose wisely.

23 April 1989   *Peter Corrigan*

CHAPTER 2

The Cup

There are now innumerable Cup competitions, but only one is instantly recognisable as 'The Cup'. The Football Association Challenge Cup is the oldest and most honoured of them all. Alan Ross thus described its special fascination in a 1954 introduction to a routine round-up of a day's results:

The Cup Never Fails

The Cup never fails. Round about now when interest begins to slacken in the League-exhausted corpse of football, its piracy and plunder act as a magic restorative. The mighty are humbled, the lowly bask in a gleam of limelight. Most important of all the turnstiles click to a quicker music.

For many clubs who have long since become wallflowers in the League – of little interest to anyone except addicts – the Cup is as good as a facelift. They have a second chance. In consequence what everyone secretly hopes is that the League delinquents will knock the lordly ones off their perch; that, apart from their own team winning, as many famous and dangerous sides as possible should be swept out of the way.

A 'good' round is a surprising round. Naturally enough though one wants Wembley ultimately to be graced by two attractive sides.

Alan Ross

That December Alan Ross was prescient enough to include West Bromwich Albion as his choice of a likely winner. The Observer was not so quick to spot the Cup itself as a likely winner with the public. It was indeed some eleven years after the historic 1–0 victory of the Wanderers over the Royal Engineers at Kennington Oval in March 1872 that The Observer *first gave even the briefest mention to any Cup Final. In those early years the Final was dated and timed so that the rival teams could first watch the Boat Race. Clearly that then had the compelling attraction which applied later to the Wembley Final. As Robertson-Glasgow wrote in a sporting print:*

Sporting Print

'One moment stood he as the angels stand, the next he was not.' Each early spring when the Oxford and Cambridge Boat Race race and the daffodils come round these words of the poet float into my mind. For in no other athletic competition are the names and qualities and weights of the contestants so long and so exactly presented to the public and then so totally forgotten . . . And yet there can be few players of other games who do not, from their soul, envy the oarsmen of Oxford and Cambridge on the great day. The banks are black with spectators. Father is Oxford because he always was. Auntie is Cambridge because she likes the colour. They're off. For twenty minutes of sweat and glory. Ah yes it's worth an age without a name.

R. C. Robertson-Glasgow

———————————

On that first Cup Final day The Observer, *which usually included only one column on sport, gave one full page of its eight to the Boat Race, but not one word of the Wanderers' win. Since then, however, it has recorded many memorable Finals with names which still live in the memory. The first mention of Cup football was in 1882. But the match at the Oval was not the Cup Final in which Old Etonians beat Blackburn Rovers. Instead, sandwiched between athletics at Harrow School and a report of the lacrosse match played before the football,*

*was an account of a game between the previous Cup holders, the Old
Carthusians and the Old Etonians with the proceeds going to charity
and the Old Carthusians again the victors.*

In May 1983 The Observer *had a leader on its sports pages headed
'Born again – the people's game in its dying hour'. This eulogised
Blackburn Olympic's 1883 Cup Final win as a seminal event in soccer
history and therefore of immense social significance worldwide.*

The people's game has suddenly made a comeback. Just as the curtain was
about to drop on an ominous, inglorious season football has become itself
again. . . .

That football should be regaining its popularity among the people,
however briefly, at this time could not be more appropriate because it is
exactly 100 years ago that the game first reached out to embrace the masses.

The FA Cup Final of 1883 between Old Etonians and Blackburn
Olympic can be marked as the match that gave football to the working class
and, eventually, to the world.

Before then organised football had been dominated by the upper class
and the first 12 Cup Finals won by former public schools players.
Blackburn Rovers, beaten by Old Etonians in the 1882 Final, were the first
working-class side to get that far.

In 1883 their rivals, Blackburn Olympic, reached the Final, also meeting
the Old Etonians before a crowd of 8,000 at Kennington Oval. The score
was level at 1–1 after normal time and, according to *Athletic News*, extra
time began with the Eton forwards 'completely done up'. After Olympic
had scored the winning goal the Cup was presented to 'somewhat reluctant
applause'.

In contrast Olympic were welcomed back to Blackburn by a wildly
enthusiastic crowd displaying their joy at what the *Blackburn Times* called
'a signal victory of the plebeian over patrician Englishmen'.

There were complaints that Blackburn had played too hard and had
spent three weeks in strict training. The *Eton College Chronicle* said
darkly, 'It may seem strange that a football 11 composed of mill-hands and
working men should be able to sacrifice three weeks to train for one match,
and to find the means to do so.'

The professionalism they hinted at became official two years later and no
public school side ever got near the FA Cup again. The people's game had
been born.

That it is now the not-so-many people's game is the concern of all admirers of football's better facets. To have a brief respite from that worry as the game celebrates a true century as our national passion is welcome.

5 May 1983

The leader doesn't mention it, but the 1883 Final was in fact the first one about which an account appeared in The Observer. *Inevitably this was somewhat more prosaic and with no indication of the great importance of the event.*

The Association Challenge Cup

Yesterday the deciding trial in this competition came off at Kennington Oval. The attendance was very large. The opposing teams were the Old Etonians and the Blackburn Olympic, and the latter won the honour of holding the cup. In the first half the Old Etonians scored a goal, kicked by Goodhart, but matters were balanced when Massie got the leather through. At the call of time the score stood at a goal each, and then the extra half-hour was entered upon. A very exciting struggle followed, and at about fifteen minutes from the call of time Costley headed the ball through, and no further score being made, Blackburn were winners by two goals to one. The Cup was presented by Major Marindin, and Mr Coddington, MP for Blackburn, acknowledged the compliment on behalf of the winners. The Etonians suffered a severe loss through Dunn getting damaged during the first half, but by way of a set-off the Blackburn team had three of their men crippled. It was a grandly-contested trial, and the Blackburn men won by fast play and good condition. Sides:—

Blackburn Olympic. – J. Yates and J. Costley (right wing), G. Wilson, A. Matthews, and T. Dewhurst (left wing), forwards; J. Gibson, J. Hunter, and W. Astley (half-backs), J. H. Ward and S. A. Warburton (backs), T. Hacking (goal keeper).

Old Etonians. – J. F. P. Rawlinson (goal keeper), T. H. French and P. J. de Paravicini (backs), Hon. A. F. Kinnaird (captain) and C. W. Foley (half-backs), W. J. Anderson and J. B. T. Chevallier (right wing), and H. W.

Bainbridge and A. T. B. Dunn (left wing), R. H. Macaulay and H. C. Goodhart (centres).

5 May 1883

The same restrained and anonymous writing pervades the account of another memorable Final eighteen years later which saw non-league Tottenham bring the Cup back south.

The Football Association Challenge Cup

Replayed Final Tie

Tottenham Hotspur v Sheffield United

At Burnden Park, Bolton, yesterday, Tottenham Hotspur and Sheffield United again met in the final tie of the Association, and after a very fast and thoroughly interesting match Tottenham Hotspur won by three goals to one. Thus for the first time since 1883 a southern club has won the cup. On the previous Saturday the teams had played a drawn game of two goals each at the Crystal Palace, and although the Everton ground had been fixed for the replay if necessary it was decided, after a protest from Liverpool, to play the match again at Bolton. The ground is hardly suitable for an important engagement, a ridge running down the centre of the field of play with strong slopes to the goals and touch lines. Fears had been expressed that the accommodation would prove insufficient for a large crowd, but there were not more than 30,000 people present, and several of the stand seats were empty. During the week the teams had been engaged in quiet work at the seaside, Tottenham staying at Southport and Sheffield at Lytham, and when, at half-past three, the game was started, the elevens were precisely the same as had appeared at the Palace.

With the wind in their favour, Tottenham had decidedly the better of the opening exchanges, and quite early Johnson cleared, when the situation looked dangerous for Sheffield. A little later, too, Thickett had to save, while at the opposite end the Tottenham backs did a lot of good work. Tottenham, however, kept up a persistent attack, but the Sheffield defence was admirable, Needham and Johnson being particularly good. Occasionally the Sheffield forwards would break away, but they were invariably pulled up by Erentz or Tait, and the play transferred to the other end. Once Kirwan sent in a shot which hit the side of the net, and Foulke had also to run out and kick away from Brown. Towards half-time, however, Sheffield played better, and more than held their own, Needham, Priest and Hedley doing any amount of fine work. Gradually the Tottenham half-backs were beaten, and Clawley was called upon to save from Needham. Nearing the interval the Sheffield goal had a narrow escape, and then after forty minutes play Needham made an opening for Lipsham, who centred well and enabled Priest to score for Sheffield United, who changed ends, leading by one goal to none.

Sheffield began the second half in vigorous style, but they were soon checked, and seven minutes after the resumption a mistake by Thickett let in Copeland. That player centred to Brown, who passed the ball on, and Cameron, with a low, swift shot, equalised the scores. From this Sheffield set up a hot attack, and Clawley had a shot from Hedley to save. Time after time a pretty piece of passing among the Sheffield forwards was brought off, but the Tottenham defence proved admirable, and danger was averted. At length the Tottenham men settled down to a good combined game, the half-backs defending cleverly, and feeding their forwards in skilful manner. It was not, however, till thirty minutes had gone by that they met with further success; then Cameron had a shot at goal, and the ball striking Boyle glanced off to one side. Smith at once dashed up and put the ball into the net. This point practically settled the result, for after a short attack by Sheffield the Tottenham forwards played up very strongly and maintained a vigorous pressure on the Sheffield goal. This soon took effect, and four minutes from the finish Brown headed the third goal from a well placed corner kick. Sheffield struggled hard, but could not get through, and thus the final score was:— Tottenham Hotspur, three goals; Sheffield United, one goal. Teams:—

Sheffield United. – Foulke, goal; Thickett and Boyle, backs; Johnson, Morren, and Needham, half-backs; Bennett, Field, Hedley, Priest and Lipsham, forwards.

Tottenham Hotspur. – Clawley, goal; Erentz and Tait, backs; Morris, Hughes, and Jones, half-backs; Smith, Cameron, Brown, Copeland, and Kirwan, forwards.

Referee, Mr. A. Kingscott (Derby); Linesmen, Messrs. C. Squires (London) and A. G. Hines (Nottingham).

28 April 1901

The first Cup Final at Wembley in 1923 was memorable for the vast crowd which poured in and the chaotic scenes before the game. No surprise that the match itself was of no great quality. But seeing what was to happen at the Heysel 62 years later it is indeed remarkable that it was all resolved without tragedy. That was clearly due to the totally different behaviour of spectators in those days and the way the police coped with an unforeseen emergency. Much credit for clearing the pitch went to the policeman on the white horse, Constable Scorey, who didn't rate a mention in The Observer *account.*

Bolton Secure the Cup

Greatest Crowd on Record

THE ENCLOSURE INVADED

❊   ❊

EXTRAORDINARY SCENES

❊   ❊

PLAY DELAYED

❊   ❊

FOOTBALL UNDER DIFFICULTIES

❊   ❊

THE RESULT TO STAND – OFFICIAL

After scenes of an unprecedented character in the long history of Cup football, the final was played at the Wembley Stadium yesterday and resulted in the Bolton Wanderers defeating West Ham by two goals to nil. The north-country team thus lifted the trophy for the first time on the occasion of their fourth appearance in the final.

The scenes before the match was begun, some three-quarters of an hour after the authorised time, were of a truly amazing character. Capable of holding 125,000 spectators the new stadium was invaded to such an extent that at three o'clock, when the match should have begun, thousands of people were on the playing pitch, and all the efforts of officials and mounted police to clear them were useless.

The teams made their way onto the ground and endeavoured to urge the crowd to leave the field of play. The teams made their way across the field to be presented to the Royal box to be presented to the King, and returning again in single file to the ground the players were at once surrounded by a huge crowd. Finally the game was begun at 3.44 but had to be stopped after eleven minutes of play, owing to the crowd encroaching again. The game, however, was continued and it is stated that the match is officially recognised as the F A Cup Final.

After the conclusion of the game the King presented the Cup to J. Smith, the Bolton captain, and the medals to the players. There was an enormous crowd in front of the Royal Box, and His Majesty received an Ovation that has rarely been heard on a football ground. The fervour with which the National Anthem was sung was in the highest degree inspiring.

OFFICIAL STATEMENT

OVER 200,000 PEOPLE AT THE STADIUM

An official statement issued by the exhibition authorities of the scene of yesterday's match is as follows:

The turnstiles were open shortly before 11.30 a.m., in accordance with the official statement issued to the Press. Between 11.30 and one o'clock the inflow of traffic was steady. After one o'clock the pressure of the crowd became very great. At 1.30 p.m. a complete inspection was made of the packing of the crowd, and at 1.45 p.m., when the returns showed that the standing accommodation was nearly full, instructions were given for all gates to be closed.

Information was telephoned through to the London termini to inform them that the Stadium was now full. During the following half-hour thousands of people continued to arrive by road and rail, and massed round outside the entrances. At 2 p.m. the police authorities were requested to telephone to Scotland Yard for a large force of mounted police. Telephonic messages had previously been sent to every police station in the immediate districts.

At 2.15 p.m. the crowd broke through all the barriers, and from then until the arrival of the King it is estimated that 100,000 people got through. The inner entrances to the Stadium and the staircases leading to the reserve seats had already been closed except to ticket-holders, many of whom were unable to reach their seats.

The pressure of the crowd was so great that some of these barriers broke down, and certain sections of the reserved seats were occupied by the people who had burst the outer barriers. In other cases a crowd climbed over the railings both of the outer and inner barriers.

At 2.45 the arrival of the King relieved the pressure of the Stadium, as thousands lined the route to cheer His Majesty.

At three o'clock the Metropolitan Railway and the London and North-Eastern Railway were asked to start running their return trains, and every effort was made to persuade those who were unable to get into the Stadium to leave by one or the other route. To facilitate the exit gates at the northern and eastern entrances were thrown open, and instructions given to remove portions of the fence separating the Stadium from the rest of the park.

The total number of people who either paid for admission or broke down the barriers may be estimated to have exceeded 200,000. The total estimated capacity of the stadium is 127,000, and probably 150,000 got a good view of the match.

After the game, the manner in which the crowd was able to disperse was very much to the credit of the arrangement, as the multitude melted away rapidly and comfortably, and it is only fair to make this statement in view of the unfortunate scenes before the game.

29 April 1923

J. A. H. Catton, the most respected football writer of his day, covered many matches for The Observer. *The following is his account of the 1932 Cup Final in which the controversial 'ball-over-the-line' incident played so important a part in Arsenal's defeat.*

Newcastle Victorious

Sports Pageant Honoured

THE KING AND QUEEN PRESENT

ARSENAL'S LUCK SLUMPS

THE BETTER SIDE GAINS THE DAY

Newcastle United 2 Arsenal 1

The Association Cup has been won by Newcastle United for the second time in post-war football. Thus the Tyneside team has surpassed all the glories of their illustrious predecessors in the long ago. Newcastle won by 2–1; a slight margin when all circumstances were considered, for, well as Arsenal played at times, they were not consistent. Had they been able to reach their own standard in their victorious final everyone would have been surprised. There was a lack of balance in the Arsenal attack. When James, the inside-left, the scheming adventurer of the vanguard, was absent, the driving-wheel was not working.

This is not said to minimise the success of Newcastle. The fact has to be recorded that Arsenal were without their greatest forward, and the arrangement of the forwards was not satisfactory. Nor can one suggest any plan that would have overcome the loss of the services of James. For once in a way a man who was indispensable and could not be replaced has been found. Arsenal have had, according to all evidence, a run of luck. Dame Fortune deserted the club for this event.

The ground was full, with its 92,000 spectators, when the King arrived, amidst a tremendous outburst of enthusiasm. The singing of the National Anthem by the crowd was done with such fervour that it made the occasion a memorable one. The King went on to the ground, where the players were presented to him in turn, to receive a handshake and a word of encouragement. His Majesty was accompanied by the Queen.

The game was well contested in the first half, and the interval score of one goal each was a fair reflection of the struggle. Arsenal relied on keeping the ball loose. Swinging passes to the wings, especially to Hulme on the right, was the mode of advance forward. Jack, Male, Jones, and everybody seemed bent on providing Hulme with opportunities.

The man who had been under suspicion of an injured leg responded gallantly. One of Hulme's cross-kicks went to Bastin at inside-left, and he shot splendidly, but McInroy was able to turn the ball over the crossbar. The flag-kick was headed out, and Newcastle made a raid on the left, but Moss cleared the centre by running out. Boyd was also prominent for his thrusts on the right. For nearly a quarter of an hour the game was fairly level. Then Hulme led another advance and swung the ball over to the left wing.

Nelson had his chance to clear, although John, the outside-left, grappled with him. Nelson went to the ground, and McInroy ran out to the rescue. The ball bobbed up in the air, and John quietly headed it into the goal without a guardian. Arsenal relied on their open game, and John was again placed in possession, but this time his effort went over the bar.

Newcastle began to get a grip on the game, and Weaver was the motive power in general, although McKenzie was also a prompter on the other wing. The Newcastle forwards were very persevering but encountered a strong defence by Roberts, Hapgood, and Moss. Arsenal were playing with one wing and Newcastle with two. Seven minutes from half-time Newcastle were able to equalise. The right wing manoeuvred and took the ball right up to the goal-line. Indeed, in the struggle the ball was forced over the goal-line. This was about twelve yards to the left of Moss in the goal. From the elevated seats of the grand stand one saw the white goal-line, a space of about six inches of grass, and then the ball, which was hooked back in front of the goal and headed into the net by Allen. The referee, who was outside the penalty area, pointed to the centre, but Moss promptly ran out to protest that the ball had been out of play. Other players were obviously of the same opinion, but as Mr Harper was firm the London players retired.

The view of the writer was clear. There was no doubt that the whole ball was over the goal-line. One cannot understand that the linesman could not see the position, for it was quite possible for the referee to be unsighted. The spectators near this deponent confirmed the impression that the ball was over the goal-line, and one of them who had refereed the Final said without prompting that the ball was one foot over the line. The goal, of course, had to stand, but there can be no doubt that a mistake was made.

This success evoked a continuous stimulating roar by the supporters of Newcastle, who were cheering their men on. It was like a sustained diapason, and to this throbbing accompaniment Newcastle responded. Roberts was a foil to their efforts and behind him Moss was magnificent. Just as the interval drew near Moss made a wonderful save. The ball came from the left wing and Boyd, rushing in, headed down. The ball was near the foot of the post when Moss dived and pushed it round the post, but there was not time to take the corner-kick before the whistle blew.

In the second half the football was not so good. The concerted movements were constantly broken up. The game became scrappy. All the same, as soon as the game was resumed Newcastle attacked and Boyd again tried to score. Moss, with another effort similar to that which he had just made, saved the situation. Indeed, Moss had much to do, for Newcastle were now the quicker in every respect and they were continually getting the ball. Occasionally McInroy was called into action, but Bastin was once half a yard too slow and Hulme got his toe to a ball which was sliced.

After Lang had wasted an opportunity Allen delivered a fine straight drive which Moss saved as it was just beneath the bar.

When twenty-five minutes in the latter portion had passed away

Newcastle got the deciding goal. There was a pass down the centre and Roberts did not meet it. He faltered. Allen sprang to his opportunity and dribbled on for a yard or two. Possibly Allen was amazed at the situation, for he seemed to dally, to delay as if he were wondering what to do. At last – it seemed a long time – he turned the ball to the left of Moss, who fell on the ground too late. The ball eluded him and rolled at an ordinary pace into the net.

Newcastle again tested Moss, but Arsenal rallied. They fought to defy Fate. A fine dribble by Jones, recalling his forward days, was supported by Jack, who gave to Bastin. He transferred to Hulme, who tipped the ball to his left foot and cross-kicked: a fine movement. There was an anti-climax, for John headed over the goal. Possibly David Jack might have equalised if even his long leg had been a trifle longer. Allen was nearly through the defence again when Roberts brought him down. The Northerners played four half-backs at times. They concentrated on defence, and succeeded, for Arsenal could never break through such a determined opposition. Thus the Cup went to Newcastle, who had the luck and made the most of what the gods sent them.

24 April 1932   *J. A. H. Catton*

J. T. Bolton followed as the main football correspondent. A good sample of his writing comes in this extract from his description of the surprise result in the 1939 Final which allowed Portsmouth to hold the Cup throughout the war years which followed.

Portsmouth (2)   4   Wolverhampton Wan. (0)   1

Once again the germ of truth, bred on tradition, which lays it down that the favourites never win the Football Association Challenge Cup, has exerted itself. At Wembley yesterday before a crowd of over 100,000, which included the King and Queen, Portsmouth beat Wolverhampton Wanderers by four goals to one, and take the Cup south of London for the first time in the history of the competition. Not for eleven years at least has any team been so strongly fancied to win the trophy as were Wolverhampton Wanderers, but they were more thoroughly outplayed, as far as the real art and craft of the game are concerned, than has any side been since final ties were first played at Wembley. Portsmouth played with less suggestion of nerves, more calm and collected football than any team before in a final tie at Wembley. It cannot possibly be said of this game – as of so many other final ties – that the better team did not win.

Let it be admitted, quite frankly, that as a team, Wolverhampton Wanderers gave a most disappointing display. So much had been expected of them: they achieved so little. Indeed, it is not much exaggeration to say that the Wolverhampton men gave the poorest exhibition of football in a Cup final of our time. They scarcely ever settled down to play what their supporters have come to regard as their normal game. The real mystery of the match is how a team which is capable of playing so well could descend to such a mediocre level. It was not a case of a side merely playing as well as their opponents would allow them to do, although Portsmouth must be given full credit for the persistence and grit which they brought to bear, and which prevented the Wolverhampton men from settling down. The Midlanders, however, contributed to their own downfall by bad tactics, and by individual errors, both of omission and commission.

In one respect the biggest attendance at Wembley since 1923 must have been disappointed. The game was over, to all intents and purposes, at half-time, when Portsmouth led by two goals to nothing, and it was certainly finished, as a contest of possibilities, immediately after the re-start. It was now third time lucky for Portsmouth, but the third time paid for all, for they have been twice to Wembley on previous occasions to finish as losers. The touch of tragedy from the Wolverhampton point of view lies in the fact that, so far as it can be said that one Portsmouth man did more than any other to bring about this result, Barlow, the inside-left, was that player. Yet two months ago Barlow was a Wolverhampton player, being then transferred to Portsmouth.

For the greater part of the game it almost seemed as if the Wolverhampton players were so convinced of their own superiority that it was scarcely necessary for them to put forth their most strenuous efforts. Time after time a player of the Midland side, safely in possession of the ball, would lose it to an opponent whose presence in a position to tackle was not even suspected. That, of course, is one way of saying that Portsmouth were more on their toes, and revealed greater pace. While the Wolverhampton players adopted the policy of waiting for the ball, those of Portsmouth ran to it, and, having done the running to secure possession, kept both the ball and their own feet. The men of the winning side on their toes; the men of the losing side on their heels. That, granting the writer a little licence, is as near a correct summary of the game, and conveying the secret of Portsmouth's success, as it is possible to get.

30 April 1939   *J. T. Bolton*

---

*Robertson-Glasgow usually confined his writing to cricket or rugby. In
1948 however he made a rare excursion into reporting soccer with one
of the most entertaining of all Cup Finals as his happy choice:*

The Cup Goes to Manchester

Manchester U.   4   Blackpool   2

Manchester United beat Blackpool in the Cup Final at Wembley yesterday
by 4 goals to 2. That they should have won after being twice a goal down is
a tribute to their courage and also a measure of their skill. Mortensen, of
Blackpool, was elusively brilliant at centre-forward, and Matthews
showed, especially in the first half, his own peculiar brand of wizardry, but
it was the team that won in the end. The King and Queen, Princess
Margaret, and 99,000 spectators watched a great match at the end of which
the King presented the cup to the winning captain.

When Blackpool were leading Manchester seemed to be inspirited by
surprise, like a master perplexed yet pricked by the unexpected excellence
of a pupil. The United forwards, in the last 25 minutes, gave a wonderful
display of control and skill. Behind them Cockburn was especially good;
and when the pinch came Carey and Aston were steadier backs than
Shimwell and Crosland, though the latter came out with credit from his
first appearance in the Cup tournament.

On the route to Wembley the first indicator to the Cup Final was a very
junior citizen of Harlesden with a very large football. He was trying to
persuade his grandfather into a *jeu de deux*. Outside the Wembley stadium
3s. 6d. tickets were being offered at £20 a go – and finding takers. One
would-be spectator was contemplating his ticket when a passer-by, doubtless considering him unworthy of so precious a possession, relieved him of
it and made off. Inside, the playing pitch presented its customary picture of

smooth perfection. Indeed, had there been no football at all, the grass alone was almost worth the visit. Nothing, so far, marred the set-up except the inevitable quackings through microphones.

Then came the band of the Grenadier Guards and, soon, those bursts of cheers and counter-cheers that are by Excitement out of Occasion. Next, to direct and co-ordinate the urge to noise, Mr Cager, resplendent in white flannels, conducted us in popular songs of past and present. After these, 'Abide with Me'.

And now, at last, the teams, both in borrowed colours; Manchester in blue jerseys, Blackpool in white. They were presented to H M the King. The bands dispersed, and, at 3 o'clock to the minute, Blackpool having won the toss, Rowley kicked off. Blackpool pressed, and both wings, Matthews and Rickett, harassed the Manchester defence. In the 7th minute Matthews, tricking Aston, gave Munro a fine chance of scoring, but he foozled the shot.

So far, mostly Blackpool. Once Rowley put Delaney through, but the latter was yards offside. By now the United were shaking off a certain early lethargy, and, from a corner by Delaney, Rowley taxed Robinson severely. Now it was all United, and they were patterns of perplexity. Twice Robinson was in trouble in goal but suddenly, there went Mortensen, clear away after a long, high pass, beating Chilton. Desperately Chilton tried to tackle him. Down went Mortensen, and the referee awarded a penalty. Shimwell took it and scored. At once the United attacked again, and from a corner Pearson headed against the cross-bar. In the desperate scene that followed, Hayward, the Blackpool centre-half, had to head over his own goal.

Mortensen made a wonderful attempt to score from a very improbable angle on the right, but it was mostly defence for Blackpool just now. Once Mitten nearly scored with a snap shot from 25 yards and both Pearson and Morris headed just wide. Then in the 30th minute United drew level. Carey, from right back, found Delaney with a clearing pass. Delaney cut in, and gave Rowley the perfect pass, and Rowley tricked Robinson to push the ball into an empty goal.

Within 10 minutes Blackpool were ahead again. From a free kick, the United only partly cleared. Dick fixed on the ball, and, once again, Mortensen was in the one place where the United didn't want him and he scored with a right-foot cross shot. Just before half-time Rickett put in a stinger from outside-left: from the corner that followed, Mortensen, gymnastic as ever, shot over the bar.

The second half began with some brisk attacks by the United, and some very neat play by Matthews on the right wing, but the first really hopping thrill was when Crompton came out somewhat too far from the United goal and only just touched the ball, which trickled slowly past the post. Excitement changed ends when Robinson failed to catch a corner by Delaney. But the impression was gaining that this should be Blackpool's match. For the first time the United forwards seemed to be losing one another, and there were open spaces where and when none should be.

But, whoever else had the impression, Manchester had not. With 20 minutes to go Delaney took a free kick on the right wing. Rowley met the ball with a head seemingly crammed with springs, and the ball went past Robinson like a horizontal rocket.

Now Mortensen again. Pouncing on some defensive hesitation on the United left, he was through like a flash, and Crompton did finely to save his fast cross-shot. So, with only 10 minutes to go, thoughts were turning to Everton and replay. Then, after a pass down the middle, the ball reached Pearson, some 15 yards out on the right; very deliberately, like a marksman on a range who needs a bull to win, he aimed and shot. The ball rebounded into the net from the far upright and several hitherto staid Mancunians expressed an agreeable insanity. Then, to seal up victory, Anderson from right-half and 35 yards scored with the sort of shot that boys dream of. I suppose it should have been saved.

Blackpool. – Robinson; Shimwell, Crosland; Johnston, Hayward, Kelly; Matthews, Munro, Mortensen, Dick, Rickett.

Manchester United. – Crompton; Carey, Aston; Anderson, Chilton, Cockburn; Delaney, Morris, Rowley, Pearson, Mitten.

Referee. – C. J. Barrick (Northampton).

25 April 1948   *R. C. Robertson-Glasgow*

Perhaps the most famous final of all was Blackpool's win in 1953. Certainly it was the most emotional as the people's favourite, Stanley Matthews, won in Roy of the Rovers style by fashioning a last-minute winner. Alan Ross reported this under the heading of 'Blackpool's Great Victory'.

Blackpool 4   Bolton Wanderers 3

The Queen, accompanied by the Duke of Edinburgh, saw Blackpool, who were making their third appearance at Wembley since the war, win the Cup for the first time in their history by beating Bolton Wanderers by 4 goals to 3. No team has more deserved their triumph, for they went to Wembley, having left Arsenal, the Spurs and Huddersfield among others, in their trail, without their inside-left, Brown. The absence of this fast, powerful player was painfully underlined as the game wore on, yet somehow Blackpool came back when the match seemed already lost. With 20 minutes of the second half gone Blackpool were losing by three goals to one. Then Mortensen scraped a beautiful dropping centre from Matthews past Hanson to make it 3–2. Bolton held this lead until five minutes from the end when Mortensen, taking a free kick from 20 yards, slammed the ball into the roof of the net.

The referee was looking at his watch when Matthews, who had trans-formed the Blackpool side in these last minutes, and whose colleagues had thrown away more perfect passes than one can bear to remember, shuffled and swung yet once more past the limping Banks. His final pass – as had done the others – went square across the goal some seven yards out. This time Perry, who, like Mudie, had a lot to answer for, coolly picked his spot. It was a fantastic dream finish, which seemed quite unreal.

Yet a minute later Johnston was leading his team up to receive the Cup from the Queen, and it was evidently true enough. Matthews, like his captain, was carried shoulder high off the arena, and no individual player has probably earned either his triumph or public love more deservedly. For his was the storybook climax to the career of perhaps the greatest footballer of all time.

Bolton, who smiled their defeat away in the bright sunlight, were, on the day, extremely unlucky. Certainly they had the easiest of paths to the final, not meeting a single First Division side, yet they led, and were the better team, for three-quarters of this match, with virtually only ten players. Bell, their left half, was a crippled passenger on the wing for all but a quarter of an hour, and Lofthouse and Banks were reduced to half speed for much of the second half.

The game had as dramatic a beginning as end, for in the first minute Lofthouse, taking a square pass from Holden, 20 yards out, sent in a low, curling shot that Farm unaccountably let slip through his hands. Twice more in this opening period Lofthouse nearly scored, each time Moir and Holden working him clear, and, on the second occasion his shot hitting the post, with Farm sprawling.

Blackpool were sliding the ball to one another neatly enough in mid-field, but near goal they were snuffed out as easily as candles by the strong Bolton backs. Mortensen fed Matthews with the care of a doting mother, but nothing could make up for Brown's missing thrust. In the thirty-fourth minute, however, Mortensen, swerved his way through, and Hassall, racing back in defence, ran his cross shot past Hanson.

Five minutes later Langton, veering to the right wing, put Bolton ahead again. He sent across a diagonal left-footed centre and, with Moir jumping across the hesitating Farm's line of sight, the ball went straight into the net. Next, Holden nearly scored, hitting the bar with Farm still as a statue. Hanson made two fine flying saves from Taylor and Mortensen, and then Holden again got clear on the right, and Bell, barely able to move, gallantly jumped to head Bolton into a 3–1 lead. Now Matthews asserted his genius, and as Bolton wilted under a series of bewildering runs, Blackpool stormed up to their miraculous victory. One of the most exciting games ever, more than likely; but classic football, no.

3 May 1953   *Alan Ross*

On 12 April that year Wembley was a magical place for another right-winger as my Pegasus team won the Amateur Cup Final by a record margin. The combined Oxford and Cambridge team seemed to exert the same spell on the public as the Boat Race still does. The only two occasions on which an Amateur final filled Wembley to capacity were Pegasus' two winning matches. For me there was a feverish start. Having reported feeling unwell in the morning I was sent to the first-aid room for a check after changing. Clumping up the stone steps in football boots I was a centre of curiosity, returning to the dressing-room with a report of a temperature of 103 and advice not to play. Fortunately our one forward reserve was also suffering from injury and though it did little for our organiser's nerves Dr Thompson agreed to my playing. In the event the fever added wings to my heels and the interval stimulants of whisky and brandy improved my swerve in the second half just as they did for Denis Compton in Arsenal's 1950 win.

Pegasus Clear Winners at Wembley

Pegasus   6   Harwich and P.   0

Pegasus won the FA Amateur Cup for the second time in three years at Wembley yesterday. The score of six goals to none in no way flattered them, for they reached their very best form and had quite their easiest match of the competition.

Harwich played sensibly enough, but they were out-gunned at all levels. They began as though they had brought a good salty whiff of the marshes to sustain them, but once Pegasus had worked off a rather casual start, scoring twice between the eleventh and fifteenth minutes, there was in truth only one team in it.

However, one-sided though it certainly was, there was no lack of interest. Pegasus showed the arts and graces that one has come to expect from only a handful of professional sides. Their defence, robustly solid in tackling, covered superbly and the ball was moved from backs to halves and then to forwards with complete understanding. It was a performance of the first quality, with hardly a kick wasted, and they looked an altogether maturer team than when they took the cup for the first time in 1951.

Pegasus, curiously launched on to a shining sunlit pitch by the 'Eton Boating Song', as were Harwich by 'Sons of the Sea', were somewhat slack in the opening stages and the Harwich inside-forwards all but worked the ball through from the kick-off. Not much later another neatly linked move between Pearson and Davis was only foiled when Vowels raced across the field to make a fine tackle as Cooper moved through the centre on an open goal.

That, in fact, though there was then no indication of it, was the last time Harwich were to have the Pegasus defence in any sort of trouble. Pegasus swept upfield and a rising drive by Sutcliffe was turned over the bar by King. Sutcliffe took the corner and Saunders, who had roamed up from left-half, headed in the kick as King moved the wrong way. Four minutes later Lunn, whose perfectly timed and angled passes were the real reason for the breakdown of the Harwich defence, sent Pawson clear of Tyrell and Sutcliffe rammed home his centre.

Pegasus now began to assert their mastery of the open spaces. Alexander and McKinna made their passes low and accurate. Vowels and Saunders flicked the ball on with the least delay, and then Lunn and Carr alternately sprayed their fast-moving wings with long diagonal kicks that left the Harwich backs hopelessly stranded.

Pawson and Sutcliffe made few mistakes and Laybourne in the centre was resourceful and intelligent. More goals had to come and Carr was the next to score, sending Sutcliffe away and moving firmly on to his return pass to drive it wide of King. At half time it was 3–0 and soon afterwards Carr took the ball through and squared it for Laybourne to crash it into the net.

The Pegasus backs now indulged in some icy intricate passing under pressure that would have warmed the heart of Ramsey, and then Pawson and Laybourne each ran half the length of the field in turn. From both their passes goals should have come, but Carr made amends when he gave Sutcliffe a lovely opening to score the fifth Pegasus goal.

Five minutes from the end Pawson suddenly turned up on the left wing and centred for Carr to flash in a low drive. It was the most civilised, polished football and it could not but have given the capacity crowd of 100,000, wherever their hearts lay, great pleasure.

12 April 1953   *Alan Ross*

Next year Kenneth Harris switched his attention from the more weighty affairs of the nation to report a semi-final won for Preston by Tom Finney's effortless brilliance.

Field Day

Preston N.E. 2   Sheffield W. 0

Preston deserved to win. 'But they would not have won if they hadn't Tom Finney,' said the man who sat next to me on the bus.

True enough. But Preston have got Tom Finney, and he was certainly playing at Maine Road to-day. He made both goals with consummately cunning passes. If his inside forwards will shoot quicker and oftener with the powder he supplies them, Preston may well beat West Bromwich in the Wembley Cup Final. Gate receipts were £15,665; 75,200 people saw the game.

The general character of the game – which was not, on the whole, inspiring – was established early in the first half. Preston settled down to play mature, cultivated, indeed rather too philosophical a kind of football. In spite of chance after chance uncurling itself from Finney's fertile feet they were an unconscionable time scoring.

Sheffield Wednesday, on the other hand, were keen, crude, and, for much of the time, rather aimless. They seemed game but green. Only their gallant left-winger, Woodhead, seemed to have a plan for scoring.

'Finis' began to be written in the last 15 minutes of the first half. Finney had now plotted his raiding lanes, and a kind of dazed astigmatic look was beginning to burgeon in the eyes of the Sheffield defence. He forced five corners in two minutes, three of them in immediate succession. His high-flighted in-swinging centres were slow torture to watch. Wayman might well have scored twice if he had not lost time by turning to shoot with his more effective left foot.

At half-time Preston had forced 16 corners – 15 of them on Finney's wing – to Sheffield's one. Thompson, in Preston's goal, was feeling chilly. McIntosh, in Wednesday's goal, was sweating like a bull, but leaping like a gazelle, and playing with courage and judgement out of the ordinary.

A second half opened much as the first had closed, with Finney dominating the game – receiving the ball in leisurely fashion, unhurriedly getting it perfectly under control, trotting forward slowly a pace or two, then accelerating like a cheetah.

Then, 15 minutes after the interval, Preston's other forwards became aggressive. Wayman ran forward to the centre of the six-yard line, and when Finney quickly placed the ball before him he flung himself high to head it and beat the goalkeeper's fist by a second. As they collapsed in a heap, the ball shot into the left-hand side of the net.

For some minutes after this, apart from a cracking shot from Woodhead, the football became scrappy. Sewell, the Wednesday inside-left, who had played a good game, collided with Docherty, the Preston right-half, and went off the field on a stretcher.

Sewell's return was the signal for another series of assaults by Finney. Suddenly finding himself unmarked, a few feet deep of the penalty spot, he beat the left-half by swerving sharply inside him. He paused, weighed the pros and cons of shooting, decided not to, and pushed the ball forward to Baxter. Standing on the angle of the six-yard line, in the inside-right position, and with the defence hypnotised by Finney's feinting, Baxter could hardly have missed. His drive into the far side of the net left McIntosh without a chance.

28 March 1954   *Kenneth Harris*

In prospect the 1958 Final was seen as an emotional climax to the resurrection of Manchester United's team after the Munich air crash. There was however no such happy ending, no such atmosphere as I recorded in this report and as Danny Blanchflower confirmed in his first article for The Observer.

Relentless Bolton Carry the Day

Bolton Wanderers 2   Manchester United 0

In prospect yesterday's Cup Final was more likely to be distinguished by its emotional impact than the quality of the football. So it proved, except that there was little of the expected excitement. Manchester rarely seemed likely to crown their wonderful recovery with this last triumph.

Bolton are essentially an effective rather than an attractive team, and they won because they were always marking more closely, tackling harder, and, above all, moving more quickly to meet the ball. Their play was, in fact, ideally suited to upset their opponents.

Manchester United, who had won through to the Final as much by their enthusiasm and spirit as by their skill, now found themselves outmatched in determination, in strength and in the will to win.

Tactically, too, Bolton were their masters, for they kept with relentless persistence to a plan that was simple and effective. Edwards, keeping always at Taylor's side, cut him off from the ball, destroying at once the cohesion of Manchester's attack.

Without the inspiration of Taylor's constructive and cunning passes, United's forwards had nothing to offer except the power and thrust of Charlton, who was left to challenge on his own the competent Bolton defence.

In attack Bolton were sensible rather than subtle, concentrating as usual on the long cross to the far post and relying on Lofthouse to charge the ball home. They had no need to change these methods, for he was playing with all his old force and fire. But the openings were made for him by a line more balanced and penetrating than United's.

Birch, on the right, was able to beat Greaves at will, shielding the ball from him with his body in the manner more often seen in Continental teams. Inside, Stevens and Parry worked industriously, making the occasional clever pass and helping to draw the defence out of position. Between them they prepared the way for the vital struggle in the centre which was the most entertaining and decisive of the match.

It was entertaining and hard-fought because Cope was outstanding in Manchester's defence, playing with a coolness and command that was lacking in the fretful play of their backs and wing-halves. It was decisive because of Lofthouse's irrepressible energy and unerring instinct for the slightest opening.

For Manchester it was a day of dust and ashes as their weaknesses were ruthlessly exposed by opponents who harried them from start to finish. It wasn't that they were overawed by the occasion, simply that they lacked the ability to counter so fierce a challenge.

This was especially so in their forward line. Dawson and Webster on the wings were too clumsy and lacked the speed to trouble Hartle or Banks, who remained unmoved by their frequent switches, finding each equally easy to deal with.

Viollet, too, was painfully slow in thought and action, without a hint of his former certainty, and clearly unfit as yet to face so testing a game.

Such forwards needed continuous support. But Goodwin and Crowther were barely able to contain Stevens and Parry, let alone dominate the midfield.

There remained Charlton to save the game for United, and it is a measure of the remarkable advance he has made that he came near to doing it. Bolton's superiority was unquestioned, but twice he nearly snatched the game from them.

In the first half he sent Hopkinson diving to save, brilliantly, a shot of tremendous power; in the second, a shot which might have turned the game thundered against the inside of the post and rebounded to the goalkeeper. A year ago Charlton would have manoeuvred the ball awkwardly and automatically to his left, but these shots were hit with equal ease and force with either foot.

In midfield his bursts of speed and close control of the ball made him a lonely threat throughout. Surprisingly, however, as the game progressed, he lay deeper and deeper, giving Bolton, who were otherwise untroubled, too much time to guard against his sudden raids.

From the start it was clear that Bolton were setting too fast a pace for United; and within minutes they were ahead. A long pass from Banks to Birch, a centre to the far post, and Lofthouse came near to rushing the ball in as Gregg hesitated.

The corner kept Bolton on the attack, and when Taylor headed clear, Edwards sent the ball back across the goal and Lofthouse, again at the far post, ran in to glide it home.

Birch continued to trouble the defence, and once when he varied his long centres by turning inwards himself and shooting left-footed, Gregg for the first time took the ball with his usual confidence.

United had their chance at last as Taylor, winning the ball for once, sent a measured pass out to Webster, and Viollet drove the ball over from close in as it was pulled back to him. In the main, however, play was disjointed and destructive, with Bolton neater and more frequent in their attacks.

So it remained till after the interval, when for a few moments United moved with rhythm and purpose. Then it was that Webster proved too slow to move on to a through pass which left him an open road to goal, and that Charlton hammered the ball against the post after a move which had swept sweetly across and through the defence.

But almost at once came the goal which decided the issue. A swift move between Bolton's forwards left Stevens running in to shoot at Gregg. The goalkeeper could only push the ball up, and as he turned to catch it, Lofthouse came crashing in to sweep everything into the net.

No doubt the fairness of the charge was difficult to assess. But Lofthouse seemed to be going for the ball rather than the goalkeeper, and to be entitled to do so as both tried to reach it first.

That was the end of the road for Manchester. The Cup went, as it did last year and as it so often does, to a side strong in defence and strong in determination.

Bolton Wanderers. – Hopkinson; Hartle, Banks; Hennin, Higgins, Edwards (B.); Birch, Stevens, Lofthouse, Parry, Holden.

Manchester United. – Gregg; Foulkes, Greaves; Goodwin, Cope, Crowther; Dawson, Taylor, Charlton, Viollet, Webster.

Referee. – Mr J. V. Sherlock (Sheffield).

4 May 1958   *Tony Pawson*

United's Lost Dream

Before the game I sat in the Press box like a Sherlock Holmes, wondering if events to come would substantiate my theories. Would United win because they had one or two personalities just beyond the ability of all the others? Ernie Taylor could pace the game to their advantage; would it be a day of favour for him?

Would Bobby Charlton crown a great season with one of his celebrated cannon-blasts?

How would Matt Busby appear, and with what effect? Would the emotional possibilities stimulate feelings and make it an exciting event; or would they deaden the nerves and dull the occasion?

After the game I sat among clattering typewriters and tried to rationalise the whole thing. It *was* a dull game; but I noticed no special feelings of emotion that one could blame for this. Matt Busby crept unobtrusively to his near-touchline seat while the attention of most was concentrated on the teams.

Bolton won and deserved to. They defended capably and without frills, and up front they had one or two tactical ideas which were practical if not always exciting. Nat Lofthouse was characteristic of the whole team. Nat is no schoolboy, but he was as alert and enthusiastic as ever.

I thought his second goal was a foul. Harry Gregg was facing the back of his own goal when Nat bundled him in with the ball. I think Nat unintentionally charged Harry in the back; it's doubtful whether Harry was holding the ball at the time.

Manchester's dreams went all astray. Ernie Taylor, that dwarf of football magic, must have felt like a giant of misery – nothing would go right for him. Bobby Charlton occasionally showed his tremendous ability; one crashing shot 'bent' the goalpost and the ball cannoned back into Hopkinson's startled hands.

Young Cope played a sound game at centre-half which more than suggests an eventful future.

It wasn't United's day. But perhaps I expected too much of them.

4 May 1958   *Danny Blanchflower*

An Observer *book entitled* Shouts and Murmurs *made up of selected writing from all its various pages included this account of the 1962 Final.*

A Soccer Classic

Burnley 1   Tottenham Hotspur 3
Robson   Greaves, Smith
£53,837   Blanchflower (pen.) 100,000

This was indeed a match fit to set before the Queen. Burnley versus Spurs is the best that Britain can offer, and not even a Cup Final could deter either team from playing clever, attacking football. From the start it was clear that both sides were going for goals, with no thought of purely defensive football. The approach to the game was summed up in the early conflict – or lack of it – between Greaves and Miller.

With that incredible little goal-snatcher lying up on the right, Miller, instead of marking him close, spent most of his time up in attack. This gave Greaves the freedom to score the vital opening goal in the first minutes, but only a great save by Brown prevented Miller countering with one of his own as his fierce drive was pushed over the bar.

Neither side had any thought of keeping to fixed formations, players moving freely where opportunity offered.

Angus sweeping up to join with his forwards much as Armfield does for England, Adamson tackling Blanchflower deep in Spurs' half, both sets of wingers constantly switching positions showed that these teams were prepared to play the fluid, inventive game that is so entertaining to watch.

Tottenham, always the more composed and skilful, were hunted desperately hard by a Burnley team that chased and fought for every ball. So Spurs achieved their second double, but Burnley were once more left chasing shadows – a galling end to what could have been a great season for them.

But while Burnley's play has faltered in recent weeks, and they often seem incapable of rising to the big occasion, yesterday they were beaten not by any shortcomings of their own, but by a Spurs team at its crushing best.

The match that couldn't possibly come up to expectations contrived to do so, and it was Burnley who helped to make it incomparably the best final I have seen. With their enthusiasm and their elegant mid-field play they threatened throughout to match Spurs if the Londoners once slipped from their high estate.

It needed Norman's confident interceptions to keep Burnley out, while Smith and Greaves, the bludgeon and the rapier, were only just good enough to beat down Burnley's defence. It was this assault down the centre that had Burnley reeling in the opening minutes as Smith and Greaves moved in happy harmony.

Smith won the space for Greaves, giving him scope for his darting runs, with a series of intelligent passes.

Almost before the opening hum of expectation had died Smith's precise header from a long clearance by Brown sent Greaves racing towards the area. Burnley's defenders converged to block the shot, but Greaves, checking and turning back, won the room to slide the ball into the net past the tangle of legs, and the unsighted Blacklaw. A goal where no goal seemed possible as, inevitably, Greaves answered the challenge of his first Cup Final with impish confidence.

But Burnley, too, were moving the ball calmly and with purpose. Miller, thrusting adventurously upfield, had Spurs defence at full stretch. So, too, did Connelly, outpacing but never outwitting Henry, and the tireless Pointer, who was forever searching for the ball or the open space.

71

Now it was that Norman, timing his solid tackles to perfection, kept Burnley at bay until Mackay drove them back, more by skilful use of the ball than by any intimidating show of strength. With Blanchflower unwontedly quiet, it was left to Mackay to switch Spurs back into attack. It was thrust and counter-thrust.

At one end there was Greaves, darting in to rob the hesitant McIlroy, and bring Blacklaw to save at full stretch. At the other there was Harris shooting wildly over the bar when Angus's centre floated gently over the defence to land at his feet.

It was this contrasting control in the penalty area that was the decisive difference between the teams. Yet, for all the probing approach work, the defenders held out till the interval. Once Miller handled in the area, and there was a great shout for a penalty, but it was clearly unintentional, and the referee was not one to be flustered into error.

Afterwards Burnley swept straight into attack, searching desperately for the equaliser. Appropriately it was Pointer who won it for them by his chasing of every half-chance. Tacking back he swept the ball out to Harris, whose low centre hit Robson on the shins and bounced off into the net.

At last fortune seemed ready to smile on Burnley, but cruelly and immediately Spurs dispelled their illusions. White's delicately accurate centre reached Smith, who swivelled clear to thump the ball happily home.

Still Burnley came back at them, Pointer just failing to gather Elder's chip in front of the gaping goal, and Connelly running a close shot into the side netting.

Smith, his socks rolled down, had been charging in with his usual disregard of hard knocks, but now he was injured as he clashed with the unyielding Cummings, and was left to limp through the rest of the game.

Jones, jinking past opponents like a snipe on the wing, nearly cut through on his own. To contrast with his dash there was the cool precision of White, his passes lobbed unerringly into the open space.

And now, as a high centre floated in from the left, Smith challenged Blacklaw and headed the ball back. The linesman flagged for a foul on the goalkeeper, but the referee gave him the benefit of the doubt.

As the ball ran loose, Medwin, making a positive contribution at last, drove in a shot that Cummings could only stop with his hand. Blanchflower glided the penalty in with cool unconcern.

Not even Burnley had any fight left after that, but they had been mastered by a great team playing with confident authority.

THE TEAMS

Burnley. – Blacklaw; Angus, Elder; Adamson, Cummings, Miller; Connelly, McIlroy, Pointer, Robson, Harris.

Tottenham Hotspur. – Brown; Baker, Henry; Blanchflower, Norman, Mackay; Medwin, White, Smith, Greaves, Jones.

Ref. – J. Finney (Hereford).

5 May 1962   *Tony Pawson*

The one absolute certainty to win a Cup Final appeared to be Leeds in 1973. They were as consistent as they were outstanding and it seemed impossible that Second Division Sunderland could beat them. So this is a fitting last sample of Cup Final reports for, as Arthur Hopcraft reported, the Sunderland dream did come true to epitomise the special attraction of the Cup.

Dreams do come true . . .

Sunderland   1   Leeds United   0

This hearteningly, unlikely outcome – not since 1931 had a Second Division club won the F A Cup – was made possible by some vivid luck, by a dazzling miss in front of an open goal by Lorimer, and by two extraordinary saves from Montgomery, as well as by the admirable diligence of this young Sunderland team.

When Mr Burns blew the final whistle Sunderland's manager, Bob Stokoe, left the bench at a sprint, in track-suit, raincoat and trilby, making immediately for Montgomery to hold him in a crushing embrace. Clearly nobody at Wembley was more aware than Stokoe of the overwhelming importance of his goalkeeper's contribution in the sixty-sixth minute: two reflex reactions by which he turned aside Cherry's flying header, then immediately finger-tipped Lorimer's shot up against the bar.

The red and white scarves of the massed Sunderland supporters swayed in an ecstatic, deep-throated acclaim as their players hugged one another, and as Don Revie's men sank to their knees in exhaustion and dejection.

Leeds might properly complain that they were denied a penalty which Watson's tripping of Bremner in the eleventh minute of the second half deserved. But Mr Burns was unhesitating in his refusal. Leeds, to their credit, wasted no time in fruitless protest.

'We want Stokoe,' the Sunderland fans chanted for minutes at the end, and the manager was entitled to every ounce of their delirious gratitude.

His side gave him all their heart, and perhaps more skill than they, or he, had any reason to expect on this most challenging of football's big occasions. In contrast there was less of Leeds' huge aggregate of talent than we hoped for. Not until deep into the second half did Revie's team start putting together the accuracy of passing and the impetus which showed how much the better side than Sunderland they really are.

But that is not to say that Sunderland did not deserve this famous victory. They were never less than their best; and in spite of the succession of near-misses around the Sunderland goal in the thrilling closing minutes, it was also necessary for Harvey to make a spectacular save from Halom a matter of seconds from the end.

The game is always going to be remembered for its result. But not much of the first half play will live very long in the memory. The first three minutes were ominous: a violent foul by Pitt on Clarke, then a repetition of the same offence. And there were three successive passes by Hunter and Bremner and Giles, which were remarkable for their massive misdirection. The inevitable, taut nerviness and enough rain on the pitch to produce miniature fountains whenever the players struck the ball hard combined to produce a great deal of error. But after a quarter-of-an-hour there came the first piece of individual enterprise; and, coming from Hunter, it was naturally menacing.

Hunter plunged deeply into the Sunderland penalty area, and managed to get that left leg of his round behind Kerr on the byline to lift the ball improbably towards the near post. Lorimer was there to try a flicked volley, and the ball flew past the back stanchion.

Soon afterwards Horswill struck Sunderland's first shot, and the ball was deflected past Harvey's right-hand post. Immediately Leeds counter-attacked, and there was Clarke spinning to Cherry's excellent pass to the penalty spot. Watson saw the danger in time to stab the ball away on the instant Clarke went for the shot.

Clarke had his name taken shortly after that for tripping Hughes from behind. Briefly it appeared that the game would develop a general violence. Among a series of harsh fouls the most alarming was a wild kick at Tueart's shins by Hunter. But this disagreeable promise was not fulfilled, happily. The game was to be an hour old before the play reached an impressively high standard. But even though Hughes was cautioned 10 minutes from the end for a foul on Cherry, there was generally an unusual scrupulousness about the tackling once that unpleasant little flurry of the first half had passed.

The goal, in the thirty-second minute, was handsome. It came, appropriately, from Porterfield, the most stylish of Sunderland's eager forwards. Harvey had been forced to tip a lob from Kerr over his bar, and Hughes placed his corner kick firmly beyond the thick grouping in the penalty area to Halom, all alone on the right of the box. Halom used his body to get the ball down at Porterfield's feet. Then Porterfield flicked the ball up with his left foot and struck hard with his right. Harvey was cleanly beaten.

Now, as Leeds found some of the urgency that had been missing, there grew from Madeley one of those exceptional personal performances which remain bright in the mind. He is naturally a graceful player: the head always held high, the ball hit with an easy accuracy. In the last 10 minutes of the first half, and throughout the second, he devoted much of his skill to prompting his forwards – a rare ability in a centre back. Just before the interval he ran 30 yards with the ball, before placing it exactly at the feet of Clarke well inside the Sunderland penalty area. One felt Clarke ought to have scored here. He is capable of sharper response than he showed. Pitt was allowed time to make ground and stab the ball away for a corner. The first half closed on a dramatic shot from Lorimer's right foot. Montgomery stopped the ball by defending his face with both palms.

Montgomery, in fact, looked frequently insecure, in spite of his several vital saves. He lost the ball just outside the goal area, after stopping a shot from Bremner, and again it was Pitt who cleared. Quickly afterwards there occurred the incident which might have given Leeds their equaliser – Watson's lunge at Bremner's legs as the little Scot hurried into the Sunderland penalty area from the left. There must have been many among the spectators who would have awarded Leeds a penalty for that. Mr Burns adjudged otherwise.

That degree of disappointment is bound to cut deeply into any team's morale. Commendably, Leeds shrugged off the effects quickly. Soon Madeley was again running smoothly at the retreating Sunderland defence. His ground pass was aimed for Lorimer's right foot, and the shot sent the ball scraping along the side netting.

Then came the remarkable melodrama. Jones, in considerable trouble with his back to a cluster of Sunderland defenders on the edge of their penalty area, intelligently played the ball back to Reaney. Carefully, Reaney crossed high for the far post. Thrillingly, Cherry hurled himself forward to meet the ball hard with his head. But Montgomery, with an unlikely flap of one hand, turned the ball away to his left. It dropped straight in front of Lorimer. The man with one of the strongest and most certain shots in football had no obstacle between him and the goal. He showed no sign of fluster. But Montgomery managed to recover position and get his fingers to Lorimer's shot and the ball came down off the underside of the cross-bar.

That was in the 66th minute, and for the remainder of the game the initiative was almost wholly with Leeds. Bremner joined the attack, and stayed. Eddie Gray, whose form had been disappointing, was replaced by the strong, if rather blunt, Yorath.

The substitute was given a perfect pass by Madeley, sending him running clear on Sunderland's left flank. Yorath's shot seemed to be passing under Montgomery's body, but the goalkeeper snatched the ball back from behind him. A shot from Madeley beat the goalkeeper, but Pitt cleared off the line.

That was Leeds' last assault. Fittingly, and to delight the Sunderland followers, the last shot of the game was Halom's, and Harvey needed all his ability to beat the ball away beside the angle of post and bar.

Leeds – Harvey; Reaney, Cherry, Bremner, Madeley, Hunter, Lorimer, Clarke, Jones, Giles, Gray. Sub: Yorath.

Sunderland – Montgomery; Malone, Guthrie, Horswill, Watson, Pitt, Kerr, Hughes, Halom, Porterfield, Tueart. Sub: Young.

Referee – K. Burns (Stourbridge).

6 May 1973   *Arthur Hopcraft*

For some teams the Cup dream is not of getting to Wembley, but of making news in an early round by upsetting their betters. David Hunn recognised this in making Eddie McCluskey's Granny his sports personality of the week after an Enfield win:

When Granny's Cup Overflowed

Will Eddie McCluskey's granny make it to Wembley? That is the question of the hour at Enfield, where the lively manager and his local soccer heroes have passed a euphoric week that left them in the fourth round of the FA Cup for the first time in their history.

76

Football the leveller; the great Danny Blanchflower playing for Tottenham's reserves.

Tottenham's Paul Allen is crowded out by Arsenal's defenders.

Eamonn McCabe came to the Heysel to photograph Platini and had to focus instead on this scene of carnage.

Brian Robson shields the ball as Manchester United win their Cup Final replay with Brighton.

The worry lines on his forehead map the anxieties of a manager, but West Germany's Helmut Schoen can afford the occasional smile. His teams' many successes eased the tensions.

The Cup that cheered. A lift for Rougvie and British soccer as Aberdeen win the Cup Winners' Cup in 1983.

Chris Waddle is caught in Sweden's defensive web as England draw their 1988 World Cup qualifier 0-0 at Wembley.

The Cup

Granny McCluskey and the Cup are both 100 years old, so a get-together in May would be most appropriate. Even Eddie agrees the likelihood of the union is slight, but it's a certainty that the old lady will remain with the team in spirit wherever they go.

'She's an Enfield fanatic,' he said. 'On Tuesday night she was sitting at home here with the radio, a rosary and a bottle of brandy. And she got us through, you see.'

The old lady should have been at the ground at Southbury Road. Normally the haven for six or seven hundred Isthmian League fans (Enfield are the League champions), it was packed with more than 6,000, some of whom were queueing hours before the third round replay. The atmosphere was unlike anything most of the part-timers had ever known, but it was their opponents, Fourth Division Port Vale, who were overawed by it.

One, two, three, the goals whipped in, assembled on the boots of postmen, decorators, taxi-drivers, surveyors and the unemployed. Port Vale offered depressingly little in reply, but Enfield's achievement makes them the Observer/Mumm sports personalities of the week. They have been quaffing champagne like cocoa in the past few days, but a case of Mumm is on the way to prolong the celebrations.

Some of their players have been with League clubs and opted out. Young Ashford was with Fulham, Holmes was at Brentford, Howell (who hammered in that last, joyful goal on Tuesday) saw service at Millwall, Brighton and Swindon. Others are eager young men hoping the phone will ring one day soon, but school teacher McCluskey doesn't think there are as many of those about as there used to be.

'Unless you're in the First Division or one of the top Second Division clubs, you're probably better off playing for Enfield and holding down a full-time job outside the game. We pay them a weekly wage and they don't do at all badly out of it. There's training on Tuesday and Thursday evenings and occasionally on a Sunday, and we have this tradition of coming in early on Saturday before an important match.

'We were inundated with League people on Tuesday. I don't want to lose any of the lads, of course, but if there are any offers it's really a bit of a pat on the back for us for getting them to that standard. The further we go in the Cup, the greater the chance of someone going, I suppose, but I don't want to think about that.'

The next stop is Barnsley, a Third Division side not noted for delicacy. They are managed by Norman 'bite-yer-legs' Hunter and have the sort of reputation that might cause a gladiator to buckle on another layer of armour. Manchester United at home might have been a more rewarding draw, but Barnsley it is and a gate of perhaps 20,000 as the best to hope for.

'We could have had a more exciting draw,' McCluskey agreed, 'but the most important thing is to win it, whatever it is. As our chairman said, we are more keen on making progress than making money. For the fifth round, we could do with the weakest club left in – but at home this time.

'Obviously Barnsley are a better side than Port Vale, but our lads are a pretty nippy lot and we might just catch them on the hop. At least we have a decent chance of winnning, which is more than you expect to say at this stage. As you see, the First Division sides are busy knocking each other out of the Cup while we creep closer to Wembley through the back door.'

With Granny in tow, of course, making whoopee with the cognac and trying to get her hands on a glass of champagne.

11 January 1981   *David Hunn*

The Cup can also give footballers in decline a chance to attract the limelight again. Stan Bowles was one of those skilful and entertaining forwards who give more pleasure to spectators than to managers demanding high work-rate and combative aggression. His love of gambling off the field also gave him trouble, but Julie Welch watched him still impishly effective in an early Cup round with Brentford as they scored seven without reply against Windsor and Eton.

Bowles a Sound Bet

Bowles looks the part of a sober 33-year-old who's done nothing more outré than make model aeroplanes.

He still bets – 'It's a disease, gambling' – but not so heavily now. Recently remarried, he says he can't afford it; 'I've got two wives to keep.' And he is sensitive to the suggestion that his once anarchic personal life might have held back his career. 'I've had a lot of private problems over the last 16 years but they've never affected my performance. I've upset a few people along the way when I could have kept my mouth shut, and I know if I'd toed the line I could have had more England caps. But everything I've done, I've done off my own bat and I've always played reasonably well, except at Forest, where I had a personality clash with Brian Clough.'

Anyway, the crowds still like him enormously. 'They've always been good to me. Probably because I'm a bit like them, I go with the same type of people. I'm not a typical footballer. I don't mix with other footballers. I don't watch football.'

His best memories are still of the 8½ years he spent at Loftus Road. 'They got the best football out of me. But Forest came in with a bid of £260,000 and I couldn't turn it down really.' Nevertheless, he doesn't regret anything – except, perhaps, that he's never played in a major final at Wembley.

Who knows, though? Brentford are still in the Milk Cup, and you can't head more emphatically for Wembley, either, than scoring seven goals in the FA Cup first round proper. You felt sorry for the small Isthmian League team Windsor and Eton that they happened on Brentford during such a purple patch. Once Mahoney had put them ahead on the half hour with a drive from just inside the penalty area, the West Londoners were the only outfit in the match.

Within the next 15 minutes, Bowles had set up the moves that made the score 3–0, with McNichol the second to beat Windsor's keeper Wills, and then Mahoney striking again with a long, low drive. After the restart, it was the same story, with McNichol putting Joseph through for 4–0, Mahoney almost immediately bagging his hat-trick. Then Hurlock got in on the act, first with a fine volley off his toecap, then a low drive from just outside the goal area.

As Bowles says, 'I've played with the best, against the best, and I've come up from the Fourth Division to the First and the First to the Fourth again. No one else has ever done that.' No one else at Brentford can quite do things his way either. Let's hope he can keep them going in the next round.

Julie Welch

Arsenal have had their share of Cup triumphs, but of disasters as well, starting with the famous Walsall defeat of their all-star team in the thirties. Trevor Bailey reported on an humiliation by Third Division Northampton.

Speed Beats Arsenal

Northampton Town 3 Arsenal 1

A delicate dainty Arsenal fell before the speed and enthusiasm of a side who are struggling in the wrong half of the Third Division. In every race for the ball and every tackle a Northampton player normally gained possession.

The conditions were treacherous. In the circumstances the long ball was obviously more suitable than the short, particularly against the determined Northampton tackling. Arsenal, however, persisted in close passing and neglected their wings, where the game might well have been won. In the second half Nutt scarcely received a pass.

As Gale, the Northampton centre-half, held Groves effectively, most of the Arsenal moves broke down in the penalty area. Northampton's methods were much more direct, and, consequently, far more effective.

Northampton started well. Their tactics were effective, rather than classical, with defenders hitting the ball hard down the field and their forwards chasing everything enthusiastically.

It was no surprise when they went ahead following a free kick which was headed home by Tebbutt. Gradually Arsenal came into the game, and for the last 25 minutes of the first half they played some good football and should have scored more than a well-taken goal by Clapton. But their shooting was woefully weak.

The second half saw Northampton take a control which they never again relinquished. The only time that Arsenal threatened was when Herd hit the post. For the rest, it was all Northampton. Both the home side's further goals came after free kicks. First Hawkins scored following a neat cross-back by English, and then Leek put the result beyond doubt. On one occasion Arsenal were fortunate when Wills headed off the goal-line with Kelsey beaten.

Arsenal never seemed to realise the urgency of the occasion, and in attack and defence they were clearly a beaten and disheartened team. What must have disappointed their supporters was not merely the result, but the lack of fight which one expects from a team with their traditions.

5 January 1958 *Trevor Bailey*

The League Cup has enough status to be an acceptable second best even if it lacks the ultimate prestige of the FA Challenge Cup. For Stoke, however, it proved a rare prize as Hugh McIlvanney recorded.

It's Stoke's Turn of the Century

Chelsea   1   Stoke City   2

The team they said could not win an argument at last took one of the big prizes of football when Stoke City won their League Cup Final with Chelsea yesterday in a Wembley Stadium that seemed to contain half the people and all the spirit of the Potteries.

In more than a hundred years of history Stoke have never claimed any honour more elevated than the championship of the Second Division.

Stoke's success will depress no one, but the manner of it will weigh on Chelsea memories. After a sickening start, the London team had the greater share of almost everything except goals. However, all their advantage in possession and pressure was outweighed by the fact that they also had the greater share of defensive errors and finishing slackness.

While Banks played up to the standards of the best goalkeeper in the world, and his defenders responded with relentless endeavour, Bonetti made one crucial mistake and was unintentionally repaid with several examples of dangerous living by the men in front of him. And while Stoke's attackers grabbed hungrily at the chances that came to them, Chelsea showed a hesitancy about shooting inside the penalty area and, in the case of Hollins, a fruitless willingness to shoot hastily from far outside it.

Cooke and Hudson channelled the play from midfield towards the Stoke goal for most of the hour and a half, but were never promised a full return for their efforts. For a time Garland, who has rarely played with more persistence or relevance, did suggest that he would make things right. But when Mulligan disappeared from his full-back position at the interval (after eight minutes' absence for treatment in the first half had failed to alleviate bruising to his ankle) the damage was, ironically, to Chelsea's front line.

Houseman was moved to left back, Harris switched to right back and Baldwin, the substitute, was drafted in as a forward. Suffering the dual handicap of a substitute's normal disorientation and a recently-injured player's lack of sharpness, Baldwin remained a sadly blunt instrument in the assault on Banks.

But all this will seem negative to Tony Waddington and Stoke. Largely they made their own luck and they need not listen to anyone's excuses.

Stoke's pursuit of a major honour, which they have maintained thanklessly since 1863, accelerated encouragingly after five minutes when they scored an untidy, but clearly important, goal. It was the kind of start to make a team rise above generations of frustration and the arbitrary predictions implied in bookmakers' odds. It was, equally, the kind of blow to subdue the surging confidence Chelsea had carried into the match.

They had begun with an urgent fluency that swept the play towards Banks and blue was very much the colour in the crowd during the opening flourishes. But provincial optimism was about to be nourished. Harris miskicked a clearance and Dobing moved out to the left touchline to offer a long throw.

Long it was, but orthodox enough, and when Bonetti jumped behind his defenders, a clearance seemed assured. The punch, however, was inadequate. Eastham steered the ball back into the six-yard area and there was hectic anxiety in the defence as Smith and Greenoff tried to force in a shot. A body, probably Dempsey, was put in the way, but when the ball spun out towards the penalty spot Conroy met it with a lunging header to lift it high behind Bonetti into the net.

It would be ridiculous exaggeration to say that Chelsea were unnerved by that goal, but there is no doubt that it made several of their players uneasy and one or two dangerously nervous. The most conspicuous victim was Mulligan. Recently the Irish full-back has emerged as one of the most improved players on his club's staff, but now he found himself releasing a series of damagingly inaccurate passes, not only serving opponents with the ball, but effectively overshooting the most creative men on his own side.

Some of the other Chelsea defenders fell into the same error and, for a time, Cooke and Hudson, although they were clearly in the mood to be dominating, were prevented from making their full contribution to the match. The corollary was that Eastham and Dobing in midfield were spared more than a little of the pressure that might have been applied to them. The veterans made good use of this situation, playing with their familiar skill and thoughtfulness, seeking above all to prompt the long threatening runs of Conroy.

Chelsea's defenders were always stretched by Conroy's speed and adventurousness and they were fortunate that their side developed sufficient flow as the match progressed to make those sorties fairly isolated. They were not, however, isolated enough to prevent Conroy from making the opening for that devastating goal 17 minutes from the end.

Much had happened before that, of course, most of it in the area in front of Banks. There was the moment soon after that first goal when Hollins's 50 yard pass was collected by Garland, who cleverly left Bloor shut out behind his back as he tried to steady for the shot. He had lost control before Bloor fouled him, so the booking of the defender was as unnecessary as it was justified.

Osgood, too, had his name taken later in the first half for a scuffle with Smith after being previously warned for a foul on Greenoff. And Pejic was similarly punished for a brutal interception of Garland.

Chelsea had the huge psychological boost of a goal in the last minute of the first half. Cooke, pressing up on the Stoke penalty area from the right, curved the ball in deep and diagonally. Webb challenged forcibly for it, first in the air, and then on the ground. When he played it with his foot the ball seemed to be driven against Osgood, who took it on his chest and swept it low past Banks's right hand as he fell. That goal inspired Chelsea to control most of the second half, with Cooke in particular running and passing brilliantly.

But after 73 minutes Conroy broke free down the left and floated his centre beyond the far post. Ritchie headed it back into the stride of Greenhoff, who brought Bonetti to a diving save. The goalkeeper could only palm the ball out and George Eastham was there to run it home.

Chelsea crowded and frightened Stoke until the very end. Cooke and Hudson made chances that Baldwin was too slow to take.

Stoke, too, had their substitute on the field four minutes from the end, when Mahoney replaced Greenhoff, who had been nursing an injured wrist for about an hour. But who was worrying? They had won the League Cup and everybody was entitled to celebrate.

Chelsea – Bonetti, Mulligan, Harris, Hollins, Dempsey, Webb, Cooke, Garland, Osgood, Hudson, Houseman. Sub. Baldwin.

Stoke City – Banks, Marsh, Pejic, Bernard, Smith, Bloor, Conroy, Greenhoff, Ritchie, Dobing, Eastham.

Referee – N. Burtenshaw (Great Yarmouth).

5 March 1972   *Hugh McIlvanney*

CHAPTER 3

The World and International Scene

In pre-war years England had a lordly contempt for the World Championship, apparently feeling it unfair on other countries if they should enter a team so certain to win. That complacency was further fostered by victories over leading European countries in 'friendly' matches then taken much more seriously than now and often anything but friendly. England's win over world champions Italy in November 1934 is still known as the 'battle of Highbury' because of the fury with which the Italians fought back after being three down in fifteen minutes. J.A.H. Catton reported two years earlier on an equally narrow win over Austria, the 'Wonder Team' of Europe. Catton appreciated that this skilful side was at least the equal of England and in skill terms even superior.

When the Austrian eleven met England in mid-week officials and enthusiastic players from Holland to Turkey gathered at Chelsea. Even Stephen Bloomer, now in his sixtieth year, had his curiosity aroused and looked on with keen eyes. There has never been a more representative assembly at any game. This was a test of the relative capacity of England and Austria, the most formidable of any continental country. England just won, but the victory was far from convincing. . . .

Some express the opinion that England did not acquit themselves as they can. There is a football proverb that teams play as well as opponents permit. Even on this basis the Englishman must admit that the margin of supremacy was trifling when conditions did not favour the Austrians. They are not accustomed to good turf, to a sticky surface and to the bleakness of a December day in our island. They were soon two goals in arrear yet were merely beaten by 4–3. In two goals the Austrians were unfortunate though such experience is inevitable in manly and moving games with quick changes.

The old game, forwards advancing in a line, with the support of all the half-backs, was used once more. Not for years has such smooth combination been seen in this country. The Austrians could give each other the ball with the accuracy of a Bloomer passing to a Bassett. They always knew where each man was in position and positional play is 60 per cent of the art of football.

Again had the old country a centre-forward like Sindelar? In Vienna he is called 'Der Papierene', the man of paper. He is so light, with spindle shanks and narrow shoulders, that it would seem as if he could be blown aside. He has the elasticity that deceives. With perfect control of the ball – this was a common characteristic of the team – he served the wings with old-fashioned passes of the sweeping type. A dribbler full of wonderful footcraft, he was 'up' for the centres and quite busy among the defenders. He is not a crack shot, but the goal he got was due to close command of the ball at his toe and sure touch in placing.

The best goal-getter is usually Schall, the inside left. Small and sturdy, he is another to have power over the ball. He is known as the 'Freispieler' of the side, with his fellows trying to manoeuvre so that Schall is free and unmarked. He is looked to as a man to shoot the goals, just as Dean of Everton was when he first appeared.

The Austrians scorned all modern crazes such as 'third back' and the W formation. Though beaten they took the honours of the game by their quality. Only constant practice can produce such combination and deft control. Most certainly ball practice is quite a minor part of a footballer's training in England and team work is supposed to grow as naturally as wild flowers. What fallacies are these! Skill in any game is the reward of constant striving.

11 December 1932   *J. A. H. Catton*

There was no mention of England's first entry into the World Cup in 1950. No doubt that was a relief to all concerned. Defeat by America was a matter for amazement and amusement abroad, but tight-lipped resignation at home. Interest was still muted in 1954 with this minimal coverage of a championship replete with goals and entertaining foot-

ball and with the 'Magical Magyars' somehow losing out in the final to
a German side they had beaten 8–3 in an earlier round.

England Lose

England's interest in the World Cup ended in the St Jakob Stadium here this evening, when they were beaten by Uruguay by four goals to two.

To the surprise of many, however, there was no exhibition by the South Americans. Indeed, for much of the game England, playing with great fire, threatened the supremacy of the current world champions. The English defence, with Wright outstanding, was more stable than in recent internationals and combined well to play themselves intelligently out of trouble. It is all the more tragic that at least two of Uruguay's goals, scored when England were on top, might have been saved by Merrick.

When all this has been said, the fact remains that the Uruguayans were technically far the better footballers. The contrast between the two teams lay not only in individual skill but in teamwork. When England's attack reached the danger zone there were usually seven or more Uruguayans to be beaten and yet in midfield play Uruguay seemed always to have a spare man. The English forwards time and again were in the wrong position and far too many attacks were spoiled by inaccurate passes.

With an early goal in the first minutes of each half through Borges and Schiaffino, Uruguay took and held the initiative at the critical moments. Matthews, or, as he is called here, Der Zauber (the magician) was once again the inspiration of the England forward line and engineered an equaliser for Lofthouse in the sixteenth minute. England might easily have taken the lead soon after when Wilshaw lobbed the ball just wide after Maspoli parried a shot from Lofthouse. As it was, within a few minutes Uruguay again took the lead, this time through a spectacular waist-high shot by Varela from fully 20 yards.

A goal by Finney brought England back into the game in the second half and Uruguay were kept on the defensive under heavy pressure. During this period again it was Matthews playing deep at inside-left, supported by Wilshaw, who was outstanding. But, in a sudden breakaway Ambrois scored a fourth goal for Uruguay and that was virtually the end.

In the second quarter-final tie played yesterday at Lausanne, Austria beat Switzerland by seven goals to five.

26 June 1954

1958 was the year England might so easily have won the World Championship for the first time, yet finally failed to make as significant an impact as Wales or Ireland. The 'if onlys' related to the sad loss of such players as Duncan Edwards, Roger Byrne and Tommy Taylor in the Munich air crash. That was compounded by an early injury to Finney. Peculiar refereeing decisions also deprived Bobby Robson of two good-looking goals against Austria, which would have seen England through to the quarter-final. The prospects had been bright enough as John Rafferty reported a satisfactory end to England's home international season.

All the Talents, but Not All the Attacks

Scotland 0   England 4

So substantial a win for England would seem to suggest an end to all their World Cup worries. Not a bit of it: the win was decisive only in the score. England still have team-building to do.

They were opposed to a poor Scottish side, condemned before the game by Scots critics whose warnings proved only too correct. Yet the game hung in the balance for a long time: top-class opposition would have made England pay dearly.

England had a forward line of all the talents: the artistic Finney, the cheeky and progressve Douglas, with three hard-hitting inside men in Charlton, Kevan and the subtle Haynes. Yet although they were faced by slow tackling wing-halves, McColl and Docherty, and should have been running riot, it was Scotland who did the bulk of the attacking.

England's trouble was at wing-half. Clayton and Slater were destructive, but they couldn't serve their brilliant forwards adequately; and forwards, no matter how clever, can do little without the ball.

But if England have problems, they are really the pleasant ones of producing a World Cup-winning side. Poor Scotland will have to struggle to find a team that won't be disgraced.

Younger and Evans were really great players, fit for any side. There the superlatives must end. Murray at inside had a good game, and wingers Herd and Ewing were really not failures. But two wing-halves and at least two inside-forwards must be found before Scotland could even make a show in Sweden.

87

In the first half England had the wind and obviously all the forward skill, yet Scotland might have scored three goals.

Mudie, who had a shocking game at centre, unaccountably failed to reach a pass from Ewing which beat the defence. Then the centre shot past. Forrest headed against the crossbar, and Hopkinson made a fantastic one-handed save to stop a Murray header. It is hard to believe that a team with so many easy chances scorned should be so decisively beaten.

Apart from their goals, England's remaining chances were well taken by Kevan and Douglas and brilliantly saved by Younger, who throughout was a confident, accomplished goalkeeper.

Those England forwards made bricks without straw. Given the goods, the results could be sensational.

They made goal-scoring seem smooth and easy. Douglas's first in the twenty-second minute was a simple affair. Docherty unnecessarily gave away a free kick. Charlton took it and swung it across goal. Douglas took it fair on his forehead, and Younger was well beaten.

The second goal was against the run of play. In the thirty-fourth minute Douglas broke away on the right and passed inside along the ground to Kevan. The big centre hit the ball in his stride and beat Younger off his right-hand post: a sweet, smooth movement.

Scotland, two goals down at half-time, were entitled to feel aggrieved. They had pressed hard and continuously, perhaps with little plan or sense, but in a way that did make openings.

Soon after the interval Scotland had a lucky escape. Douglas came along the by-line and cut the ball back. Kevan, with the whole goal gaping, hit Haynes on the heels with the ball.

England's third goal was worth seeing. Finney moved artistically along his wing. Parker couldn't get in a tackle, and the winger sent over a knee-high cross. Charlton hit it on the volley and scored a goal as spectacular, and certainly as hard hit, as Hampden has ever seen.

Only then did England take full command and Scotland's fervour altogether waned.

More was seen of Clayton and Slater in attack, and England's football became neat and cohesive. Still, it's easy to be clever when three up. Kevan's second (and England's fourth) goal would not have been scored if Scotland had really been in the game. The centre-forward moved in on goal from the right. He was unchallenged, and shot easily past Younger.

Scotland. – Younger (Liverpool); Parker (Falkirk), Haddock (Clyde); McColl (Rangers), Evans (Celtic), Docherty (capt.) (Preston N.E.); Herd (Clyde), Murray (Hearts), Mudie (Blackpool), Forrest (Motherwell), Ewing (Partick Thistle).

England. – Hopkinson (Bolton W.); Howe (West Bromwich Albion), Langley (Fulham); Clayton (Blackburn R.), Wright (capt.) (Wolverhampton W.), Slater (Wolverhampton W.); Douglas (Blackburn R.), Charlton (Manchester U.), Kevan (West Bromwich Albion), Haynes (Fulham), Finney (Preston N.E.).

19 April 1958   *John Rafferty*

For this championship in Sweden The Observer *had its men on the spot. They included the Irish captain, Danny Blanchflower. Always his own man this highly intelligent and articulate footballer chose* The Observer *to emphasise that his articles were his own and not the work of a 'ghost' as with most famous sportsmen. He was prepared to make the point at some expense to himself as the 'populars' would have paid much more handsomely. The point was driven home to me. As his main partner in reporting the championship I had a letter from my sports editor confirming that I should cover the event on the understanding that my fee and expenses did not exceed £50 for the three weeks in Sweden!*

With Blanchflower as captain the Irish were an entertaining and popular party with Danny the joy of the press. Used to being bored by earnest tactical descriptions from managers, they relished his light-hearted comments. Asked the basis of his winning tactics he claimed it was just a case of equalising before the other side had scored. His originality is further evidenced in these samples of his articles with Brian Glanville and myself adding an overall view. It was a pity the final was on a Sunday so that we could watch, but not report, the match in which the young Pele, Vava and Garrincha displayed dazzling skills as Sweden were beaten 5–2 by Brazil.

Soon after arrival, Blanchflower mused on Irish prospects while Glanville weighed up the opposition to the British teams, all four of whom had qualified. My own articles then covered the general impressions of the week with no Saturday matches to report until the play-off for third place.

Will Cinderella Get Caught Out?

Waiting for the World Cup games to start, I feel rather like a lead character from 'Cinderella' who has got mixed up in a production of 'Alice in Wonderland'. Northern Ireland is the Cinderella of the soccer world and that we are here competing with the *élite* of international soccer is an 'Alice in Wonderland' tale.

When we finally qualified for this World Cup series by defeating Italy the whole football world was shocked. Football fortunes are precarious everywhere, but for little Cinderella to overcome the mighty Italians could, in terms of a 'Wonderland' character, only make an unpredictable game 'curiouser and curiouser'.

While the world at large may have raised its eyebrows at this success it wasn't much more than we in the Irish camp had expected. It was a just reward for the all-round efforts we have made in recent years. I say this with no arrogant air. I know better. In a lifetime of chasing a football around I have experienced those 'curiouser' fortunes.

Usually the ball has responded reasonably to my desires. At times it has seemed to anticipate my every wish and flowed so smoothly that I thought it a part of me and that the whole wide world lay obedient at my feet. But there have been times when it would bounce awkwardly and I had despairing days fighting the unseen forces that bedevilled it.

Such were the times when I first began to play for my country. We were weak and small and poor and rare of talent and so confused that we were just a run around for our much stronger opponents. Occasionally we had a good day and lost 4–0 instead of 10–0, and everybody but our opponents would be happy.

Then one day along came our Prince Charming – Peter Doherty. He brought us a wealth of gifts like discipline, organisation, faith, adventure and determination to fight the great odds against us. Gradually confidence grew and we made a fight out of the impossible. We did not go out and conquer the soccer world; but we whittled down those defeats to the odd goal, drew many of our games and had an occasional win to gladden the heart.

This year we have reached a great peak with an unbeaten season of five games and qualification for the World Cup. Now the soccer experts of the world watch over us and wonder how much longer we can keep at bay those forces of destruction gathering to wreak vengeance on us for daring to achieve so much with so little.

I wonder, too. What effects will the taste of this great competition have upon us? Will the partaking of it make us shrink as Alice did – or grow as she did?

Or will we like Cinderella get caught out after midnight?

7 June 1958   *Danny Blanchflower*

Foreign Challenge

In 1954, though it was not possible to forecast the winners of the World Cup, it was easy enough to prophesy the outstanding team – Hungary. Now, four years later, one can only say that this seems the least distinguished field in the history of the tournament. Hungary, deprived of their great inside-forwards, Puskas and Kocsis, are a shadow team; South American football is in twilight.

The present favourites must be Yugoslavia, thanks to their recent 5–0 win over England. Yet this team depends too much on the whims of Milutinovitch, its 22-year-old centre-forward. When he's in form the whole attack moves like angels. When he's not, the wingers seem lethargic, and too great a burden falls on the little Sekularac, at deep inside-left. But the half-back line of Boskov, Zebec, the former left-wing, and Krstic, improving with every game, is formidable.

The Czechs are less endowed with stars, but their general level of play is excellent. Forwards such as Moravicka and Kraus, defenders such as Hertl and Novak, are of fully international standard; there are none of the alarming fallings-away in certain positions, such as beset, say, England and Wales.

Of the South Americans, it's generally agreed that Brazil are the best prospects, if only for their sheer unpredictability. Both they and the Argentinians play a style of football which is heavily influenced by South American crowds' demand for spectacle at all costs. There is much individualism, brilliant ball control, but little consistency.

Argentine, who lost four major forwards to Italy last year, are inclined to be too academic. Their play lacks bite, and it's doubtful whether Rossi, the key attacking right-half, can provide the necessary inspiration. He is 33 now, and that is old for a Latin player.

Russia, poorly though they played against England, must still be taken into account. In Netto, the blond, attacking left-half, and Yachine, in goal, they have two of the world's great players, while their stamina and fighting spirit are beyond question. What they lack is inspiration.

Sweden, reinforced by Hamrin, who has had a magnificent Italian season as Padova's outside-right, Liedholm, the 36-year-old Milan half-back or inside-forward, Gustavsson, a mighty centre-half, and Skoglund, the erratic 'Inter' Milan left-wing, may do better than anyone expects. They have, after all, the advantage of home ground.

Germany, strong at wing-half, with Eckel and Szymaniak, cannot expect Fritz Walter (now 37) to inspire them as he did in 1954. Austria have a clever attack, but a far from sufficient defence; the French team is in a frenzied process of rebuilding.

It is, in fact, anybody's Cup; on paper, at least, it's the most democratic there has yet been.

7 June 1958   *Brian Glanville*

Enslaved their Captains in Chains of Fear

Good soccer captains, like dinosaurs, are threatened with extinction. They are being hounded into a state of nervous nonentity by a huge pack of master minds who inhabit the high, drier lands of the grandstands.

There was a time, so we are told, when a football captain was a magnificent animal. He set his charges a fine example; led them with a rod of iron; and solved every problem on the field with quick and imaginative decision.

I do not quite believe that the old crew were really such a dominating race: legend has its own way of exaggeration. But they must have played a bigger part in the scope of things than do the present pretenders to the throne. It is not that they were better men; but rather that they prospered in times better suited to their individuality. (Perhaps the parallel lies in the field of politics.)

But evolution has changed all that. With the development of the game twin tribes have been fostered – the officials of the game, and those public guides the Press experts. They have tasted the power and fascination of the great game and suffer its hallucinations. Together, with careless abandon, they have 'safari-ed' into the game's mysterious and dangerous lands which were once the accepted province of the manager and his aide, the captain. They have civilised the manager and enslaved the players and their captain in chains of fear.

In most soccer camps the captain has become a peacock figure strutting vainly to mimic old traditions that no longer exist. He is permitted no liberty of decision or action and yet he is judged as if he were. After a game has been lost the Solomons of his camp will criticise him for not making certain positional or tactical changes; yet if he bravely does these things in vain endeavour to save a lost battle these same second guessers demand his blood.

What football needs most is players of skill, initiative and confidence. It needs captains of character who have the encouragement and authority to act according to their own judgment. Because when all is said and done it is down on the field that the game is lost and won. Yet, here in Sweden, evidence suggests that fate is pushing in the opposite direction.

Scotland had trouble in the 1954 world series when their manager resigned on the spot. This time enthusiastic goalkeeper and captain Tommy Younger was dropped because it was said the captaincy was affecting his play.

And as if the football world isn't crazy enough the Brazilians have brought along a psychiatrist. Apparently he chooses the music they should listen to. I prefer disc jockeys. He encourages them to wear their favourite coloured clothes. This used to be called superstition. And he helps in selecting the team according to the players' mental condition. Now we can add psychiatrists to the list of selectors alongside greengrocer, butcher and builder, etc.

As I see it what the game needs is good managers and captains. Anybody who consults a psychiatrist ought to have his head examined.

21 June 1958   *Danny Blanchflower*

The third-place match in Gothenburg gave me an unusual reporting problem. By the time The Observer *decided to give it brief coverage it was too late for me to get there from Stockholm. The solution for so short an account seemed to be to watch the game on a cinema-sized screen in the Stockholm press centre, with* The Observer *booking a call there as the final whistle was also the deadline for copy.*

That plan took no account of the room being in darkness, the commentary in Swedish which I didn't understand, the two teams I

93

hadn't watched scoring nine goals between them and incompetent TV camera work which panned in late on a mass of players hugging each other. In the circumstances getting the nine goals correct was a minor triumph in adversity. The article did at least accord with my sports editor's principles: 'As a first priority meet your deadline, as a second get your facts right, and after that you can indulge in fancy writing if you wish.'

France Earn a Place

In today's match at Gothenburg for third place in the World Cup, the fine French forward line played well enough to bring a 6–3 victory over a German side in which there were a number of changes. The French with their flair for attack have scored many more goals than any other country and the German defence was no match for their speed and skill.

It was a forwards' game throughout, but at the start it was Germany who swept easily past the French defence down the wings. Their finishing, however, was not as certain as usual and excessive endeavour often led to mistakes.

Soon their defence, whose fierce tackling at first subdued the French, began to give opportunities which Kopa and Fontaine were quick to exploit. These two outstanding players have been largely responsible for the success of a side which has many weaknesses and soon they put France ahead as Kopa contrived the opening and Fontaine shot home.

Germany equalised when Cieslarczyk scored with a left-foot drive, but the French forwards took complete charge after Kopa had scored from a penalty when Wiesnieski, a dangerous outside-right, was brought down as he raced through the centre. On the slippery ground France's quick moves continually caught the Germans out of position and before the interval Fontaine scored again.

After the interval the forwards of both sides continually baffled the defences, and France went further ahead with a goal from Douis. Thereafter the issue was never in doubt, and a further two goals from Fontaine confirmed France's superiority and his own position as leading goalscorer in the competition. Germany showed the weakness of the French defence with goals from Rahn and Schaefer.

France. – Abbes; Kaelbel, Lerond; Penverne, Lafont, Marcel; Wiesnieski, Douis, Kopa, Fontaine, Vincent.

West Germany. – Kwiatkowski; Stollenwerk, Erhardt; Sturm, Wewers, Szymaniak; Rahn, Schuclinger, Kelbassa, Schaefer, Cieslarczyk.

28 June 1958   *Tony Pawson*

Our Final preview from Danny Blanchflower drew the right conclusions.

Brazil Should Win Today

It is reasonably accepted by the experts assembled here that the two best teams in the World Cup competition have won through to to-morrow's final. And of the two, Brazil unquestionably have made the greater impression.

Technically they are all good players. They are easy masters of the ball and against France in the semi-final belied the opinion that they cannot shoot. Their positional play is very intelligent and they appear ever alert to the changing demands of attack and defence.

Santos is a fine full-back; coal-black 'Didi' of the lightning reflexes and swerving shot is the recognised master of the team; 17-year-old Pelè had a wonder game against France; and right-winger Garrincha with animal-like speed and instinct is a bewildering player whose shadow must lead a frustrating existence trying to keep in touch with him.

Tactically they employ a system which best suits their character. The two full-backs play very wide and the left-half drops back to play a dual role with the stopper centre-half: in simple terms, it is a line of four full-backs. The two wingers and twin centre-forwards operate as a front-line attacking force of four. Between these lines of attack and defence Didi and Zozimo supply a wandering half-back service.

The general rhythm of the team is a casual pleasant one; but occasionally some combination explodes with lightning effect to startle and excite the onlooker.

Their weaknesses are not easy to define. They beat France easily but will find Sweden a more difficult adversary. France appeared to penetrate better through the middle but that may have been due to their brilliant Kopa and Fontaine.

By reputation the Brazilians are temperamental and easily upset. They will not like the psychological disadvantage of playing before the home crowd. And despite their skill they fear the rain.

So if it doesn't rain too much and the Swedish crowd does not upset their mood too much the Brazilians ought to win the World Cup here at Solna Stadium to-morrow.

28 June 1958   *Danny Blanchflower*

Swedish Drill

Sweden have always played well enough to justify the confidence of their team's English coach, George Raynor, that they would reach the final. In addition they have had the natural advantage of playing at home and the good fortune of being drawn in a weak group which gave time for the professionals returning from Italy to blend with the players from Sweden's own amateur clubs.

The fact that a number of amateurs are playing in the final of the World Cup need cause no surprise for, since there are no professional clubs in Sweden, their leading players, though all amateurs, have the same training and competition as professionals in other countries.

The Swedish team, for all its individual ability, has undoubtedly been helped by Raynor's leadership. His instructions to players are simple and direct, and even at Press conferences where others are non-committal or evasive he is frank and clear. He talks of his team as a slow side who rely on the ball to do the running. This is certainly true of Gren and Liedholm, the insides who build the attack, but there is speed where it matters most in defence and on the wing and the whole team is quick and intelligent in its reactions.

28 June 1958   *Tony Pawson*

For McIlvanney, the 1966 World Cup finals came alive in the first week with a wonderful exhibition of football by Hungary against Brazil, who later failed to qualify for the quarter-finals when beaten also by

Portugal. *The atmosphere at Goodison Park also made a major contribution to a memorable occasion.*

One Legend Dies,
Another Revives

Now no one will dare to ask what all the fuss is about. Friday night at Goodison Park gave a gloriously comprehensive answer. The professional cynics have had to swallow their sarcasm; the honest doubters have been reassured. One match does not make a World Cup but one match as superb as Hungary's historic defeat of Brazil does convey the unique essence of the greatest team competition in sport.

It was an incredible occasion, so filled with the archetypal elements of the great game – skill, heart, atmosphere, an awareness of immortality being earned – that it would all have belonged more naturally to the pages of *The Wizard* than to a rain-darkened night in Liverpool.

Yet if any place in England deserved to be in on the real beginning of the 1966 World Cup it was Merseyside. Beyond their insatiable appetite for football, the crowds there have a heightened sense of drama, a flair for audience participation that is not inhibited by the knowledge that none of the central figures was born within a thousand miles of Lime Street.

On Friday they decided, with a predictable affection for the outsider, that they were for Hungary, and when they are for you it does not matter very much who is against you. Their support must have contributed significantly to the demise of one legend and the reincarnation of another. For more than eight years Brazil had so dominated the world game that the yellow jersey had come to be in football what it is in cycle racing: the symbol of leadership.

They had not lost a World Cup match since 1954 when Hungary, the peerless Hungary of Kocsis, Hidegkuti and Puskas (though he did not play that day), the finest side ever to fail in the World Cup, beat them 4–2 in a game that ended in a pitched battle. It is unlikely that the garnet red of Hungary will ever again be carried by such a consummately gifted team but no players could have worn it more worthily than the attacking geniuses Albert and Bene, and they could not have asked for more sustained support than they had from Farkas, Meszoly, Sipos and the rest.

The result was a performance that did not merely overcome but rather overwhelmed Brazil. In the end Hungary would not have been flattered if they had won by six goals. Albert, picking up the ball in deep positions and wheeling effortlessly away from tackles to swoop in on goal with an assurance that created an impression of inevitability, looked one of the world's greatest players. 'Albert, Albert,' the Merseysiders roared at the end, and he stood for several minutes in front of the stand, drinking from a bottle of water, waving and beaming. He was not acknowledging their tribute so much as simply sharing their exultation.

They are still a fair bet to be in the quarter-finals, for their greater determination and physical competitiveness should see them through on Tuesday against Portugal, with or without Pele. The Portuguese have one or two players, including Eusebio himself, who have been known to shrivel slightly in the fire of a crucial match.

Sadly it is not yet certain that we will see Hungary in the quarter-finals, for a narrow victory over Bulgaria could still leave them behind both Portugal and Brazil on goal average. However, every one of the 51,000 people who saw them at Everton on Friday will hope that this apprehension proves unfounded, and none will hope more sincerely than those of us who were sufficiently misled by form to underrate them at the outset.

Now it is clear that there is no side better equipped to counter the threat of negative play that hung a cloud of anti-climax over the initial exchanges of the competition. Perhaps Albert and Bene would not be able to run with the same free grace through the moving-forest defences of Uruguay, England and Italy but it would be a stirring experience to see them try.

It might be a reasonable gesture to give free tickets for Hungary's next game to all who endured England's goalless draw with Uruguay last Monday. Here was the classic illustration of what happens when defensive football is taken to its illogical conclusion.

17 July 1966   *Hugh McIlvanney*

John Arlott accurately described the Argentinian team after the preliminary matches.

Hard, Fast Argentina

Argentine football has been transformed in the past two months. Losing finalists in the first – 1930 – World Cup, they have never again so much as reached the quarter final. They came to this final pool by winning the weak No. 13 group from Bolivia and Paraguay. During the past year two coach-managers – Minnella and Zubelbia – resigned because they felt their powers were not adequate. Argentina appeared a poor prospect.

Two months ago Lorenzo Guacello was appointed coach with sole control of selection and direction. A dumpy, unhurried, thoughtful man of the Ramsey type, he coached the 1962 Argentine side in Chile. Then he went to Italy to manage Laszio, took them up from the second to the first division and then, as no player or official *ever* does, crossed the city to Roma: he made them Italian Cup winners.

In this time his views on football changed and he has changed the methods of the Argentine team accordingly. They made an impression on Wednesday, not merely in beating a Spanish side by no means short of talent – their win might well have been more decisive – but by their style. They even *look* different.

Formerly they were reminiscent in manner of the Uruguayans: they massed in defence, slowing down the game there and, much influenced by Brazil, like all South American teams, their midfield play tended towards relaxed rhythm.

Oddly English-looking on the field (the English contingent in Argentina is the largest in the world outside the Commonwealth) – in striped shirts, hairstyles, incisive movements and explosive tackling – they have been given a fresh character by Guacello. The change was deliberate.

In Guacello's own words: 'We had lived too long in South American football: we built up slowly; playing the ball often square and using many short passes. Europe taught me that more direct, and forward-moving methods and longer passes – 40 or 50 yards, not 10 – are more effective: and Argentinians can play in that way. For this type of football you must move and tackle and advance more quickly. I have young men who are strong and fast and can play this way.'

He has indeed – with Rattin, a solid master of positioning at their core. Mas is a younger version of Gento on the wing: Onega a gifted, sensitive inside forward: Ferriero a back superbly fast in movement and thought, quick to overlap in attack.

Argentine may prove the hardest and fastest competitors in this series: certainly no team will beat them which shrinks from harsh contact or high pace.

17 July 1966   *John Arlott*

They were indeed fast and very hard giving England a difficult time at Wembley and the referee an even harder one, as Harry Weaver indicated in summarising the progress to the semi-final matches.

Europe Dominate the Cup

It is 32 years since there was an all-European World Cup semi-final, and now, after a sad day for the image of football, we are to have two – Russia v. West Germany at Goodison Park on Monday and England v. Portugal at Wembley on Tuesday.

The end of the South American era, for the time being at any rate, came as a shabby postscript to so much past brilliance.

Two Uruguayans, Troche their captain, and Silva were sent off at Hillsborough where West Germany went on to coast to a 4–0 win.

And, at Wembley, Rattín, the Argentine captain, was sent off . . . the game was held up for 10 minutes when he refused to go . . . three Argentine players had their names taken. . . . German referee Rudolf Kreitlin had to be escorted off by police at the end as Argentine reserves jostled him.

The FIFA disciplinary committee, which suspended Argentinian Albrecht for one game a week ago and warned the whole team, meets today to deal with yesterday's incidents.

England scraped home to their first World Cup semi-final in a disappointing game through a header from Hurst, replacing the injured Greaves.

Mr Ramsey, the England manager, explained later that England will do better when they come up against a team which 'comes out to play football, not act as animals'. He added that Greaves is unlikely to be fit for Tuesday.

North Korea, the long shots (in both senses), looked like delighting underdog fanciers when they led World Cup favourites Portugal 3–0.

Eusebio, who promises to be the player of the tournament as well as winner of the £1,000 prize for top scorer, shattered their vision with four goals, two from penalties, and Augusto added a fifth.

Eusebio was hurt in a tackle which led to one penalty and there is some question about his fitness for the semi-final.

Last night one London bookmaker was offering the following odds: Portugal 2–1, Russia 11–4, West Germany 11–4, England 3–1. Another, however, made England joint 5–2 favourites with Portugal.

24 July 1966   *Harry Weaver*

In the run-up to England's triumphant final there were other fasci-nating matches to record as in the following description by John Arlott of that extraordinary match between Portugal and North Korea. There were also many interesting aspects for us to reflect on.

Four-goal Eusebio

Portugal emerged as a complete football team, as fine in temperament as in technique – and Eusebio stood head and shoulders above everyone else on the field – in this quarter-final. To be three good goals down in a match on this level, to come back and win handsomely, must be near indeed to the peak of footballing achievement.

The Koreans' newly made friends from the North-East had barely begun their chant of 'Kor-ee-ah', in the unmistakable tones of Tees and Wear, when their 'diddy men' scored a goal. It was the first move in the first minute: Li Dong Woon hammered his kick against the defensive wall, it bounced off: Han Bong Zin, on the right, pushed it back to Pak Seung Zin, who took two strides to the back of the penalty area and struck a rising shot into the top left corner of the Portuguese goal. The crowd cheered and laughed.

Portugal came back coolly and strongly, sending the ball up for Torres's head. But though he was a foot taller than the Korean defenders he could climb no higher than Ha Jung Wong and Rim Yung Sun, who jack-knifed into the air like cats on a hot hob.

In midfield the Koreans stroked the ball, tricked and juggled with it; cross-passed and doubled back. The Portuguese defence was suspicious and uneasy.

Still within the half-hour, Pak Doo Ik pushed a forward ball to Yang Seung Kook: Li Dong Woon took his precise cross, sighted the goal and shot into it. 'We want three,' called the crowd, and a minute later they had three.

Yang Seung Kook took Han Bong Zin's short ball, pushed it past two men, used the last fraction of a second to take aim, and drove right-footed into the roof of goal. Three–nil to North Korea: Goodison giggled with disbelief. Yet few defences would have kept out these sharp, gimlet-like attacks. But Portugal steadied themselves.

Eusebio now was grafting like three men. On the half-hour he gave the ball to Simoes, took the return and as the Koreans hesitated cut right away, found an avenue for his shot and fired it home.

It was all impossible. Portugal, to their credit, continued calmly to attempt to disprove it. In the minute before half-time Shin Yung Kyll, a hard, strong back, tripped Torres as he burst through. Eusebio sent the penalty fiercely and steeply beyond Ri Chan Myaung's spreadeagled leap.

Portugal began the second half with ominous efficiency, but this was Korea's great spell. Small but wiry; fit and devoted; they were sharp and quick as needles. Only genius would penetrate, and the genius was in the Portuguese line. Simoes directed the ball low across goal, and there was Eusebio lancing through to meet it with a glorious shot in mid-leap. Level at three all; half an hour left.

No sooner were Portugal again in possession than he was there again, this mighty, lithe man of bursting vitality, taking on three men, racing down the left, round the outside and into the penalty area where a despairing leg fetched him down from behind in his shooting stride. This time he changed his approach to the penalty kick, but hit the same uncoverable point in the net.

Now Portugal could slip into their normal gear, pacing and commanding the game. Eusebio could relax. Yet surely the Koreans, like the rest of us, knew that at need he would do it again. In case they doubted he made his point when, from a dozen yards outside the penalty area he powered a shot so fiercely from his amazing right foot that it tore through Ri Chan Myaung's hands and bounced leadenly away from his body.

Seven minutes from the end, Portugal made certain with their stock move. Eusebio crossed from the left; Torres rose up and nodded it precisely back for Augusto to head the last goal.

Portugal. – Pereira; Morais, Baptista; Vicente, Hilario, Graca; Coluna, Augusto, Eusebio, Torres, Simoes.

North Korea. – Ri Chan Myaung; Rim Yung Sun, Shin Yung Kyll; Ha Jung Wong, O Yoon Kyung, Pak Seung Zin; John Seung Hwi, Han Bong Zin, Pak Doo Ik, Li Dong Woon, Yang Sung Kook.

Referee – Ashkenazi (Israel).

24 July 1966   *John Arlott*

Before the Final Hugh McIlvanney found the Germans paradoxically worried by English militaristic nationalism.

Deserving of Kipling

England in the World Cup Final was a phenomenon that deserved to be chronicled by Rudyard Kipling and, having read the sports pages last Wednesday morning, I am prepared to believe that it was.

But not everybody was proud to be English. The Scots and French, for example, did not feel that way at all. Scottish reporters sat in a smouldering sulk in corners in the Press Centre in Kensington and insisted that they did not know what all the carry on was about. People like myself who betrayed their birthright sufficiently to acknowledge that England played rather well to beat Portugal in Tuesday night's semi-final were accused of defecting to 'the caramel chewers'.

The English sour grapes discharged even more acid. *L'Equipe* carried a vicious cartoon showing Bobby Charlton and Nobby Stiles (bereft of front dentures and looking like a vampire) driving a Rolls-Royce while referees in policemen's uniform held back the Argentine, France and a few other rivals. The caption said 'Let us pass please'.

Such ungenerous reactions probably called for the corrective of some chauvinism. It came in a great smothering flood and its dubious origins were emphasised by the fact that the opponents to be met in the final were the West Germans. The Germans themselves claimed to be bewildered and appalled by the militaristic nationalism of the English.

Ulrich Kaiser, who works for a sports information agency in Dusseldorf, said the whole thing alarmed him. 'I know that if we win some of our people are going to say "We have beaten the world." I hate that. I will not have beaten the world. Eleven German footballers will have won a cup and I will be glad to see it. But I am not saying I have beaten anybody. Of these eleven players how many at home would I have in my apartment for coffee or beer? Maybe two of them. I am not looking down at the others but we are in different areas of life you understand. We have different friends, different interests, different thoughts. How can I say "We have beaten the world." It is nonsense and I don't like it. I think it is dangerous.'

Werner Schneider, who is one of the best-known television commentators in Germany, was equally disturbed. 'Everywhere you look in the newspapers they are saying "England is going to win, England is going to rule the football world." This nationalism is surely more than football. Perhaps we have learned our lesson because of the Second World War. Perhaps we think more than other people of how mad this thinking is. You would expect this from countries who have nothing else. You could understand it in Ghana, or in the South American countries like the

Argentine and Brazil where football is just about all they have. But in England it is strange and sad.

'They want to fly flags and beat drums because they are winning at football. Look at that band at Wembley. Tin soldiers, I call them. It is said that the Germans are the most militaristic people in the world but it is not so. The British are. Even winning at football is treated like a victory in battle.'

The case was apparently proved when the crowd watching the third-place final between Portugal and Russia at Wembley on Thursday began to chant 'England, England.' But the Germans on the terraces responded with bellows of 'Uwe, Uwe,' which seemed to combine the worst elements of nationalism with the cult of personality.

In fact the man the official German party were expecting to win the day for them was not the veteran Seeler but the 20-year-old Beckenbauer, the superb half-back from Munich Bayern who has emerged as one of the indisputable stars of the World Cup. Beckenbauer was a great player as a schoolboy and from his first match in his club's senior side at the age of 18 his progress has been a triumph to compare with the tragically curtailed career of Duncan Edwards. At a cocktail party in the German Consul's home in Kensington last week all the talk about the final was talk about Beckenbauer. FIFA's decision to erase the second caution which might have kept him out of the game was an unavoidable act of good sense but the German relief was prodigious.

'It means a great deal to us,' said Helmut Schoen, the team manager. 'Beckenbauer is one of the greatest talents of Europe. And he is better than he shows. There is more to come from him.'

Schoen, a tall, bald man with flawless manners, obviously meant what he said when he expressed surprise at reaching the final. 'Next year we will have a younger, better team. We have players like Jurgen Grabowski ready to come in. He is a brilliant winger, but he is only 20 and not quite right for this. Not everybody can be a Beckenbauer.'

Schoen won 17 caps as a stylish centre-half with Dresden, and when he stopped playing he managed the Saar's team for a time. In the qualifying series for the World Cup of 1954 the Saar played West Germany and Schoen found himself opposed to the greatest figure in the history of German football, Sepp Herberger. Later, when the Saar was returned to Germany, he became Herberger's assistant and after about five years he took over the job of manager.

For a small man, Herberger casts a big shadow and there are many who say that Schoen has still to merge from it. Certainly at the cocktail party the old master's audience was as large and attentive as his successor's. He was describing how Germany might succeed in breaking down England's

wonderful defence where Portugal had failed. 'Portugal use the Mediterranean individualism,' he said, 'They ask Eusebio to do it alone. We will
not do that. We will have at least two strikers running parallel, with
powerful units backing up from behind.' The script might have been by
Rommel.

Across the room the editor of *Kicker*, which claims to be the biggest
football magazine in Europe, was back on the subject of Beckenbauer. 'He
is the greatest German player since that man gave it up,' he said, pointing at
a dapper figure with a ruddy face and unexpectedly brown eyes. It was
Fritz Walter, the most celebrated of German players. Walter said that
Beckenbauer for his age was almost a sensational talent. 'Almost but not
quite. He still shows signs of immaturity. But he is going to be very, very
great.'

The England players, convincingly simulating coolness at their Hendon
hotel, clearly did not think that anybody was great enough to stop them on
the run in. In beating Portugal they had come to a confident awareness of
their strength. George Cohen tried to indicate how they felt but had to fall
back on vague gestures. 'We feel really good,' he said at last.

No doubt the man who felt best was Alf Ramsey. Nothing that
happened in the final could deprive him of a massive satisfaction. Some of
the criticisms levelled at him still appear valid but they are now utterly
unimportant. The achievement is tremendous and the only thing to do is to
applaud it.

24 July 1966   *Hugh McIlvanney*

---

*The 1970 World Cup Finals were also full of colour and excitement
with England so unlucky to go out in the quarter-finals as an illness to
Gordon Banks deprived the team of his great talent. As McIlvanney
reported, even the Scots could scarce forbear to cry at the injustice of it.*

Even the Scots Had
Tears in Their Eyes

If anything could restore spirits bruised by the sad and undeserved
expulsion of England from the World Cup it was the sight of Brazil

surging, like a man o' war with nuclear armament, into the final of the competition for the fourth time.

Whatever happens in the Aztec Stadium here tomorrow, and clearly the most likely occurrence is a Brazilian victory, Pele and Tostao, Gerson and Rivelino, Jairzinho and the rest have demonstrated that the richest flowering of football is still to be found in the southern latitudes.

That statement is no slight on the deposed champions, who will accept it as sufficient tribute that the most exciting and dangerous team in the world regard them as equals, to be respected to the point of apprehension.

Judged by all objective criteria, England should be in tomorrow's final with Brazil, meeting fire with ice in a classic collision of the European and South American philosophies of the game. Italy are there, and no one should carp about their presence. But the contrasting memories of how they struggled from beginning to exhausted end against West Germany and the ease with which England dominated the Germans, until the wide crack in Bonetti's nerve let them through, make it impossible to believe that Italy would have beaten England.

Sir Alf Ramsey's team are out because the best goalkeeper most people have ever seen turned sick, and one who is only slightly less gifted was overwhelmed by the suddenness of his promotion. In sport disaster often feeds upon itself but this was a sickeningly gluttonous example.

Those who ranted smugly in distant television studios about the tactical blunders of Ramsey were toying with the edges of the issue. Errors there were, and Ramsey in private has acknowledged one or two, but the England manager is entitled to his claim that his side were felled by something close to an act of God.

There are people who would offer prizes to anyone who could quote an occasion when I have been sentimentally pro-English, but I was one of many outsiders who were moved by the champions' harsh experience in Leon and by the way they took it. 'I had a lump in my throat. I had to get out of the stadium before anybody noticed tears in my eyes,' said one Scottish international player. 'You just had to be affected when you saw a team with all those qualities – fellows like Mooro and Ballie and big Geoff and Mullers – getting the message like that. I'm telling you this competition lost something special when it lost them. Anybody who calls it nobility isn't far wrong.' Those who wince at that as soggy chauvinism should have heard it delivered in a West of Scotland accent.

That Scot, and quite a few Englishmen, had the good fortune to be moved in a more uplifting way three days later when Brazil, whose fuse had gathered sparkling momentum with each succeeding match in the tournament, exploded thrillingly to fragment Uruguay's stubborn defence.

The 3–1 victory was much more than a reiteration of all the virtues

Europeans identify with Brazilian football: it was marvellously persuasive evidence that this side, like the best of their predecessors, reinforce genius with good sense, grace with athletic strength and art with tactical calculation.

Much of this was represented in their response to the goal they lost to Uruguay after 18 minutes. A carelessly misdirected pass by Brito was punished by the inspired cunning of a centre from Morales, but Cubilla, in controlling the ball, was forced to an inhibiting angle, and his shot was hit slackly. When Felix, an emotional choice on whom Mario Zagalo has expended an excess of loyalty, reacted by dancing along his line like a novice ice-skater and allowing the ball to bounce languidly into his net, despair might have been general.

Gerson did clutch his head as if he had heard a terrible noise, and even the powerful captain, Carlos Alberto, looked broken for a moment. But Pele ran through the demoralised lines to retrieve the ball and bring it back for the kick-off. In this, an unforgettably brilliant World Cup for him, he has shown an uncanny awareness of what is relevant (the crowd's cheers are no more than a bonus far out on the borders of his mind), and in that instant he knew the most meaningful thing was to play ball-boy.

'My first concern here, in Mexico,' he said afterwards, 'was to play a full World Cup. I have never been fit to complete all of Brazil's matches before. But now we have got this far I am determined to win. I am told I seem to be some kind of father figure now. If that is true it is only because I have the greatest experience of the World Cup. But, of course, I do have a special place in Brazilian football. I can talk to the other players. I can get them to do things that perhaps no one else could. This is something that has come naturally, not something I have worked to create. But I am happy to make use of it.'

In his efforts to calm and steady the team, Pele has the required quorum of rationalising influences. Three is an acceptable number and in 1958 Brazil had Didi, Zito and Nilton Santos. Now Tostao, who has all the cool, imperturbable shrewdness expected of men from Minas Gerais, a state that produces politicians as freely as others produce coffee, is an obvious lieutenant. And Gerson, though his volatile nature is inclined to dramatise disappointment, is too intelligently attuned to the realities of the game to be misled for long.

It was Gerson who first exposed the crippling flaw in the man for man marking of the Uruguayans. From the start he had been subjected to the ruthless proximity of Cortes, who stayed close enough to use the same shaving mirror. With Pele similarly crowded by Montero Castillo, the effects could have been serious. But Gerson has the uncommon advantage of thinking as fluently as he talks.

'First I went to the left, then I went to the right. Then I moved up to the edge of their penalty area and still he stayed with me. So I decided there was one place to take him. They were interested only in defending, so I took him back to our penalty area. That meant one body out of the way of our attackers. I told Clodoaldo to go forward and do my job, that I would stay behind with the number 20. Clodoaldo scored our equaliser from my position. Then the whole game was changed and we could not lose.

'At half time I asked Zagalo if he approved of what I had done. He had no complaints. The only other change he wanted was that Rivelino should move a little to his right in midfield to give Pele and Tostao room to make their moves on the left. They made good use of the room.'

Tostao in fact has spent the last year learning to employ his humbling talents without the luxury of space. Since his prodigious beginnings in the game he had functioned much as Pele does, seeking the ball in the middle of the field and moving forward to beat tackles, creating trouble from deep positions.

'But when I came to play regularly with Pele in the national team I realised I would have to change my style completely. There was too much risk of duplication. I saw that I would be far more effective if I operated as a pivot for the attack, staying forward as much as possible and giving first-time passes to the others as they came through.

'I developed the knack of playing with my back to the goal. My main function is to offer the maximum number of options to the other attackers, to draw defenders out of position and exploit the gaps with those one-touch plays.'

That he is now arguably the most consummately skilled exponent of this technique is no surprise to those who have followed his career. He is, in equipment and attitude, an astonishing amalgam of the finest in the European and South American approaches to football: the best of both worlds, an artist who turns economist if the going gets hard.

The will needed to transform his style in one year was no greater than that which enabled him to overcome the injury inflicted on his left eye by blows from a knee and a football. Detachment of the retina was minimal but it necessitated an operation in Houston, Texas, and the loss of vital months of action on the run-in to the World Cup.

As recently as the week before the tournament started, Tostao, disturbed by painless but unsightly haemorrhaging in the eye, had a psychological crisis and was ready to return to Brazil. A telephone call to Doctor Abdala Moura, the Brazilian ophthalmic surgeon who operated on him in Houston, brought reassurance.

The doctor, a football addict and supporter of Tostao's club, Cruzeiro, flew to Mexico to watch the young forward play against a Leon side and told him that even if he had more bleeding in the eye he could turn out in a match the same day. Tostao's confidence was renewed and Brazil felt they were on their way to winning the World Cup.

Whether they do or not, Tostao will return to Houston to have the cause of the haemorrhaging removed. It is deduced to be the result of an allergy to the catgut sewn in during the operation.

The prospect of more surgery was only a fringe shadow on the bright optimism of the Brazilian camp after the defeat of Uruguay. They appreciated that Italy are formidably calculating, but are content to suspect that they will be faced by the man-to-man covering favoured by Uruguay rather than the more subtle zonal marking of the English defence Zagalo has defined as the best he ever saw. Any advantage the Italians gained by playing all their earlier matches at substantially higher altitudes has, they are sure, been balanced by the draining effects of those murderous two hours against Germany. Whoever wins tomorrow will claim permanent ownership of the Jules Rimet trophy, for both have two successive victories to their credit, but Brazil's dominance is a postwar phenomenon and they have the right to consider themselves favourites.

Pele is now hard pressed to restrain their exuberance. As he stood in the sunshine by their motel swimming pool in Guadalajara before they left for Mexico City one had time to notice a great deal more than the remarkably low instep and the wide spread of toes that give him unlikely feet for the world's outstanding footballer. He took trouble to emphasise that Italy, with their frustrating competence at the back and Riva at the front, have still to be beaten. But he found it difficult to forget how great Brazil are.

Watching the Brazilians reach tentatively for a dream made us remember the scene in Leon on Sunday night when the England players had reconstructed a nightmare. As in all nightmares the central figures and events were at once familiar and unfamiliar. Bonetti was somehow not Bonetti.

'The cat didn't look like the cat out there,' somebody said. 'That first goal were a Weetabix goal,' one of the players added. 'And the second wasn't all that much. But you've got to feel sorry for Peter. Banksie seemed to have got over Montezuma's on the Saturday night and he was playing about with the ball on Sunday morning. He was in the side and then keeled over at the team meeting and Peter was told he was in about half an hour before we left for the ground. No wonder he was a bunch of nerves. If he'd had a lot of the ball early on he might have sorted it out, but there was hardly anything to do before Beckenbauer stuck that one in. In that sort of situation goalkeepers have no chance to find their feet.'

Sunday afternoon did nothing to improve Banks's condition. He was watching the quarter-final on a delayed television transmission. And

England were a goal ahead when his room-mate, Alex Stepney, came in with the shattering news. The team doctor, Neil Phillips, who had seen his obsessive conscientiousness come to nothing, had the additional pain of telling Banks that Stepney's report was all too accurate.

Outside at the swimming-pool the players tried to make themselves believe they were out. Naturally, they wondered about the timing and the nature of Ramsey's substitutions. Several could be persuaded to agree that Bobby Charlton should not have been called off, that Lee should.

Perhaps neither Lee nor Peters should have been fielded in the first place, but for me the only specific criticism to be made of the England manager is that, once he had Bell warming up on the touchline, the player should have been pushed on without delay instead of being withheld until Germany had scored and the change assumed the appearance of a panic measure.

Sadly, all that is now a footnote to this World Cup. Tomorrow belongs to Brazil and Italy, and principally I believe, to Brazil.

21 June 1970   *Hugh McIlvanney*

For McIlvanney the final was flawed by Italy's poor performance, but illuminated, as the whole championship had been, by Brazil's marvellous talent.

Brazil's Marvellous Talent

The World Cup of 1970 was one of those events that should be left in the bright colours of immediacy, not greyed by an excess of retrospective analysis.

Naturally, however, there must be some overspill of argument and recrimination and it is as well to get the unpleasantness out of the way first. The Italians, for instance, cannot possibly escape being criticised for the meek sterility and downright folly of their tactics in the final.

In a nation that has long had an almost paranoid obsession with tactical theory, their blunderingly unimaginative response to the vast problems presented by the brilliance of Brazil was as surprising as a wooden leg in a long-distance runner. Perhaps coping with the Brazilians was too much to

110

ask of any team in the competition, but few of us had the nerve or foresight to predict, as a friend from Rio did, that the Italians would leave a player as devastatingly resourceful and accomplished as Gerson unmarked in midfield.

'They will use man-for-man covering on our forwards and leave Gerson free,' he said. 'Gerson will come through to shoot, probably he will score, and he will control the pattern of the match.' Those of us who did not frisk him for a crystal ball silently assumed that Italy could not be naïve enough to make good his forecast.

We were spectacularly mistaken. In their familiar determination to keep an extra man at the back, the Italians allowed Gerson to roam unhindered and lay the basis of a superiority in the middle of the field that left even the splendid, tireless Mazzola without decisive influence. There was one cage too few. A lion was left on the loose.

Against such opposition, no one expected Valcareggi – or the more shadowy men credited with usurping his function as manager of the side – to abandon the established policy of having only two players, Riva and Boninsegna, thrust forward. But adding surrender in mid-field to that accepted limitation was bound to be disastrous.

The extent of Italy's confusion was demonstrated when, having decided to introduce Rivera at a time when any hope of winning had disappeared, they withdrew Boninsegna, the one man who had measured up to the excellence of Mazzola's example. Such peculiar decisions must be related to the widespread and reasonable suspicion that the Italians were so glad to reach the final, after the humiliation of 1966, that they suffered from a resigned lack of ambition in the match itself.

They certainly did sufficient to earn a home-coming much more agreeable than that of four years ago, when they were pelted with rotten fruit. Brazil's only resemblance to North Korea was that they had the same number of limbs. And there were times when even that seemed doubtful.

Most Brazilians now acknowledge that the present side is better than the winning team of 1962 but not quite as comprehensively talented, from deep defence through to the spearheads of the attack, as the one that took their first World Cup in Sweden in 1958. They consider that Djalma and Nilton Santos, Bellini, Orlando and Zito gave Gilmar more impressive protection than Felix had, though the defence showed more skill and organisation in this year's tournament than most people admitted, and might have been still steadier if Felix himself had looked as much like a goalkeeper in the earlier matches as he did in the final.

In any case only the Brazilians, whose three victories in the last four World Cups have entitled them to permanent possession of the Jules Rimet Trophy, can afford the luxury of such refined comparisons. Even they do not strain too hard to identify any previous combination of inspiration and athletic power that did more damage or gave more entertainment than the collective gifts of Gerson, Clodoaldo, Rivelino, Jairzinho, Tostao, Pele and, intermittently but dramatically, Carlos Alberto.

Mario Zagalo had been accused of a defensive approach to the challenge in Mexico but in the event his team scored 19 goals, more than in 1958 or 1962, and an average of better than three a match. In the process they beat three former champions, Uruguay, Italy and England, convincingly swept aside the tired fallacy that Brazilian football is always a wild force of nature, incapable of accommodating any tactical awareness, and proved that their players could be persuaded to train with the intensity needed to match the physical endurance of Europeans. Brazil's stamina was a vital factor, along with the confident patience that spread outwards from Pele, Gerson and Tostao, in enabling them to score important goals in the last 20 minutes of their games.

Zagalo managed another more personal achievement. He overcame at last the resentment of him that had persisted among the men, notably Pele, who had played with him in 1958 and 1962. No one questioned the value of his contribution in those years ('Zagalo was the one who showed the world 4–3–3', says one Brazilian, 'who made it clear to all of us that a footballer must have two shirts – a defender's and an attacker's.') But his team-mates felt that his luck, which is legendary, had kept better players out. In 1958 and 1962 Pepe, the great goal-scoring winger of Santos, was removed by injury and Germano was similarly unfortunate in 1962. Pele was one of those who believed that the Zagalo luck had put a jinx on his rivals.

It was an intriguing scene, therefore, when Pele and Zagalo came face to face, alone for the moment, in a corner of the dressing rooms at the Aztec Stadium after the final. Pele put down the glass of water he was drinking and, without a word, they ran to each other for a long, tearful embrace. Later Pele gave the manager his shirt.

At roughly the same time the President of Brazil, General Garrastazú Médici, was draping a national flag round his shoulders and going out of his palace to play informal, euphoric football with the crowds in Praça dos Tres Poderes, the main square of Brasilia. The one player President Médici strenuously advocated, Dario, a Negro centre-forward, did not help directly in the winning of the World Cup, but he helped to keep it. Carlos Alberto, while making his jostling lap of honour with the Cup, failed to notice that the gold top of the trophy had slipped on to the ground at his feet. Dario, following on behind, saw a small boy pick it up and after a brief chase was able to retrieve it.

Paulo Cezar had to survive a chase to hold on to another prize, the match ball, which he snatched on behalf of a friend who is a fanatical supporter.

When he was pursued by an Italian player, Paulo Cezar had an unanswerable advantage – he had been resting on the substitutes' bench throughout the match.

Long after the final was over, and they had congratulated Zagalo on his refusal to be diverted from the view that Carlos Alberto would play a big part in winning it, some of the Brazilians still found difficulty in absorbing what had happened. Pele says that when he woke on Monday morning he seriously wondered if he had been dreaming. The sight of his medal at the bedside only partially reassured him and he telephoned his wife, Rose, at home to ask: 'Are we really the champions?' Rose, who is six months pregnant with their second child, told him she had felt a severe pain when he scored the first goal. She must have been one of the few people in Brazil who did.

If Pele has played his last World Cup, and it is impossible to dispute his own conclusion that at 33 he will be too old to do himself justice in Munich, then we must be grateful that Mexico provided such an exhilarating demonstration of his uniqueness. Who will now suggest that he is less than the greatest footballer we have seen. The mature completeness of his game, the cunning, implacably relevant exploitation of bewildering skill and superb athleticism, recalled a tribute by Jose Saldanha, who should be remembered with sympathy as the man who chose the players (all except the dispensable Felix) Zagalo led to success.

Said Saldanha: 'Ask me who is the best right-back in Brazil and I'll say Pele. Ask me about the best left back or the best midfield man, or the best winger, or the best centre-forward. Always I must say Pele. If he wants to be the best goalkeeper, he will be. There is only one Pele.'

28 June 1970   *Hugh McIlvanney*

At the end of the 1982 Finals in Spain The Observer *listed these quotes from those eventful weeks.*

The Brains in Spain

'Next week World Cup superstars Zico, Maradona and Hamilton will have gone home, and Spain will be bankrupt.' – *Barcelona newspaper.*

113

'Zoff's alright on the high stuff but with low shots he's been going down in instalments.' – *Ian St John on Italy's World Cup captain.*

'This fellow Tardelli, he's likely to leap out of the TV at us. He's put more scar tissue on people than the surgeons at Harefield Hospital.' – *Jimmy Greaves.*

'Communism v Alcoholism.' – *Scottish supporters' banner at Scotland v Russia game.*

'Don't worry lads, Ally McLeod's in Blackpool.' – *Scottish banner in Seville.*

'I cannot feed my child on glory.' – *Paolo Rossi during his pay dispute with Juventus.*

'Two months ago he was over the moon – now he is asking for it.' – *Juventus official on Rossi.*

'I've never met a team which squeal like the Germans. That Breitner especially. Once I put my hand out to hold him off, and he went down screaming as if I'd dropped him one.' – *Bryan Robson, after England v W. Germany.*

'I felt sorry for Herr Derwall and Herr Schmidt. Two such honourable men should not be asked to justify the unjustifiable.' – *Algerian FA president Hadg Sekkal, after the dubious Austria v W. Germany match.*

'There is no FIFA rule which says teams cannot play as they please.' – *Hermann Neuburger, German FA president and FIFA vice-president, after the Austria–W. Germany match.*

'FIFA are worse than the Mafia.' – *Sheikh Fahd Al Ahmed Al Sabah, Kuwait FA president, after disputed goals in match against France.*

'Argies Smashed.' – *The Sun, after Argentina's defeat by Belgium.*

'Irish frivolity masks both fitness and resolve.' – *The Times.*

'You are not at the seaside now you know.' – *Billy Drennan, Irish FA secretary to players who complained about their World Cup hotel in Madrid. The players had nicknamed the hotel 'El Dumpo'.*

'What do you think of Brazil?'

'I think he's a great player.' – *Interchange between Brazilian journalist and Kenny Dalglish during the World Cup.*

The road to the World Cup finals gets harder all the time. On the way to their disappointments in Mexico, Scotland and England both tasted success in November 1984. Ronald Atkin witnessed a resurgence of Scottish spirit and skill on an emotional night at Hampden Park.

Scotland v. Spain, 1984

Grown men hugged and pummelled each other at Hampden Park last Wednesday and that was only in the press box. The Scottish media, who rejoice in the description 'supporters with typewriters' were quite beside themselves as they watched the goals going in, while on the terraces the paying punters loudly assured the boys in blue of their enduring affection.

Scotland's defeat of Spain was a memorable occasion, memorably celebrated. As Jimmy Reid said at one of the late-night Glasgow-wide sessions 'this is the only time you can kiss another man in Scotland and not be called a poof'.

Even the team manager, Jock Stein, whose level of discernible emotion is normally on a par with the faces carved into Mount Rushmore, leapt off his bench and hurried to the touchline anxious to add his congratulations to the kisses being bestowed on Kenny Dalglish for the stupendous goal which sealed his side's victory.

By press conference time, however, Stein had battened down any temptations for a repeat of such a frivolity. Stirring sugar into his tea, he pronounced himself 'quite satisfied' and assessed Graeme Souness, the inspirational captain of a mightily impressive team, as 'not a bad player'.

The Spanish manager, Miguel Munoz, looking as if he had just walked away from a rather nasty road accident, was asked what he thought of Scotland's performance and the young local interpreter translated his reply, rather freely but perhaps understandably, 'magic, tremendous'.

Taking his ease in the Centenary Room of the Scottish FA offices the following morning Stein offered the opinion that the Spaniards had under-estimated his men, and it was difficult to argue against this.

Clearly, they could not fathom the absence of such as Archibald, Strachan, Hansen, Nicholas, and Wark from the Scotland line-up. 'They thought they could subdue the outside left (Davie Cooper of Rangers) and they didn't expect so much from Jim Bett,' said Stein. 'They thought Dalglish was very much on the wane and that we had defensive weaknesses they could capitalise on.'

Munoz and his players were disastrously wrong on every count, except possibly the last. Scotland's dread disease, the fumble-fingered goalkeeper, was again in evidence as Leighton thought about coming out for Camacho's free kick, changed his mind and was beaten by Goicoechea's bouncing header.

Elsewhere the defence, with the Aberdeen pair Miller and McLeish solidly at its heart, looked just about bomb proof, except for the tendency of the otherwise admirable Nicol at right back to get himself too far forward rather too often (understandable perhaps because he doesn't play in that position regularly for his club, Liverpool).

Stein was keen to stress the influence of Souness's captaincy. 'He's very important for us because he pulls the stings,' he said.

Moving to Sampdoria has been good for him. 'Now he plays 30 games a year, whereas with Liverpool it was more like 70. Graeme has been a revelation. That one game a week has made the difference. At Liverpool he was involved in so many things but with Sampdoria he has different aims. They haven't been promoted long and their ambition is to establish themselves in the top six.'

Bett, the tall midfielder who plays in the Belgian League with Lokeren, was another revelation. Spain were initially distracted and finally destroyed by his plundering runs, the most punishing of which swept him past Urtubi's challenge and dropped the ball on Maurice Johnston's head for the second goal.

'When Bett left here for Belgium he thought he was saying goodbye to the international team,' said Stein. 'But he's so versatile, you should see him play right-back. He's shy and reticent but we are getting him out of his shell a wee bit.

'I spoke to him about his tendency to make a careless start and told him he ought to try to start on a high key. There is no doubt he started in the right key last night.

'He is also a very good influence on the outside-left. Cooper had this great way of showing the Spanish exactly what he intended to do and then going ahead and doing it anyway. The Rangers chairman said to me afterwards: "Why doesn't Cooper play for us like he does for Scotland?" '

Stein also paid sincere tribute to the predatory skills of Johnston. 'A lively bugger, isn't he? He threatens defenders even when he isn't scoring. He has the natural goal scorer's instinct for rebounds.'

But the manager's deepest admiration was reserved for the 33-year-old Dalglish. 'He's a very brave player. Most forwards don't like getting kicked but Kenny kept getting himself into positions to get kicked. But he has this skill of running across the front of people in the box knowing they aren't going to touch him for fear of a penalty, and that's how he got his goal. Yet he didn't train at all before the match because he had a sore knee. If he had trained he wouldn't have played.'

In fact the Scots did very little training. 'We thought they would out-gun us physically anyway so we talked a lot instead,' said Stein. Much of that talking was done by Aberdeen's excellent manager Alex Ferguson, whose arrival as national coach has produced three wins and 12 goals at Hampden this season.

That run, and solid, settled look of his squad has transformed Stein's fortunes. The legendary big man was under severe fire from the supporters with typewriters for his team's dismal failure to qualify for last summer's European Championships. 'I have come from a villain to a king in two games,' he smiled.

'But you can't become good enough overnight to beat a team like Spain by two goals. We have been building steadily, bringing in people like Nicol, McStay, Johnston and Cooper. Now players like Hansen and Wark, can't even get on the bench, they have to watch from the stands.

'As far as I'm concerned, beating the European finalists who had all their players to choose from was better than beating England. Don't get me wrong, I like to beat England as much as anybody else but our players got more out of last night's win.'

Stein will also hope that Wales, who nudged aside Iceland nervously to record their first win in Group Seven, will be able to inflict enough damage on the Spanish when they meet again next April, while succumbing to his own team home and away. Topping their section would remove the anxiety of further qualifying processes against the winners of the Oceania Group.

Meanwhile, beating England next spring is certainly not beyond Stein's excellent and exciting side. That, together with further solid progress down the World Cup qualifying road will no doubt ensure further outbreaks of hugging and kissing in the press-box.

18 November 1984   *Ronald Atkin*

As England took the fast lane to Mexico that same November, Hugh McIlvanney evaluated a result deserving to be remembered for more than being just an example of Turkish inadequacy.

Turkey v. England, 1984

People were making cracks about the Turkish football team long before they produced their own bad joke at the Inonu Stadium on Wednesday afternoon.

'The sons of the Prophet are not doing well as footballers,' a leading backer of the sport in Istanbul announced wryly at the dinner table on the previous evening. 'It seems to be a better game for Christians.'

Islam has exerted its share of questionable influences over the centuries but even Kemal Ataturk, the father of modern, secular Turkey, might have balked at lumbering the old faith with responsibility for the historic ineptitude of England's mid-week victims. A bunch of bit-players from Kismet, complete with curly slippers, would have looked more like World Cup challengers than the strugglers whose awe-inspiring incompetence justified Bobby Robson's claim that in winning 8–0 his team had let them off the hook.

However, Mr Robson is entitled to be resentful of any tendency to use the weakness of the Turks as an excuse for failing to give England proper credit for a memorably effective and encouraging performance. The manager and his players had to accept that critics would queue up to pummel them recently when permutations of inadequacies led to poor results. Now they have a right to expect praise for the concentrated efficiency that has enabled them to begin their series of qualifying matches in the World Cup with two uninterrupted slaughters, four points and goal figures of 13 for and none against.

Ruthlessness is always a sign of health in England football teams. For them, far more than for players of some other nationalities, the natural expression of superiority is a hatful of goals. If the Scots are clearly on top, their inclination is to declare the fact with extravagant flourishes of technique, to hold the ball and seek to torment the opposition, in short to take the mickey. Jock Stein will want a more hard-headed approach from the richly gifted squad now in his charge but the traditions classically embodied by Jim Baxter don't yield easily to adaptation.

In contrast, the more the English are in command the cooler, more practical and more deadly they become. Opponents who are outclassed are liable to be crucified. The reassertion of that characteristic in Istanbul, even against a team ready to hold out their hands to take the nails, must be regarded as significant.

Qualification for Mexico is now surely a formality and the principal relevance of Wednesday's result is as a generator of morale, of self-belief among the men Robson will lead into the Finals there. He was right to emphasise the importance of the mood in the dressing-room during the interval, when the score stood at 3–0. If the players had opted to sit on their lead, no tangible harm would have been done. But without doubt that would have been a misuse of the Istanbul experience, because an opportunity to draw nourishment for the future would have been lost.

Since the Turks were too feeble to improve England's work with the cape, the best way to benefit from an hour and a half in their company was to sharpen the sword and practise kills. Being merciless, like nearly everything else, is partly a matter of habit and that smooth exercise on a raw afternoon by the Bosphorus may eventually have helpful echoes in North America.

One man who felt that it represented rather more than the predictable acquisition of two points was Peter Shilton. While obliged to acknowledge that he might have been subjected to greater strain if he had been working against a team recruited from Burton's window, the goalkeeper was considerably impressed by the sustained application of England. 'Everybody, from the back four through the midfield to the forwards, maintained concentration all the way to the end and that's why we kept up our pressure. No slackness was allowed to creep in. Every player was still trying to do the job right when the Turks were dead and buried.

'I love to see that attitude. As long as we've got it, we'll do well, even when the opposition is a hell of a lot tougher than it was here.'

Shilton was so enthusiastic about what was happening in front of him that before the finish he was convinced England had scored nine goals and was making himself hoarse exhorting the attack to go for double figures. He was not alone in thinking that the record total of 10 (inflicted decades ago on Portugal and the United States) might well have been passed.

18 November 1984   *Hugh McIlvanney*

The European Nations Championship has so far eluded British teams. In 1984 McIlvanney watched France win a final despite a lacklustre performance from one of the great players of the decade.

Idol Striking in
a Low Key

It is only a minor sadness that all the exhilarating football provided by the 1984 European Championships should have led in the end to a flawed, anticlimactic final at the Parc des Princes in Paris on Wednesday night.

The quality of what had gone before was much too substantial to be belittled in the memory by one persistently moderate match. Some of the action in the earlier stages of the competition was so imaginative, fluent, dramatic and graceful that it restored to recently abused lovers of football the right to claim that theirs can be the most beautiful of all team games. Even those of us who were limited during those early phases of the Championships to the heavily edited coverage offered by British television were left with plenty of exciting images shimmering in the mind.

Many of the most satisfying we owed to a French team brimming with sophisticated talents and aggressive zest and such disappointments as we had to bear at the Parc des Princes were considerably eased by the fact that the final had the virtue of putting the best possible name on the trophy. France had stood enough of being admirable, romantic losers and when they survived a night of edginess and occasional incoherence to defeat Spain, the great neutral majority of football supporters around the world could only applaud.

Yet there was a sense in which Wednesday's final left a slight sediment of uneasiness. It concerned the performance of Michel Platini, France's captain, the reigning European Footballer of the Year and the man whose thrilling and deadly forays from out of the French midfield brought him a total of nine goals in the competition and, understandably, encouraged many observers to declare categorically that he must be rated the finest player now at work anywhere.

Clearly it would be both foolish and unjust to use Platini's downbeat, largely anonymous performance in the final to chip at a reputation so genuinely earned but if comparisons with the truly great attacking foot-ballers of other eras are to be attempted – with such as Pele, Di Stefano, Cruyff, Best and Beckenbauer (he was a magnificent attacker before defensive responsibilities became his chosen priority) – there is justifica-tion for asking why Platini was so inconspicuous for long stretches of the final and of the semi-final in which France moved past Portugal towards the Championship.

The severely muted nature of his contribution in Paris was quite remarkable considering that he was a national idol being cheered on by an adoring home crowd against opponents who had been drastically

120

weakened by the enforced removal of three of their best players and were seen by the bookmakers as remote outsiders. Given such an ideal context for the flourishing of greatness, would Pele, or Cruyff or Best have been invisible for so much of the evening? It seems almost unthinkable that any one of them would.

Naturally, credit must be given to Camacho, the Spanish No. 3 who was allotted the task of policing Platini. Camacho did not opt for relentlessly adhesive, skin-tight marking but sought instead to ensure that he was positioned to block the Frenchman's route to goal, to try whenever possible to steer Platini towards the more harmless areas of the field. The defender did a splendid, intelligent job but the passivity of Platini must surely be traced to something beyond his opponent's resourcefulness, to something in his own nature.

He is a highly individual footballer. Even his appearance sets him apart from most outstanding practitioners of his trade. There is a strange, rather unathletic line to his shoulders and upper body and his feet, too, look a bit unlikely until they start doing outrageous things with the ball.

He is very much a sporadic player, one who has no consistently discernible theme or pattern running through his play. His great weapon is the sudden, electrifying surge that sweeps him through the demoralised ranks of the other side and into their penalty box, where the brilliance of his finishing makes him as welcome as an assassin. When he has completed one of these bursts he withdraws quickly to a deep position and is then mainly concerned with finding the next opportunity to launch into a run.

Of course, there are other notable elements in his game, not least the superb heading ability and judgment of precisely when and how to meet centres that have confused defenders, but what is certainly true is that Platini is not the kind of footballer who keeps himself constantly involved in the action, constantly relevant to the workings of his team.

That may be seen as an inspired calculation of the best way to utilise his tremendous gifts. But it may be more realistic to see it as representing the absence of one of the basic qualities identified with the very greatest attacking players and definitely with the handful of marvels mentioned earlier. There are many ways of defining this quality but what it comes down to is an unremitting assertiveness, an absolute refusal to be rendered peripheral. Di Stefano was that attitude incarnate. Glenn Hoddle, on the other hand, seems to suffer from a terrible shortage of it.

After all that Michel Platini has achieved since leaving France to join Juventus, and especially after his triumphs of the last two or three weeks, it would be criminal and crazy to start concentrating on deficiencies in his play. But the unmistakable evidence of Wednesday in Paris was that in certain circumstances he can be pushed out to the edge of events.

If that suggestion is answered by a reminder that Platini scored the goal which swung the final France's way, the riposte must be that Arconada should be credited with an assist. When the generally impressive Spanish goalkeeper saved Platini's modest shot and then let the ball squirm over the line, he was emphasising that the French captain was merely telling the truth when he said before the match that these days just about everything he tries comes out right.

Platini talks like someone riding one of those tides in the affairs of men that Shakespeare wrote about. Practically every decision he takes or move he makes, in football or elsewhere in his life, seems to prove dead right – and if it isn't, there's someone like Arconada around to make it so.

On Wednesday most of the people who swelled the happiness that is engulfing Platini in his thirtieth year were in the blue shirts of France. That marvellous little ally Giresse was patently wearied by the exertions of the previous fortnight but still a handy man to have about you and so, conspicuously, were such as Bossis, Fernandez and Bellone.

But for this latecomer to the feast, the star of the final (and a figure whose influence on the tournament as a whole was no less than Platini's) was Jean Tigana, the slim black midfield player from Mali who combines a wealth of refined skills and dazzling ingenuity with an endless appetite for the fray and tireless running over almost every yard of the pitch. In addition to his competitiveness and virtuosity Tigana has the classic, head-up awareness of where men and spaces are that is always found in truly constructive players.

Tottenham must be sorry that the negotiations that might have brought him to White Hart Lane after the World Cup of 1982 fell through but his present employers, Bordeaux, will have no complaints. Nor does Michel Hidalgo, the civilised orchestrator of France's wonderful revival as a power in football. 'When Tigana is playing well the whole team benefits,' says Hidalgo who is in the process of moving on from his job of manager of the national side to oversee the development of the game at all levels through France. 'He is the heartbeat of the team.'

It is a joyful heartbeat and we should be grateful that it was characteristic of the European Championship of 1984.

1 July 1984   *Hugh McIlvanney*

*In the European Cup, however, there have been other triumphs to
follow Celtic's first win. Here Hugh McIlvanney analysed the wildly
dramatic semi-final in 1968 as Manchester United surged past Real
Madrid on their way to final victory later over Benfica.*

The Tank of Resolution
Crushed Real

With Manchester United and the European Cup it is always difficult to
identify the boundary between the dream and the reality; to separate
genuine optimism from wishful thinking, or an objective expectation of
failure from a dark, mystical suspicion that a mocking providence must
always thwart Matt Busby's ultimate ambition.

What happened in Madrid on Wednesday evening did nothing to clarify
these distinctions. The match that saw United through the semi-final of the
competition at the fourth attempt was in many important respects the most
bizarre, the most unnaturally (almost super-naturally) dramatic I have
experienced. It was, for me at least, unique, with an essential pattern that
denied comparison with any other game I have seen.

It could be suggested that the emotions of the past 11 years, the
memories of those major and minor disasters this club has known in its
association with European football, rose like sediment from the bottom of
a glass to cloud perspectives, tempting us to impose profundity on
ordinary fluctuations that would have been readily accepted on a less tense
occasion.

But that interpretation will convince no one who sat through the stifling
hour and a half in the Bernabeu Stadium, whose sheer sides seemed to
imprison the clamour and the stale air under a blue ceiling of cigarette and
cigar smoke.

Those who can make persuasive analyses of the action lean heavily on
oversimplification. For instance, it is true that United, by their own highest
standards, played moderately; that Real Madrid played worse; that
inadequate defence had more significance in the match than inspired attack.
However, all this is only a limited version of the truth. The discrepancy
between the events of the first half and those of the second was so
staggering as to be unreal.

After coping skilfully, if rather uneasily, with Real Madrid's swift,
controlled aggression for slightly more than 25 minutes, United's reinforced defence all but disintegrated. Pirri was pursued too late when he

123

sprinted towards the near post to meet a free-kick from the right and he had time and space to strike a fine, powerful header beyond Stepney.

Brennan, going to make an easy interception, was unfortunate to find the ball bobbing over his foot and Gento was left to race in unhampered. He shot earlier than anticipated and Stepney, who was in the act of taking up a new position, could not prevent the ball from spinning between his legs.

Zoco, incredibly transformed from the strong man of Old Trafford to a confused, nervous, incompetent, restored hope briefly by slicing Dunne's free-kick past Betancort, but the speed of the great Amancio's reflexes brought a third Spanish goal almost immediately.

At half time, anyone who wanted to bet on United might have been trampled down in the rush, and by British feet at that.

What occurred subsequently was barely comprehensible. It was natural that United should commit themselves unreservedly to attack, with Sadler surging away from Foulkes' side, Charlton eagerly seeking openings for shots and Crerand moving through like an inside forward. But for all their admirable adventurousness there was no impression of overwhelming menace about them and when the Real defence suddenly opened up to let them through it appeared to be a process as arbitrary as the parting of the Red Sea.

It was as if some outside force had chosen to reward United for their greatness over the years and at one stroke had drained all resistance from their opponents. Zunzunegui and Sanchis, so superbly assured earlier, now found themselves unable to balance the disastrous uncertainty that spread from the hapless Zoco and in goal Betancort began to behave like a man in a trance.

There must be praise for the cool alertness that gave Sadler and Foulkes their decisive goals and even more for the brilliance with which Best prepared the way for the winner, but a sound defence would probably have prevented both. 'We played the double centre half plan in their penalty area', said Pat Crerand afterwards, condemning the opposition with a joke. So what did happen? There is a choice of practical explanations. 'We went out and played them,' Nobby Stiles shouted from behind a towel in the steaming, swigging, hugging, tearful hysteria of the dressing-room. 'We went out and bloody played them and they cracked.'

Crerand elaborated. 'When we came in at half-time, Georgie Best said, "We're as well losing 10–1 as 3–1. Let's have a real go at them." The boss felt the same way. He told us to get at them. They made it easier by letting us have the ball in the second half. They must have thought they had done enough. Whenever we got moving they were knackered. You couldn't breathe out there because of the humidity. You'd have thought they'd have stood it better, but they didn't. They kept running over to the trainer to get drinks and have water splashed down their necks. They just didn't stay with us.'

Bobby Charlton, having struggled to emerge from a state of shock ('I'm going mad, me, going mad. This game will drive me bloody crackers'), saw it similarly: 'There was no air at all. You couldn't sprint because it took you five minutes to recover. We didn't play well, not nearly as well as we can, but the lads deserved it because they kept going. They had the heart to come back when most would have slung it.'

This takes us some way towards the basic truth about the match. United drove themselves well beyond the point that most teams would have seen as the limit of hope and endeavour, certainly far beyond the limit that Real Madrid had subconsciously set for themselves. In the end the victory was one of will. United's determination to win the European Cup, to have done with the frustrations and the condolences, has accumulated into something more potent than even they realise. Their collective faith and sense of purpose is much greater than the sum of individual ambitions.

When they went out for the second half they rode their resolution like a tank and Real, sensing a spirit they could not equal, capitulated.

19 May 1968   *Hugh McIlvanney*

Aberdeen moved more smoothly to the Cup Winners Cup in 1983 with none of the desperate moments Manchester United had to survive before they beat Benfica at Wembley. Hugh McIlvanney paid tribute to their night of triumph in Gothenburg.

Aberdeen's Night to Wave the Flag

Glasgow comedians working slanderous mischief around the invented theme of Aberdonian meanness used to be fond of telling how the advent of a flag-day would clear the handsome streets of the northern city more swiftly and thoroughly than an air raid. Well, they had a flag-day of sorts up there last Thursday and not too many of the locals went into hiding.

Twenty-four hours after he and his Aberdeen players had waved the

European Cup Winner's Cup from an open bus struggling to maintain a crawling pace through the happy delirium that choked Union Street with red and white scarves and banners, Alex Ferguson was still quietly awed by the reception. 'They said on television that 60,000 turned up. They've got to be joking. There were 60,000 around the bus. I've never seen anything like it.'

The town has rarely seen anything to compare with the team that represented it so thrillingly in the battering rain of Gothenburg last Wednesday night. To say merely, as the record books will, that Real Madrid were beaten 2–1 in extra-time is to blur and belittle an achievement that would not have been exaggerated if three goals had separated the sides at the finish.

Real were threateningly in control during the latter part of the first half, after McLeish's extravagantly under-hit pass to his goalkeeper precipitated a penalty that let Juanito score an unearned equaliser. And, if Leighton's brilliant reflex save had not denied Santillana's sudden, violent shot in the second half the Spanish would have taken the Cup. What is beyond question, however, is that such a result would have been the most desperate larceny.

Ferguson's men performed with a mature self-belief, with so much purposeful composure and sound, disciplined technique (the occasional aberrations of McLeish notwithstanding) that, as the evening wore on, winning began to seem their mature right. Real Madrid under the symbolic leadership of the great Alfredo Di Stefano, brought an intimidating weight of tradition to the Ullevi Stadium but Aberdeen – the challengers from so far out on the periphery of the European game that some claim to suspect them of playing their home matches on an oil rig – deployed clearly superior equipment on the night.

'I don't think they are an ordinary side but our commitment and strength and ability made them look that way,' said Ferguson as he recollected the emotion of mid-week from the comparative tranquillity of Friday lunchtime. It was a legitimate answer to those who felt that the famous opposition had fallen miserably below expectations.

Perhaps it is a fact that Juanito should be able to do far more with the depth of skills he possesses. No doubt the richly gifted Stielike (who had just recovered from injury but was easily his team's outstanding creative attacker until cramp put the leg-irons on him) and his most consistently aggressive allies Gallego and Santillana, should have been given more widespread and sustained support.

But Real's weaknesses were, to a considerable extent, a direct reflection of Aberdeen's exciting strength. No-one should talk about the Spaniards losing this Cup. It should be recognised that the Scots won it with the kind of conviction and quality of work that have come to be identified with players sent on to the field by Alex Ferguson. At 41, Ferguson is as impressive a young manager as there is in British football and one of the ambiguous fruits of Aberdeen's success is the likelihood that powerful attempts will be made to tempt him elsewhere.

Ibrox Park, where John Greig has been a somewhat beleaguered figure in the manager's office of late, has been mentioned as a possibility and that is hardly surprising, since Ferguson is a Glaswegian from Govan, the Rangers' heartland, and was unmistakably saddened when his spell as a hustling centre-forward in the old club's colours was abruptly terminated. Obviously, Greig will be especially relieved if Rangers can give Aberdeen a frustrating jolt in the Scottish Cup Final next Saturday.

There may, of course, be English clubs who would pay a lot of money for the services of a man who had proved his value even before he went to Pittodrie. Ferguson's accomplishments at St Mirren verged on the miraculous. Staff at the Paisley ground had become inured to attendances of 800 or 1,000 before he went there – they could almost recognise everybody who came through the turnstiles – but when he left under bleakly acrimonious circumstances there had been something like a tenfold improvement in gates, the team had been promoted from the First Division to the Premier Division of the Scottish League and they were heading towards participation in Europe. As a case of revitalisation it lost out to Lazarus, but only in a photo-finish.

Since he joined Aberdeen in 1978, taking the place of Billy McNeill, who appeared to be fulfilling his destiny by returning to Celtic Park (Aberdeen have the proud distinction of never having fired a manager in the 80 years of their history), Alex Ferguson has dramatically confirmed the promise he had shown at St Mirren and earlier when in charge of the minimal resources of East Stirlingshire. In fact, his extraordinary drive and application had been revealed much earlier and not just in his days as a player, when his extreme competitiveness had the dual effect of making him a prolific goalscorer, notably with Dunfermline, and a severe irritant to opponents and referees. . . .

Unsurprisingly, when he lists his priorities, Ferguson places heavy emphasis on developing young footballers, bringing them along to the point where they realise the full worth of what's in them. 'You acquire the ability to blend talents but my attitude was to improve players before I thought about improving teams. And not just their technique – their stamina, their discipline and, maybe above all, their ambition.'

He doesn't have to look far for an inspiring example to offer his boys. Willie Miller, the captain and controlling influence in the defence, was superb in Sweden but, then, it seems he always is. 'I can't remember one

127

bad match he's had this season,' insists Ferguson. 'We make notes on everybody after each game but with Willie it's just one word – "Magnificent," "Excellent," or, if he's a bit off, just "Good." That's the worst you can give him. He's amazing.'

You can say that with admiration of Aberdeen FC as a whole, and of their manager, and their happy crowd. Last week was a cheering time.

15 May 1983   *Hugh McIlvanney*

Until Cup competitions became so important 'friendly' internationals were played hard with pride and prestige at stake. John Arlott sums up a fine 5–0 win over Russia in 1958.

Not a Quirk in Sight

Russia had good reason, after the death of Stalin, to abandon 'the cult of the individual' in the political field. There was less wisdom in the thoroughness which seems to have extended that attitude to the football field.

The Russian team which lost so heavily to England on Wednesday was a painstakingly drilled cadre. Each member was fit, capably two-footed, well trained in positional play, passing and covering defence. Not a single one of them, however, left any impression as an individual player or ones capable of surprising opponents already disposed to counter the expected.

For the first, dull, forty-four minutes of the match, England went through a whole series of text-book advances. The thoughts of the Russian players almost could be followed as they identified each movement and carried out the counter-move with precise, mass discipline at drill-pace.

When Douglas made the initial pass in the English attack which ended the first half, he did so at practice-ground speed. Finney and Haynes carried it on at the highest tempo of footballing instinct, which is crucially faster than footballing thought, and they were through the Russian defence before it could reform, by numbers, to stop them. Haynes scored his – and England's – third goal from a situation out of which the instruction book prescribes that he should make a cross-pass to a colleague in front of goal. The well-drilled Russian goalkeeper, accordingly, moved out to cover that pass; whereupon Haynes, who works out his football for himself, promptly shot a goal through the gap Belyayav had left behind him.

Before the magnificent Hungarian team of 1954 came to England, someone described its players as 'Communist automata'. On the contrary, although they were highly trained in the skills of the game, they thought out their movements flexibly and rendered them effective by exploiting the outstanding, and sometimes unorthodox, aptitudes of particular players.

It is a disappointingly obvious judgment to make but, in fact, the Russian team at Wembley *was* like a well-drilled machine – undeviating, incapable of improvisation or originality. Surely *one* of their players had, deep inside him, an idiosyncrasy, a quirk, an unusual characteristic. Certainly their predecessors had. Yet none of these men even hinted at the unusual.

On this evidence, they will be no danger in the World Cup of 1962. Some other teams – like Austria, Argentina and Hungary – are suffering lean periods: but in the next four years they well may discover outstanding players who could fit into their patterns to take them again to the peak of international football. The problem for Russia's football administrators is not that of finding great players – their essential greatness would be emasculated by such regimentation as this team seems to have suffered – but the deeper matter of a complete change of mental approach. Surely the great traditional gusto of the Russians should be expressed in their football. Yet these might have been men of any nation – or no nation – which latter point may be politically significant.

England beat a better technically equipped Russian team through individual players who, within planned movements, applied personal brilliance. Modern defence 'by the book' is only conclusively beaten by invention which *creates* a defensive error, as distinct from hoping for one.

Here, after many years, was an overseas football team which could learn from the English. Perhaps, however, they have already learnt from England the excellent foreign relations move of losing heavily, but courteously, in the other man's country.

26 October 1958   *John Arlott*

In home internationals Ireland have given England many a difficult match and there has never been any holding back in these encounters. John Arlott reported one Ireland should have won.

129

England Attack had no Spearhead

Ireland 3   England 3

Tactically Ireland won – only to be denied their deserts by the incomparable shooting of Charlton.

A spectator from Wales or Scotland must have called this a fine game of football. As the turf of Windsor Park was slowly churned, under the steady rain, from green meadow to grey morass, play continued bright, varied and intelligent.

There were constant flashes of sharp attack, and there was resourceful defence.

However, once the spectators had sung 'The Queen' with apparent determination to be heard across the border, they settled down to a parochial matter: helping Harry Gregg from Magherafelt, Danny Blanchflower from Ballymacarrat, Billy Bingham from Glentoran and their mates to beat the Englishmen.

The players, similarly assertive, picked up the game where they had put it down after their well-planned win over England at Wembley a year ago, moving back into that control of the midfield which means mastery and should mean victory in any football match.

Steadily Blanchflower and Peacock collected the ball and pushed it forward to McIlroy, under whose prompting Bingham, McParland and Cush ran penetratingly in on the English goal.

England surrendered their tactical advantage without a struggle. Confronted with the twin problems of the mud and the pace of the game, McGuinness, playing in his first International, never found his feet; while Clayton, as if always conscious of having been dropped from the English team last May, was unambitiously cautious, rarely venturing out of defence.

Thus Haynes, under the constant pressure and screening of Blanchflower, Peacock or any Irish player who might be within worrying distance had to improvise attacks out of hasty clearances.

To be sure, Charlton once struck Gregg with a strong shot; and when Broadbent volleyed the rebound back at the Irish goal, Keith kicked it clear from the goal-line. But the English advances sprang out of quick flashes and unco-ordinated brilliance. The Irish pressure, on the other hand, was measured and consistent.

Their first goal was a microcosm of their play. Peacock pushed the ball square to Blanchflower, who held it momentarily while McIlroy 'lost' Clayton and was ready to receive it; McIlroy twisted clear of McGuinness and darted a through pass to Cush, who neatly opened the angle through which he shot wide of McDonald.

The English attack had no spearhead, no one to carry out the less glorious but essential duties of a centre-forward by occupying the attention of the opposing centre-half, taking the bumps and tumbles of goal-mouth scrambles. Only Broadbent ran ahead of the man with the ball; otherwise the main object of the English line seemed to be to tee up a long-range shot for Charlton.

This Haynes eventually contrived to do, whereupon Charlton duly swung his right foot and raked the ball into the top left-hand corner of the goal. So despite the hammer blow from Cush, which McDonald's finger-tips touched on to the goalpost, the score was one-all at half-time.

So into a second half in which skill narrowly overcame mud, pace and effort. Again Ireland produced a perfect move when Bingham touched a short pass to Blanchflower, ran ahead for a long, curved return ball of perfect length, and shot a long centre across goal to McParland; his quick jab reached Peacock in perfect position to shoot Ireland's second goal.

Again England equalised when, at length, Cunningham slipped, from grace and balance, for Finney to run on to the loose ball and put it into goal.

Within a couple of minutes, as the steaming crowd roared its players back into attack, McDonald caught a long shot – but couldn't be rid of it before Casey bumped him over his goal-line. Still (and often) Blanchflower drove his forwards past Clayton and McGuinness, so that Wright – quick as ever in thought, if not in movement – Howe and Banks had often to stretch their legs further than allows a considered or constructive clearance.

Again, however, England's one logical expectation of scoring matured when Finney moved inside to take Haynes' pass and pushed it outside Keith. Charlton, spurting through the mud, once more swept a rising drive into the roof of the Irish goal.

Still, when Banks limped out to the left wing, Broadbent fell back and Brabrook disappeared from the game, it seemed that Ireland might yet achieve the win they had earned.

Again and again Bingham tripped down his wing. But now Wright had moved out there, and shepherded trouble away from his goal until both sides could lift their weary feet, for the last time, out of the Irish bog.

Ireland. – Gregg (Man. Utd.); Keith (Newcastle Utd.), Graham (Doncaster R.); Blanchflower, D. (Tottenham H.) (capt.), Cunningham (Leicester C.), Peacock (Glasgow Celtic); Bingham (Luton T.), Cush

(Leeds Utd.), Casey (Portsmouth), McIlroy (Burnley), McParland (Aston Villa).

England. – McDonald (Burnley); Howe (WBA), Banks (Bolton W.); Clayton, R. (Blackburn R.), Wright (Wolverhampton W.) (capt.), McGuinness (Manchester Utd.), Brabrook (Chelsea), Broadbent (Wolverhampton W.), Charlton (Man. Utd.), Haynes (Fulham), Finney (PNE).

4 October 1958   *John Arlott*

England had a purple patch between 8 October 1960 and 10 May 1961 when they scored 40 goals in winning six successive matches. Most striking was a 9–3 victory over Scotland to surpass the famous drubbing England received from the 'blue devils' back in 1928. This was my account of an unique victory.

England v. Scotland, 1961

The Scots were butchered to make an English holiday as Haynes' triumphant team swept decisively to the Home Championship and into the record books with this massacre of their bewildered opponents. Appropriately this was the anniversary of Culloden, perhaps the only other battle in which the Scots have been as savagely mauled. 9–3 is their biggest defeat since the first International was drawn 0–0 in 1872. It is also the highest score ever at Wembley Stadium.

The Scots, however, were not disposed to go quietly as they struggled to free themselves from England's grip at the start of the second half. But no sooner did they pull back two goals and threaten England's authority, than they were beaten into abject submission by six more scored in half-an-hour.

There was no questioning the wisdom of keeping together this England side which played so well last autumn – and looked as if they had been playing together ever since. Their understanding and anticipation was uncanny, and this was the foundation of their success, the secret of the casual ease of many of their most delightful moves.

Thirty-two goals in their last five matches indicates where England's strength lies, but their forwards have never yet played so commandingly and so attractively. This wealth of goals was no easy offering, for Scotland pride themselves on a sound defence and, before the game, were more concerned about the ability of their forwards.

England's 4–2–4 formation, in its normal interpretation, is a defensive system yet it has been brilliantly adapted to form the springboard of attack. With Swan and Flowers blocking the centre it is Robson and Haynes who act as the transformers, changing the current of play in midfield and switching the ball instantly to the feet of the other forwards.

The killing power of the line is in their universal ability as goalscorers, and in their speed of thought and movement. All have that sense of position which carries them into the open space and they can rely on getting the ball placed perfectly into their stride at the precise moment the defence is split.

This was teamwork such as we have not seen from an England side before. The understanding was apparent as a long pass from deep in England's half reached Greaves moving unchallenged through the middle. For once he dallied too long and McNeill caught him with a saving tackle.

The respite was brief. Greaves flicked on a pass to send Smith free on the wing, and moved up to take the return. With the centre blocked Greaves pulled the ball back to Robson, striding up to the edge of the area to drive the ball low under Haffey's dive. Then Haynes, as if equipped with some private computer, calculated the pass to the exact inch to meet Greaves, stealing in between backs and goalkeeper to turn the ball into the empty net.

Scotland were passing just as neatly, but they lacked the changes of pace and direction which gave England's happy wanderers the knack of roaming to the right place at the right time. The best example of their close co-operation came as Douglas raced back to tackle Scotland's left-winger then pushed the ball forward for his own back to run the length of the field.

Armfield's low centre slipped past Haffey, but Smith, his head still singing from a clash with McNeill, failed to give the touch that would have turned it in. But Smith never lacks persistence and at once he drove in a shot which poor Haffey could not hold. Greaves, inevitably, was there to tap it home.

At the start of the second half the Scots marking was closer with Mackay and McCann not so often caught out of position in midfield. For a time they seemed to gain the measure of England as Law, Mackay and McNeill, accepting that Scotland could not match England's skill, tried strength, their tackling ferocious, often illegal. Soon Mackay drove a free kick at the wall of defenders to see it deflected past Springett into the net. With

133

England unsettled Wilson quickly squeezed the ball past Springett glancing in one of McLeod's centres.

Now as McLeod's dainty dribbling took him all too frequently past Middlesbrough's McNeil England were at their testing time. The response was swift and final. As Wilson tried to delay a free kick on the edge of the area Greaves suddenly flicked the ball to Douglas, darting in behind the wall to shoot gently past Haffey. The goals then came almost too swiftly to record. A pass by Greaves, a side-step and powerful shot from Smith and it was 5–2. Then Wilson sent the ball trickling through a maze of legs to roll past the unsighted Springett. Before the echo of the Scottish cheers had died Haynes had moved up to drive home two powerful shots from the edge of the area.

Immediately Greaves with insolent ease, Smith with hearty gusto, took advantage of two defensive errors to make it 9–3.

Other goals should have followed had Greaves not given the ball an affectionate pat with his hand before hooking it into the net or Charlton's certainty of shot deserted him after two swerving dribbles had taken him clear of challenge. Nothing further would have been added to the picture of England playing the football their Manager, Walter Winterbottom, must have dreamed of and has worked so patiently to perfect. No wonder Johnny Haynes, the England captain, was chaired from the field after receiving the International Trophy from the Queen.

My colleague John Rafferty picked Greaves and Haynes as the decisive influences.

'These men, Greaves and Haynes, won the game and had they been in Scottish jerseys the result could well have gone the other way.

'They were a perfect blend. Greaves was ever running clear inviting the ball to be sent ahead of him. Haynes, lying deep, had the spirit to fight for the ball, the speed to work clear, the precision to lay on the chances for Greaves. The Chelsea man has the sublime forward virtue that he seldom misses. It all seems so simple and, indeed, it is if you know how – but the simplicity conceals the intelligence and accuracy with which the pair works.'

10 May 1961   *Tony Pawson*

CHAPTER 4

Football's Characters

Many outstanding players have been the subject of The Observer
*articles. Sir Stanley Matthews was the first footballer to have the rare
distinction, for a sportsman, of a 'Profile'. But for me this selection has
to start with the greatest English sportsman, in the round, of my
lifetime. In any sport. The honours system, like the spectating populace,
was so dazzled by Matthews' spectacular dribbling that he is a knight,
Finney only an O B E. But 'gentleman' Tom Finney deserves every
word of Hugh McIlvanney's massive tribute which starts this chapter.*

*Matthews mesmerised with his dribbling, destroyed with the pen-
etration of his passes. He was a marvellous attacking right-winger, but
not much given to heading the ball or tackling or scoring. Finney by
contrast was the complete player, equally good as right or left outside,
or either inside, or attacking or deep-lying centre-forward. He did his
share of the hard graft, taught himself to be as strong with his right foot
as natural left, headed the ball well by comparison and was a
dangerous goalscorer, particularly when cutting in from the right wing
to shoot with his left. He was a one-club man with total loyalty to club
and country in an age when players were paid a pittance. The perfect
gentleman on and off the field, Finney was as self-reliant in his work as
in his play and made as great a contribution to his community as to his
club. There is no one who better disproves that trite American saying
that nice guys don't win anything.*

*Certainly he won my admiration from the start when we ended the
war together with the Sixth Armoured Division in Austria, Finney
having somehow survived after courageously volunteering to drive
honey tanks, those most suicidal of fighting vehicles. I taught him a bit
about fishing and he taught me all I know about wing play. What
particularly impressed was his sheer love of the game. Whatever the
match Finney played his heart out whereas most professional footballers then took no risk of jeopardising their future career by injury on
poor pitches against rough players. My abiding memory is of a game in*

Padua against an all-star exhibition team sent out from Britain to entertain with their brilliance us troops waiting for 'demob'. On an icy surface Finney held nothing back, organising and directing the other ten enthusiastic amateurs to a 5–0 win over stars who were not going to risk injury on that surface. That match allows me to say I was once preferred on the wing to Finney. Well I was the officer in charge. But as both player and person Finney far outranked me as, in my view, he outranked all others.

Hugh McIlvanney's 1983 tribute to Tom Finney, the player's player, was titled 'Marauder of North End'.

Once the case has been made for Stanley Matthews and George Best there is hardly another winger in the last 50 years of British football who belongs in the same parish as Tom Finney.

That assessment implies an insult to a dozen memorable talents from Cliff Jones and Jimmy Johnstone to Bobby Mitchell and Cliff Bastin. It is simply a fact that no one – not even Best (who was for two or three seasons probably the most comprehensively brilliant footballer these islands have produced) could equal Finney in combining ball skill, imagination and demoralising pace with the ability to infiltrate from the edge of the game and score vital goals.

He hit 30 in 76 full internationals for England and only a couple were from centre-forward. Seven more were struck in his 17 Inter-League appearances and overall he took 247 goals in 565 matches in first-class football. For any forward these would be wonderful figures. For someone who, until the age of 35, was a marauder from the periphery they are monumental.

When the scale of his achievements as a scoring winger is mentioned to Finney, the reaction is characteristically objective and practical. He reflects quietly that perhaps he shouldn't have been a winger at all.

'If I had my career to play over again I'd be a centre-forward,' he said last week. 'With freedom of movement and the variety of openings I'd have found there I'm sure I would have done more damage, scored more goals, than I did from the wing. Mind you, apart from the odd bad memory of days when I contributed less for Preston or England than I wanted to give, I've no serious regrets about my years in the game.

'In a true sense fellas of my generation had the best of it. I can't believe that English football will ever again be as exciting, or as full of outstanding performers as it was when we were in our prime. There was one more great period after the men I was brought up with had gone, something you could look back on as a sort of golden era. That was when Greaves and Law, Bobby Charlton and Best, the tremendous Tottenham team that did the double and a lot of other class players were around. But real quality has become scarcer and scarcer since the late 1960s.

'Of course, terrific footballers still emerge. Kenny Dalglish is a marvel and would have been recognised as special regardless of when he'd played, but I don't think I'm being prejudiced when I say that if he'd come through in my time his brilliance wouldn't have been nearly as isolated as it is now.'

The thread of understatement running through that last comment is not there for sardonic effect. Finney is always concerned with being an entirely fair witness and his utterances are not blurred by nostalgia, whether he is recalling dramas he helped to shape 30 years ago or seeking to relate his experiences to what is happening in football today.

Lunching with him on Thursday at a pleasant restaurant outside Preston imparted a genuine sense of privilege which even the recollection of all the horrors he inflicted on so many Scotland teams could not diminish. No star of the past ever had more right to distorting vanities or ever showed less trace of them.

He is 61 now, and the hair that was conspicuously thick, fair and crinkly in the photographs of three or four decades ago, is receding. But the face is unmistakable, and the body remains trim. That is no surprise, for this is a man whose retirement at 38 was considered premature by many of those best placed to judge.

No one was less surprised by Finney's longevity as a footballer than Bill Shankly, who believed that one of his duties in life was to tell the world that Tommy (always Tommy) Finney was one of the supreme geniuses of the game Bill regarded as too important to be described as a matter of life and death.

When the teenage Finney made himself a regular member of North End's first team in 1940, the rasping Ayrshire voice of Shankly was transmitting brusque counsel from the right-half position. Their relationship became warm enough to survive even Sunday tea in the Shankly's little terrace house in Deepdale Road, where Finney's young wife Elsie, who has never been in the least passionate about football, found her sanity threatened by Bill's inevitable insistence on dissecting the previous day's action relentlessly from the moment his guests came through the door.

Long afterwards, when Shankly had made himself a legend as manager of Liverpool and Finney travelled to Anfield now and again to report matches for the *News of the World*, the hard miner's arm would be thrown round the younger man and all within earshot would be bombarded with eulogies.

A colleague of mine once had the temerity to ask Merseyside's favourite

Scotsman (such as St John, Dalglish and Souness wouldn't hesitate to grant him that status) if Finney would have been strong enough for the modern game. Shankly spun on the doubter with the familiar Cagneyesque hitching of the shoulders. 'Tommy Finney, son?' he said, letting the syllables curdle with disbelief. 'Tommy Finney was grizzly strong. Tommy could run for a week. I'd have played him in his overcoat. There would have been four men marking him when we were kickin' in.

'When I told people in Scotland that England were coming up with a winger who was even better than Stanley Matthews, they laughed at me. But they weren't bloody laughing when Big Geordie Young was running all over Hampden Park lookin' for Tommy Finney.'

Many a Scottish defender was embarrassed in that way, especially at Hampden, where Finney was never on the losing side. Typically, he is quick to point out that the results didn't favour England as consistently at Wembley. He suggests rationally that the wide open spaces of the old Glasgow ground suited the English style of play better than it did the Scots, whose close-passing game was, he thinks, more comfortable on Wembley's slower, truer turf.

There is nothing forced about his concern for Preston North End, the club that has never had a serious rival for his allegiance since he was lifted over a turnstile as a five-year-old to be enthralled by the virtuosity of Alex James. He was just a year into his apprenticeship as a plumber when he was offered £2.50 a week to join the Preston ground-staff, but his father encouraged him to go on working at his trade for six shillings a week and sign initially as an amateur.

Considering that Tom's mother had died when he was four leaving six children, and that his father's second marriage had produced two more, it was a major sacrifice to forgo the two-and-a-half pounds a week and the son is still grateful. So are the other members of the close-knit Finney clan who are among the 80-odd people earning a living from the family plumbing firm started by Tom and his brother Joe, who died tragically young.

For the man whose name is above the door, the successful business, which he still opens up every weekday at 7.30 am, has meant security and freedom from any temptation to contrive an involvement with football after he stopped tormenting defenders. His only formal connection with the sport now is as honorary President of Preston North End.

There were two points in his career when the link could have been broken but two chairmen of the club prevented a parting that might have led to civil disorder in that corner of Lancashire. The first brief crisis came after Preston were relegated to the Second Division in 1949. Finney feared that the descent might make it too easy for the England selectors to overlook him but he was persuaded to dismiss thoughts of a transfer, new players were bought to strengthen the team, and within two seasons North End were back in the First Division.

The pressure to move was more dramatic in 1952 when, at a banquet following England's 1–1 draw with Italy in Florence, he was approached by the president of the Sicilian club Palermo and promised £10,000 to sign, plus wages of £130 a month, huge bonuses, a villa on the Mediterranean and a car. It is not hard to calculate the impact of such guarantees on a player who was still receiving only £20 a week in season, £17 a week in the summer, and bonuses of £2 for a win and £1 for a draw when he retired eight years later.

The injustices of the maximum wage system, especially as applied to the footballer of extraordinary ability, will never cease to rankle with him and in someone to whom bitterness is an alien currency, the memory of how meanly England rewarded service to the national colours is painfully fresh. His 76 internationals were paid at rates ranging from £20 to £50 a match in an age when vast grounds were filled to overflowing. Equally significant was the rule that on trains, players should travel in the same class as they did with their clubs, which meant that only those from Arsenal and maybe one other heavy battalion were allowed to go first. After helping to beat Scotland at Hampden one year, Wilf Mannion had to stand in the corridor throughout the wearying journey home.

In the context of all this exploitation, the Sicilian proposition seemed to be an offer he could not refuse. But Nat Buck, the local builder who was chairman of Preston then, simplified the issue. 'What's 10,000 quid to thee, Tom?' he asked without a smile. 'Nay, lad, tha'll play for us or tha'll play for nobody!'

The way he performed for them through 20 years at the highest level is one of the abiding wonders of British sport. As has been said of Paul Scofield in the theatre, he was the players' player. But he was the audience's too, able to exhilarate them without engaging in self-indulgent displays of his prodigious technique. When Finney dazzled, he did it with a deadly sense of relevance.

He was naturally left-sided but made himself two-footed in his teens, in the same painstaking practice sessions that developed his intricate control and sharpened his speed off the mark sufficiently to bring him respect as a decent sprinter during his wartime years in the Army, when he spent enough time in the front line to make nippiness an asset. One of his basic strengths on the field was the economy with which he collected the most awkward ball. 'You didn't have to pass to Tom,' Tommy Docherty declares. 'You could drive the ball at him and he took it as if you had rolled it underhand.'

His feinting, swerving dribbles bewildered defenders and once he was past them they were usually spectators. 'I liked to give them the impression of running flat out when in fact I had another gear left. They would think they were going to get to me and suddenly I'd be away, out of reach. I always preferred to go on their outside, get to the by-line and steer the ball back low for somebody coming in. When you got that simple move to work smoothly there wasn't a lot the opposition could do.'

Since he was unostentatiously fearless, violence didn't provide a way out for the persecuted full-back. Usually Finney ignored the threatening mutterings in his ear but sometimes he permitted himself a response. 'How the Hell did you ever get all those caps?' one defender asked with a show of contempt. 'Mainly by playing against silly buggers like you,' was the reply. It's the kind of answer that works well in his Lancashire accent.

A pedant scrutinising Finney's superb playing equipment for a weakness might claim that his heading didn't amount to much. But if that was a handicap it bothered him hardly at all, as was emphasised when Preston switched him to centre-forward at 35 and he was so devastating that he scored 28 goals in a single season. Tommy Thompson, the Geordie who in those days formed a partnership with him that is still celebrated at Deepdale, has his joiner's shop in the yard of Finney's plumbing business. Tom Finney never found it hard to make or keep friends.

He has stayed close to his roots, in contrast with the nomadic, perhaps lonely life of Stanley Matthews, who figured with him for so long in one of the most exaggerated rivalries ever nurtured on the sports pages of this country. Finney did not enjoy the outside-left position that Matthews' towering presence frequently obliged him to occupy. But he would gladly have played anywhere for England.

The success he enjoyed when given a brief taste of being inside-right to Matthews, and the pleasure he took from it, convinced him that they could have established an exceptional alliance. 'What is there to say about Stan's qualities that hasn't been said before? At his best, he was unstoppable. His control was so ridiculously good that he could take the ball right up to a defender until you were sure the fella just had to reach out and snatch it away. But Stan was like a mongoose. When the defender lunged, he wasn't there. And he had a fierce killer instinct. Once he had the better of an opponent that poor man would suffer desperately all afternoon. There was no mercy. Stan was marvellous and he was unique.'

The definition is no less applicable to Finney. George Eastham senior, father of the player whose court case precipitated the demolition of the maximum wage 20 years ago, was one of many given proof of that. In 1963, the older Eastham was managing Distillery in Northern Ireland and preparing them for the preliminary round of the European Cup against

Benfica. He decided that his friend Tom Finney, who had been retired about three years, could integrate and inspire his young hopefuls to make a show.

Some prolonged pestering, and a desire to have a belated experience of the European Cup, eventually coaxed the veteran into saying that he would turn in the first leg at Windsor Park. Whatever happened in that match there would be no question of playing in the return. Eastham gladly agreed, and the great Germano was among the Benfica players astonished to find such a famous face in the otherwise anonymous ranks of Distillery. Footballers from Portugal had good cause to know Finney, who had been one of the principal assassins when England slaughtered the national team 10–0 in Lisbon.

He did a fair job in Belfast and Distillery (who were to be taken apart 5–0 in the second leg) were lifted far above their normal standards to claim a 3–3 draw. Tom Finney had made a mark on another great competition. He was 41 years old.

17 April 1983   *Hugh McIlvanney*

In January 1957 The Observer *'Profiled' Stanley Matthews after his CBE award.*

Stanley Matthews

After a quarter of a century in professional football, Stanley Matthews stands out as the most remarkable, if no longer the best, player in the world. The award of a CBE in the New Year Honours List has been received by his admirers with qualified delight. They will not be fully satisfied until he is given a knighthood.

Current literary fashions have inured us to the hero with feet of clay. Matthews, however, has never disappointed his idolaters with outbursts of petty temper on the football field. In his most recent match for England at Wembley, he did not even show emotion when the Yugoslav left-back, quite desperate, stopped him by clinging to his knees.

Two qualities distinguish Matthews as a footballer: his elusiveness and his longevity. He will shortly celebrate his forty-second birthday, but the years show no decline in his transcendent ball control, nor has there been any appreciable falling off in his great speed off the mark. It is bad enough for a left-back to be beaten by Matthews; worse still is the knowledge that he will seldom have the chance to recover. Even now, few outside-rights are so fast, over the first, vital twenty yards.

Matthews has a superb body balance and technical equipment, and his self-confidence is immense. He can bring the most difficult pass under control in a moment, and then he is away, slowly, at first, the rather slight figure hunched over the ball, tantalisingly kept between his two feet. He invites opponents to the tackle, a spider beckoning a fly, and when they are lured he is past them with a wriggle of the hips and a flick of the inside or outside of the foot.

His body swerve is his most bewildering weapon. Even today, with the prestige of twenty-five years' sorcery behind it, it seems remarkable that defenders should fall to it so often. Where they waver and hesitate, Matthews is utterly sure of his ability to pass them, and once he has done so, he seldom wastes the ball. His centres are cunning and precise, gently floated to elude the hands of the goalkeeper.

Matthews was born in the Potteries, the son of Jack Matthews, a prominent boxer known as 'The Fighting Barber of Hanley', who was a favourite at the National Sporting Club. His son has paid tribute to his father's insistence on physical conditioning; he would make his children stand by the open window to carry out deep breathing exercises, regardless of the weather. To-day, Matthews is as fit as a man ten years his junior. He has always made training a fetish, and he has been amply repaid.

His promise was very soon evident, even in the Potteries, where good footballers grew like dragon's teeth in every street and alley. Once, in a schoolboys' match, he scored ten goals from centre-half, and as soon as he left school he signed for Stoke City. At the age of seventeen, he was a regular member of their League side; at nineteen, he was an English international.

It is strange, in view of his later flair for the great occasion, that he should begin poorly in England's colours. After an early, disappointing game against Italy in 1934, a journalist wrote, 'I saw Matthews play just as moderately in the inter-League match, exhibiting the same slowness and hesitation. Perhaps he lacks the big match temperament.'

That was his second international, and it was not for three seasons that he really established himself in England's team. His reputation was assured by a brilliant exhibition against Czechoslovakia, at Tottenham, in 1937. England were forced to reorganise their team through an injury to Crayston, now manager of Arsenal, and Matthews moved to inside-right.

He scored three fine goals, every one of them taken with his left foot, and England won the game, 5–4. The match is sufficient answer to those who have maintained that Matthews cannot score goals, though it is true that, as time went on, he became increasingly interested in making them for others – surely a sign of maturity.

The following year, he bewitched the Irish defence at Manchester, enabling his partner, Hall, to score five goals. Meanwhile, his popularity in Stoke was such that when he asked for a transfer from the club, the Town Hall was hired – and packed – for a meeting of protest.

In 1947, however, Matthews did leave Stoke, going to Blackpool, for whom he had played regularly, as a 'guest', during the war. He has been there ever since, representing the club in three Cup Finals, the third of which is remembered for perhaps the finest display which even he has ever given. That was in 1953, when Blackpool, with twenty minutes to play, were losing to Bolton Wanderers. Matthews sensed that possibly his last chance of a Cup-winning medal was slipping away from him. He proceeded to transform the game, dribbling the Bolton defence off its feet, and Blackpool won by four goals to three.

It is an irony of his career that, despite his celebrity, he is not a rich man; far less wealthy than many, more obscure, footballers playing in Italy and Spain. He has always been shrewd to exploit his name, with articles in the press, two autobiographical books, and sponsorship of many different products, ranging from breakfast cereals to parlour games. During the close season he goes abroad to countries in the Commonwealth, to play series of exhibition matches, for which he is liberally rewarded. Yet although these supplementary earnings make his income far larger than the average British professional's, it is still negligible by comparison with a boxer, professional baseball or tennis player of equal status.

He trains throughout the year, living most abstemiously. He and his wife, the daughter of a Stoke City trainer, once ran a boarding-house in Blackpool, though they eventually gave it up. His daughter, Jean, is a promising tennis player – a game at which Matthews himself is proficient – and his small son was taught to kick a football at the earliest possible age.

If Matthews has a 'secret' he has never analysed it himself. Once, when a journalist who had been a footballer asked him to demonstrate his swerve, he replied, 'Honestly, I couldn't do it in cold blood. It just comes out of me under pressure.' He is not one of football's thinkers; he is an interpretative artist rather than a teacher. Trends and tactics appear to interest him very little, and he is too shy a man to command a team.

Reserve, in fact, is the principal impression which Matthews leaves, off the field. He is quiet and withdrawn, unwilling to talk to the Press, though he showed at a recent dinner at the National Sporting Club that he is quite a proficient speaker. These qualities have only increased his reputation in a country where admiration for modesty is carried to excess.

One rare occasion when he unburdened was after the match between England and Brazil at Wembley, last May. The choice of Matthews had been criticised by certain newspapers on the grounds of his age, yet he played magnificently, turning a game that might have been lost by England without his presence. 'Too old,' he remarked, with sober disgust. 'Do you know, there have been times when I've read that, and I've wanted to tear the paper across!'

6 January 1957

John Rafferty was inspired by Hunter Davies' book to remember some giants of the past and their approach to football.

Giants in Their Days

The impetus to talk was Hunter Davies' book *The Glory Game*, a sneak view of the private lives of football players written after living for a year with Spurs.

Gerry Dawson was saying; 'From what I hear you would think that strain on players was something new. It seems to have been forgotten that in my day our names were household words and that we were straining to maintain success always in the public eye and subject to temptation. Do you think George Best is any better known now than Alan Morton was in his day?'

Gerry Dawson is, of course, the former Scotland and Rangers goalkeeper and when there is any talk of great goalkeepers he must always be under consideration. Along with him was another famous goalkeeper of the past, Jimmy Brownlie, whose bowler hat is still happily noticed around football grounds. He is 88 next birthday and the oldest living British international player. He had some things to say about that phenomenon, tension, which seems to have just been discovered.

'At the start of the century I began my apprenticeship, but I quit after a month to play full-time for Third Lanark. We were the idols of the town and we had a lot of money by ordinary standards, but we did not let it go to our heads. We were not allowed to. We were disciplined in the club and disciplined at home.

'Maybe we did not go out as much, for at nights we were content to be at home with our families. But we had big men then who were stared at everywhere they went. Jimmy Quinn was the king of Scotland and there is nobody now as well known and as popular as he was. He was able to live with that, for he came from good mining stock.'

I had a memory of Quinn which confirmed Jimmy Brownlie's ranking of him. It concerned my father patiently working me through a crowd at Hampden until I was standing beside a square, greyheaded figure. My father stooped and whispered, 'You're standing next to Quinn.' From the tone of his voice it might have been King George himself or maybe the King would not have so impressed him. Thus had lived on the fame of Jimmy Quinn.

Gerry Dawson thought of his days in the glory game. 'We never called our manager The Boss. That did not suit him. He was always Mr Struth to us, for he always acted like Mr Struth. We were at the top of Scottish football at the time and were in demand everywhere. We were invited to parties and dances and there was much temptation. Privacy was difficult. It was no different then.

'But Mr Struth always talked to us about our public image. He insisted that even walking along the street we were representing the club and we must never do anything to tarnish its image. We were brought up to that way of thinking and so we dressed in a Rangers way and acted in a Rangers way in public. That was his way of disciplining us and making us come to terms with our special position.

'Of course, we were not angels and we liked a wee drink sometimes and a bit of fun, but we were discreet. We had this influence from the club and another from the home guiding us. Some say that players are paid so much nowadays that this raises more temptation.

'They forget that when I played I was maybe paid some weeks only £6, but I was a millionaire then with that money. I had a car when nobody else I knew had one. I could go where I liked and I dressed well. I had all the money I wanted. There is no more strain or tension on a player now than we had, no more temptation put in his way.'

Jimmy Brownlie agreed: 'I don't think it's football which puts the strain on, it's just the way people live nowadays. There does not seem to be any home life for some players now. They go out too much, but everybody does and not only football players. Maybe they train too much nowadays and that adds to their troubles.'

In the days of Dawson and Brownlie the private lives of players were not as assiduously probed, and probably there was a lot going on under the surface which the football followers did not hear or see and they would be none the worse for that. They were not all exemplary in the old days, just as they are not all fast living and up-tight nowadays.

Steve Murray of Aberdeen can be seen on team journeys studying for a degree. Billy McNeill is building a business empire and still playing good football and raising a family. There are many more well ordered young men playing football than there are tearaways and some are beginning to be rewarded for their good qualities.

The huge majority of football players still go home eagerly to their families and live moderately. It would be quite wrong to imagine that they all crushed into bars, entertained dolly birds, drive fast cars, and shrink from going home and develop tensions. Most appreciate their obligations to their employers and their public and to their own dignity

29 October 1972   *John Rafferty*

In a series on 'My Hero', a husband and wife team chose very different characters, Ronald Atkin was enchanted by the flair and ebullience of Peter Doherty, Julie Welch by Norman Hunter, the hard man with the soft side.

Paradise and Peas

Paradise came cheap when I was a lad. A shilling, to be precise. Ninepence to stand on the terraces at the City Ground, Nottingham, and threepence for a bowl of mushy peas at half-time.

And if Forest were playing Derby County, as they frequently did in those end-of-war and immediate post-war years of regional leagues, that meant Peter Doherty was thrown in at no extra cost.

Doherty, the spare, upright, dazzlingly talented Irishman from County Derry was my hero. My Pele, my Cruyff, my Best. The man who made monkeys out of half-backs, who left full-backs straining red-faced in his slipstream. Doherty did what so few footballers are capable of doing nowadays – he floated like a butterfly *and* stung like a bee.

In Derby's FA Cup-winning season of 1945–46, Doherty scored 10 times in 10 ties, including one of the four against Charlton at Wembley. This, says Doherty (now 68 and living near Blackpool), 'has to be the highlight of my career, even more satisfying than winning the League Championship with Manchester City in 1937'.

He scored five goals in a Midlands Cup Final against Aston Villa in May 1945, as Derby followed up a 3–0 win in the first leg by taking the second at the Baseball Ground 6–0. You see, Raich Carter had got all three at Villa Park and the friendly rivalry at Derby between these two being what it was, Doherty simply had to go one better, or in this case two better.

Doherty needed to be a genius to stand out in an era of forwards like Lawton, Matthews, Finney, Drake, Mannion and, of course, Carter. In fact, he needed to be a genius to stand out in Derby's attack, a forward line that many Midlanders of my generation can still chant like a 10-times table: Crooks, Carter, Stamps, Doherty, Duncan.

To have watched those five going forward was indeed paradise for a shilling, plus the bus fare from Nottingham to Derby as the compulsion grew to watch Peter Doherty as regularly as possible – dribbling, sprinting, scoring and spurning the opposition.

It was one of the few sensible decisions of my life, since Doherty didn't stay long within the range of my pocket money. Derby secured permission in August 1944 from his club Manchester City, to use him as a wartime guest player (he was based nearby with the RAF). He signed for Derby, at a fee of £7,000, the following year and by December 1946 had moved on to Huddersfield Town for £10,000.

Doherty knew two jobs briefly before embarking on an association with football which ended only a year ago. He was a conductor with his uncle's bus company in Coleraine and then a building labourer until he signed for Glentoran in 1931.

Blackpool bought him two years later for £2,000, a move which Doherty insists was the making of his career. 'The manager was called Sandy MacFarlane, a marvellous man who gave me the discipline and tactical ideas I needed.'

While still at Blackpool, Doherty played his first match for Northern Ireland (against England at Goodison) in 1935, and altogether earned 18 caps, the last of them in 1950.

His arrival at Manchester City for £10,000 in 1936 boosted that club to the League Championship within a year, when Doherty's skills were netting him £8 a week. 'But I loved football so much I would have played for nothing,' he insists.

'Manchester City in those days were a great team but Derby were the best side I ever played for. It was a joy to be with them and the dressing room was a happy place. I had a great understanding with Raich Carter. Between us, Raich and I had the will to win and to be better than anybody else.'

'I was probably a bit arrogant,' Doherty admits now, a view reinforced by my memories of him sidefooting penalty kicks inches inside an upright, or beating an opponent, waiting for him to catch up and then beating him again.

After Huddersfield, Doherty went to Doncaster as player-manager and got them promoted from Division Three North with a points record. Then he worked for Bristol City ('joining them was a mistake, the worst day's work I've ever done'), Aston Villa, Preston and Sunderland, managed Northern Ireland's team in the 1958 World Cup and finally retired as Blackpool's chief scout a year ago at 67.

As one might expect of an arrogant genius, Doherty is scornful of the modern game. 'Football has gone to hell. It's being destroyed by the 4–3–3 system. All the spaces are closed down and the players aren't skilful enough to overcome that. It was a sad day when we won the World Cup in 1966. That started it all.

'Players pass the ball three yards to somebody else, saying in effect "Go on, you've got more courage than I have." If they came with a Rolls-Royce to take me to Wembley I wouldn't go after what I've seen.

'It makes me so angry that I'd like to go out again and bloody play. I probably could, I'm still fit.' If he ever did I'd be there, mushy peas or not.

Ronald Atkin

Norman Revisited

Off the pitch, you'd never hear a word said against him. On it, he had the reputation of a man who ate powdered glass sandwiches, chased his beer down with paraquat and picked his teeth with a masonry drill. The harder he tackled, the more maniacally friendly the smile he bestowed on his victim; in fact, he gave the impression that after he'd broken both your legs he'd call the stretcher personally and ride with you in the ambulance.

They say his Mum used to watch him from the terraces and hit anyone who criticised him with her handbag, though it was rather hard to think of Norman Hunter as having anything as soft and cuddly as a Mum, the general effect being that he was thought up by Barnes Wallis in a playful mood and bolted together before matches. Mrs Hunter and Son even had a joke going the rounds about them – 'My Norman came home last night with a terrible leg, all covered in bruises' – 'Oh really? Whose was it?'

I can't quite explain why he was my hero, but you could keep your geniuses like George Best and Denis Law, your goody-goodies like Bobby Charlton and Kevin Keegan; Norman Hunter of Leeds United and England got my vote every time.

Maybe it was because he invoked this great sense of fun in a humourless profession, or because he was loyal and brave and honest and modest, the good clubman who never pretended to be more than he was. Some were picked for their skill, some were in there for their star appeal; Norman came from the stair-carpet school of footballers, chosen for their hard-wearing, stain-resistant qualities.

Certainly I can't ever remember him moaning about his wages or droning on to the newspapers about reconsidering his future; he never ducked out of a challenge (though plenty ducked out of his) and if he was fit enough to pull his socks on, he was fit enough to defend. And defend he did, 543 times for Leeds from the day he signed for them in April 1961 till the day he left them for Bristol City in October '76, by which time he'd scared dozens of strikers witless, given thousands of spectators their money's worth, helped Leeds from the Second Division to the First and, for what it's worth, scored 18 goals in the process.

He wasn't, in fact, all that big for a defender; at 5 ft 11½ in. and 12 stone 5 lbs he was fairly streamlined and the top of his head was just about level with Jack Charlton's Adam's apple. But he was agile as well as courageous, and though he always maintained he couldn't play, the daft thing was that he could, very well indeed; his right foot might just have been something to fill in the space between his ankle and the ground, but his left foot was a winner.

When people talk of that Leeds United championship side, it's usually John Giles or Billy Bremner or Sniffer Clarke they mention, but he was every bit as good as them in his own way, and every bit as vital to that team.

Above all, he had – still has – a lot of class as a person. When you meet them, heroes have a nasty habit of becoming human before your eyes but Norman Hunter just became – well, more Norman Hunter. He was the first footballer I ever interviewed and it was with some trepidation that I walked through the doors of Elland Road that day; would I find him arm-wrestling with the club gorilla? Would he snap my biro in two and start ripping up my notebook?

Instead, he was sitting in the hall in his tracksuit clutching a tin of Johnson's baby powder, and that's how I'll always remember him, not scoring for England or flooring adventurous strikers. He was, quite simply, one of the most amiable footballers I ever met. I hope Barnsley know how lucky they are.

Julie Welch

Roy Perrott remembered Duncan Edwards who was set to be one of the great players of his generation, indeed was already close to being so, when the Munich disaster cut him down before his prime.

Duncan Edwards

Whenever, some time in the future, soccer old-timers are trying to remember what that Manchester United side was really like, one eager, chunky figure will tend to come pounding into their minds. Duncan Edwards, perhaps more than any of his team mates, represented the spirit of the side.

Watching him, you always felt that he would be glad to join in a scratch game between coats in the local park and would play there with the same unflagging concentration and exuberance that he put into a floodlit European Cup game. The whole team was rather like that but this young buccaneer most of all, and it put him deeply under the skin of the Old Trafford crowd.

As a player he certainly had a long way to go before he absorbed all that Busby had to teach him about technique; there were several half-backs who excelled him in style and polish. But in his combination of rock-like strength, his eye for opening out a game, his fine positional sense, there were few or none better. He played as though he owned the field. Quite often he did.

Since the emotional side of football is such a puzzle anyway, it would be hard to measure just how much he gave the crowd. Perhaps more than anything Edwards conveyed the enormously boyish idea that anything was possible.

We shall go on seeing him striding up with the ball from the cable factory end at Old Trafford as though it was a piece of colossal cheek to come beyond the halfway line, massive intentions about a goal written on his face and on his boots. When, as sometimes happened, he struck home with a shot fit to break the net the crowd hardly knew their way out.

22 February 1958   *Roy Perrott*

———————————————

In 1959 this was my tribute to Jeff Hall after his untimely death. Hall was the quietly effective partner of Roger Byrne in a period of English success.

The Quiet Man

Jeff Hall's death from polio brings to a tragic end one of England's most successful partnerships. For 17 successive internationals Hall and Byrne were England's full backs, and during that time only one match, against Wales, was lost, while the dozen victories included wins over such leading sides as Brazil, Yugoslavia, Spain and Germany.

Both were cut off in mid-career, Byrne a victim of the Munich air crash, now Hall dead at the age of 29.

By contrast with the dashing Byrne, Hall was a quiet, unassuming player, too often underrated because he was efficient rather than spectacular. Slight of build, and only 5 ft. 7 in. in height he was typical of the modern back, achieving results by speed, positional sense and anticipation rather than by physical toughness.

He was not a defender to overawe and dominate his opponent, but he was at his most effective in countering the swift and tricky Continental wingers, who found him difficult to elude.

The wide-eyed, startled expression that was habitual to him on the field may well have deceived opponents, who found in practice that he was hard to surprise. It was on the basis of this sound defence that England enjoyed two of her finest seasons and was a match for any team in the world.

But the limelight tended to be on the more dashing figures like Byrne, Edwards or Taylor, and Hall never quite established himself as one of the great players in this class of football.

As a club player his value was not only on the field. The quiet, steady, dependable player is of immense value to the team over a long season, and

Hall was of a character to make any manager's job easier. A fine person and nearly one of the great players, football may well mourn his loss.

5 April 1959   *Tony Pawson*

Before Gordon Banks and Peter Shilton there were goalkeeping problems for England. Clement Freud considered the 1959 claims of one whose ability never quite matched his self-belief.

Tony Macedo

There was a time when the England team selectors sat down at a long table, wrote the name of Frank Swift on the team sheet, and then, with a sigh of relief at the completion of a job well done, said to one another: 'Now whom shall we play in front of him?'

Alas, those days are a decade away and the choosing of an England goalkeeper is now one of the real problems that confront Mr Winterbottom and his men.

For Wednesday's international against Sweden they rely once more on Hopkinson of Bolton; a 'keeper whose worst is remarkably good, whose anticipation and positioning are brilliant, but whose handling of the high ball is definitely suspect – a weakness that is well advertised and an open invitation to opposing forwards to shoot towards the crossbar with hearts full of hope.

Apart from Hopkinson and Colin McDonald, whose all-round excellence in the 1958 World Cup in Sweden made us feel that here, at last, was our man, but who is now in a rehabilitation centre with a slow-healing leg that he broke playing for the Football League in March, there are five other international goalkeepers playing League football.

On the grounds that the devil you know is better than the devil you don't, they might all have been considered by the selectors; on their showing for England, they could only have been rejected. They are Merrick of Birmingham, who conceded six goals against the Hungarians at Wembley and never recovered, internationally speaking. Wood now of Huddersfield, whose feats for England fell short of those that had made him the idol of Manchester United.

Baynham of Luton, who was in and out of the England side without really having a chance to prove his worth, but may have lacked the necessary big-game temperament. Hodgkinson of Sheffield United, whose success as an Under-23 cap was not repeated as a full international, and Matthews of Chelsea, a man of erratic brilliance perhaps better suited to the unpredictable 'Pensioners' than the national team.

Over the seven capped goalkeepers looms the shadow of a man whose selection can only be a question of time. A man who on Friday was tipped by over half the nation's sportswriters, and most of the country's players, to play against Sweden – Tony Macedo, of Fulham.

Macedo has run on the fringe of the international stakes since 1957–58 when his acrobatics helped Fulham into the FA Cup semi-final, where they were beaten by Manchester United in a replay. Perversely it was for this replay, in which he conceded five goals, three of which might well have been stopped by a schoolboy, that he is remembered. He went off in tears, much photographed.

'Didn't you feel badly,' I asked him after the game, 'letting down your team-mates?'

'If it hadn't been for me they wouldn't have got as far as they did, so they've got nothing to kick about.'

And what about the tears? 'I cried,' he said, 'because I had played the worst game of my life and I'd never play as badly again. It was relief, see?' Perhaps the selectors did not see.

There was much speculation in that spring of 1958 about Macedo's future. Was he, a son of Spanish parents, eligible to play for England? The answer was 'Yes'; his father was born in Gibraltar and held British nationality. Sir Stanley Rous was quoted as saying that he was eligible, if selected; but McDonald and Hopkinson were capped, Hodgkinson chosen to keep goal for the Under-23s.

Last season he helped Fulham to win promotion to the First Division. He got engaged to a local girl, and was widely quoted as saying that he would marry when he was awarded his first England Cap. If this was an appeal to the hearts of the selectors, it misfired. McDonald continued to keep goal for England, Hopkinson took over when he was injured and Hodgkinson remained in goal for the Under-23s.

Yet some honours came his way, for at the close of the season he was chosen to represent Young England, helping them to draw against the senior side. If it did not permit his pride to marry, it was official recognition, a promise of things to come. This season he was picked for the Under-23s against Hungary.

It was hard on him that a week before the match he should have had to face Wolverhampton at their fiercest and fish the ball out of the net nine times, but he is one of the few goalkeepers in the world who could do this and still believe wholeheartedly in his quality.

Macedo is cocksure, the undisputed master of his penalty area, which he governs with shouts and gestures, even barging his own full-back off the ball to clear it upfield. His father is an ex-footballer of the Spanish League. The son is an admirer of Spanish football, and has styled himself on the flamboyant exhibitionism of the Continentals, underwriting this with his natural speed and sureness of touch that is the legacy of an apprenticeship in our League.

He exudes nervous energy, bites his nails. 'If I stopped biting my nails,' he says, 'it would all go. Everything.' And he waved his arms in an eloquent gesture.

In Fulham's team he was for some time the odd man out, a boy with the confidence of a man. Now his behaviour has been granted artistic licence, his individuality accepted by virtue of his talent. He is still improving. Two years ago he kicked only in emergency, throwing the ball in the manner of the Continentals. Now his place kicking is as good as anyone's, his punting better than most.

He trains when he is able, privately in a gymnasium, feeling that a goalkeeper needs different preparation for a game than the rest of the team. He is very much a specialist.

Against Sweden, who delight in drawing the defence to leave a man clear for a duel with the 'keeper, Hopkinson's sureness of positioning and good judgment of when to come out of goal may well have tipped the selectors' scales in his favour. But Macedo's time will come, and once in England's goal it will take much to shift him.

A few days before the selectors met to announce our team for next Wednesday, he was asked whether he was worried about his international prospects. 'I'm not worried,' he said, 'but Hopkinson is.'

25 October 1959   *Clement Freud*

For some Pat Jennings may be the sports personality of a decade. Ronald Atkin included him in The Observer's *usual Sports Personality of the Week series after he had helped Northern Ireland qualify for the 1986 Finals.*

Jennings, Keeper of a Heritage

As pastimes go, waiting for Pat Jennings to exhibit signs of fallibility could be compared to watching celery grow or living in the expectation that gold will one day become a worthless commodity.

Arsenal's reserve goalkeeper George Wood, a patient fellow, had simply had enough when he asked for a transfer a few days ago. 'I can see no future at Highbury,' he confessed.

In his 19 years as a professional with Watford, Tottenham and now Arsenal, Jennings has seen quite a few rivals come, and has watched all of them go. 'I don't think any of them left with any bitterness towards me,' he said. Bewilderment possibly, bitterness never. 'I have had a good relationship with all the lads who have left. But there is not very much I can do about it.' Apart, that is, from doing the unthinkable like losing form or making a mistake now and then.

Jennings, who will mark up his 700th league game this season, has just achieved what even he is the first to acknowledge as the unexpected climax to a brilliant career by helping to take Northern Ireland into the World Cup Finals.

He played in six of the eight qualifying games and let in two goals, which might reasonably be termed a useful contribution. Thirteen league matches this season have seen Jennings beaten only ten times, fewer than anybody else in the First Division except the leaders, Manchester United. The fact that Arsenal are floundering isn't his fault. After all, he can't be expected to score them as well as stop them.

Last Wednesday night the biggest hands in British football were clamped around a glass of champagne after the Irish had beaten Israel to take runners-up place to Scotland in Group Six, and next week Jennings will have the chance to repeat the finger-chilling exercise. His meritorious services to the profession of keeping goal earn him the Observer/Mumm jeroboam of champagne as sports personality of the week.

Jennings claims he was 'more relieved than surprised' about getting into his first World Cup. 'I thought it had all passed me by,' he admitted. 'But I knew this was my best-ever chance' (not 'last chance', please note) 'and if we had slipped up with a fixture like Israel it would have hurt.'

As qualifications go, Northern Ireland's was constructed along lines roughly comparable to England's roller-coaster progress to Spain. When they were beaten 1–0 in Sweden last June, Jennings said 'I thought that was us out.' Then came the momentous match with Scotland in Belfast, a 0–0 draw which left Jock Stein's team celebrating a place among the World

155

Cup's final 24 and the Irish, in Jennings's phrase, 'drowning our sorrows back at the hotel'. Then came the news that the Swedes had won in Portugal. Suddenly there was a better reason for getting drunk.

Jennings has made 89 appearances for Northern Ireland and, Boycott-fashion, is probably building towards his second hundred rather than his century. 'I don't really keep count of how many games I have played' he says, though he recalls smartly enough the big ones, like his six Cup Finals (four FA, two League) with Tottenham and Arsenal. He categorises the other Wembley occasions as 'a load of international and representative matches'.

Since he lets in so few, the question of tabulating goals is an even simpler matter. 'In the World Cup games it was a penalty in Sweden and a goal against Scotland at Hampden. That's about it.'

That realistic attitude extends to his assessment of Ireland's chances in Spain. 'It is a unique achievement to qualify when you look at the size of the country and the players at our disposal. We are never going to win it but we won't just be going for the ride. There's no pressure so we can enjoy ourselves.'

Enjoyment is not the first adjective which springs to mind about keeping goal for a tiddler nation which tends to lose far more frequently than it wins. 'If the opposition, say England, is on top form there is no way you should be able to live with them,' he says. 'You just hope they have a below-par day and you play out of your skin.'

Playing out of his skin is a habit Jennings has cultivated to the point of his skills being perfected to the stage where they are simply taken for granted. 'I would be kidding myself if I said I am as good now as I was five or six years ago, but I still feel I have been doing a good job over those last five or six years.'

The man who launched his career as a goalkeeper at the age of 11 in a Newry Street league is 36 now but insists he hasn't even started to think about retirement. He has made no plans for his future, and is happy enough to remain a senior and enormously respected member of that strange collection of brethren, the goal-keeping Mafia.

'It's a funny position,' is how Jennings describes it. 'We all know each others' problems. It's my turn to make a mistake one week and somebody else's next.'

Possibly, but Arsenal and Northern Ireland could be forgiven for estimating the odds on Jennings as a good deal better than even.

20 June 1981   *Ronald Atkin*

In September 1972 Terry O'Neill interviewed Liverpool's new star, Kevin Keegan:

'Hey, just look at that. It's Beatlemania all over again,' said a policeman, his gaze reluctantly leaving a row of beauty queens. 'Look, just look at him, he's being mobbed like he was the four of 'em rolled into one.'

The centre of attraction of a howling mob was 21-year-old Liverpool player Kevin Keegan. True to tradition, the public crucifixion of Superstars has left the throne of George Best vacant. Keegan is the heir apparent.

Best was an unprimed prototype, he learned the hard way – from his own mistakes. Keegan, a compact, handsome, earnest young man, has carefully taken note. 'I've had offers from every top agent in football. They all want you to sign contracts, and they'll promise you the world. "I'll earn you this" or "I'll get you that." I prefer somebody like Vic, who says "I can't get you this" or "I can't get you that, but I'll try." There's something genuine about that.'

Vic Hugling, his agent and close friend, guards Keegan's interests carefully. 'This boy is great, all he needs is protecting. He could be anything from 1974's trendy top model to a third partner for Morecambe and Wise. He's a complete gentleman. His only fault, if it can be regarded as such, is he thinks too much of other people before himself.'

Keegan is the new breed of footballer on whom England's prestige may depend. His explosive runs against the polished military of the senior back 'fours' have made him the most marked man of the year. After only one top class season he is on the verge of a full senior cap. Sir Alf Ramsey says, 'His play reminds of Geoff Hurst, he uses the whole width of the pitch. He and Geoff are among the few players who recognise this method of play.'

The reason behind this method is simple, 'Ambition, that's what drives me, I'll run till I succeed. I'm relieved when it's Saturday, you know? It's pressure all week but I react opposite to most when I get out there on that field, it's a relief. You're your own boss, there's no turning back, you've just got to get on with the game. All the talking's OK but I think, *this* is what I'm here for, to *play*.'

His keeness is ill-disguised. He is the first ready for training and first at Anfield on match days. Liverpool manager Bill Shankly says, 'He's a whipper of a player, like a weasel after rats, always biting and snapping at your legs! He reminds me of Denis Law when he was 16. He's got everything, fantastic ability, two good feet. He's brainy and courageous and has the will to win. He's a perfect size, a fully fledged middleweight – the greatest fighters of them all!'

Keegan's nickname at Liverpool is 'Handy Andy'. His idol when he was younger was Alan Ball, but now, 'I like the great ball players like Cruyff, Beckenbauer and Netzer. I admire Ian Callaghan very much for his skill and the example he sets in the game, and if you could graft a new pair of legs on Ian St John what a player he'd be.'

The skill he enjoys most is heading. He practises for hours, jumping against Tommy Smith and Larry Lloyd at a suspended ball that is progressively heightened, and from all accounts he more than holds his own. 'I love it best of all, I don't know why. It's the thing I work at most, that and my speed.'

He hates arrogant people, and detests 'the sneaky players who go over the top. If it's one of the hard men you expect it. I'd rather not name them, but we all know who they are all right, the ones you least suspect. Always smiling and friendly.

'I don't like playing against big, physical players either. They just use their brawn, it's fair play all right, but it's my size you see, when I go up for the ball they just knock me off it and if they're *too* physical I get a real seeing to.'

His destiny, he feels, is at Liverpool. 'The worst thing that could happen to me is that I'd have to leave here. Mind you when I first got here everything went wrong for me. It seemed everyone was shouting at me, even the players, "No, Rubbish. Rubbish. Get hold of it!" or the coaches game after game, "Cut this out. Cut that out." It was a living nightmare.

'I said to me Dad, "I don't know what I've let myself in for here, they know the way I play. They must have seen me, yet I get all this." But I don't think I could play anywhere else, I've grown to love everything here so much. I signed my contract sitting on a dustbin, you know.'

When he played for Scunthorpe his wages were low and there were no win bonuses, so in the close season he took a job as a porter at a hospital for mentally handicapped, thalidomide and spastic children. He still spends every Thursday evening with them.

The pressures of fame are building. 'But,' he says, 'when you're getting pressure it means you're successful. One goes with the other, and I think the players who moan about it, well they've dug their own grave. I hope one day I get the pressure George Best got. Or Bobby Moore. I think every young lad does. I just hope I can live with it that's all. I don't envy anyone who's not got there, but those who have and are grumbling about it are fools, I think.'

He has three current targets, to play at Wembley, to improve his temperament ('if somebody kicks me I must curb my feeling to kick him right back') and to get a full England cap. 'I'm not greedy though, I can wait.'

Meanwhile his emotions are cradled in the loving hands of the Kop. 'The only thing I fear in life is missing an open goal in front of them. I'd rather die than that happen. It's funny; empty, the Kop doesn't look anything but when it's full you feel there's a million people there. When they start singing "You'll Never Walk Alone" it makes my eyes water. Sometimes tears have been streaming down my cheeks. I've actually been crying while I'm playing.'

17 September 1972   *Terry O'Neill*

In 1983 Hugh McIlvanney gave this account of a goalkeeper whose self-confidence was matched by selfless dedication and enduring skill.

Whole World in His Hands

It is only the deep-rooted sense of decorum natural to Scottish football supporters that prevents them from asking Peter Shilton how he feels about being an artificial insemination donor. They are entitled to suspect that having his genes in a test tube might be the best insurance against experiencing another 9–3, 7–2 or 5–1 at Wembley around the year 2005.

The old game may be sorely pressed to last into the next century as a major professional sport but for us as long as it is played in anything resembling its present form Shilton will occupy a special place in its lore and its record books.

He is, beyond all worthwhile argument, the best goalkeeper now practising the trade anywhere in the world. And to Scots in particular, with their psyches scarred by a long succession of goalkeepers who have looked (at least when transported to London) as if they could not keep a size five football out of an egg cup, his gifts are so unfamiliar as to seem like the properties of an alien species.

Even in the English First Division this season, he is, to a remarkable degree, a man apart. Before his club, Southampton, kicked off at Leicester yesterday they had lost only two goals in eight League matches, one to Liverpool at Anfield and one at Villa Park. That gave them easily the best defensive statistics in the country. It would, of course, be an over-simplification, and a silly insult to the rest of the team, to suggest that his

159

excellence explains Southampton's challenge for the leadership of the League. But anyone who does not accept that his is the paramount contribution should not be allowed out in traffic.

Southampton's manager, Lawrie McMenemy, isn't inclined to blow bugles on behalf of individual players under his control but he has too much sense to have any truck with the phoney egalitarianism that sees each man as no more than one-eleventh of the team. On the contrary, McMenemy is happy to acknowledge that the thought of how unusual Shilton is can still give him a little romantic *frisson*.

'When we were sat together in a plane recently I found myself looking at him from the back and thinking just what a wonderful thing it is for a person to be accepted as the best in the world at anything – not in Hampshire or in England or in Europe but on the planet. It makes you shiver. Even if there is some little fella in Mongolia that we have never heard of who is plucking them out of the air, who is a genius, then the worst you can assume is that Peter is one of the two best in the world. And the world is a pretty big place.'

When people try to catalogue the qualities that have raised Shilton to a status that remains unthreatened at the age of 34, extreme dedication to his job, the powerful obsessional streak in his personality, is inevitably high on the list. There is a slight echo of that commercial in which the elderly tourist in New York asks the hard-hat worker how she can get to Carnegie Hall and is told: 'Practise, lady, practise.'

It is true that most of his strengths, physical and technical, have been developed by a remorseless concentration on improving exercises, that his single-mindedness is sufficient to justify the title of a book he has done with Jason Tomas: 'The Magnificent Obsession.' (There will always be those who insist that there is nothing very magnificent about preventing a ball from passing through a rectangle eight yards wide by eight feet high, but that prejudice can be left aside for the moment.)

What makes the commitment to the sort of conservative perfectionism essential to great goalkeeping especially fascinating in Shilton's case is that it coexists in his nature with a quite separate, almost contrasting element, an appetite for letting himself go, for taking chances, that is most strikingly represented by his liking for the chanciest of all recreations – betting horses. He has also been known to take a refreshment, which is the Glasgow euphemism for having a whole-hearted skirmish with the bevvy.

Says McMenemy: 'In terms of dedication and the intensity of the preparation for his work, he is, I believe, the equal of Geoff Boycott. But he has got an advantage Geoff does not have. Peter is able to have a day at the races or have a bloody good drink now and then. You have got to think that this capacity to relax has been a big factor in helping him to maintain such tremendous standards over so many years at the top levels of the game.'

Another distinction that must emerge from any comparison with Boycott is the fact that Shilton, for all his unmistakably (often aggressively) high opinion of his own talent, never loses track of his responsibilities to the team.

His manager again: 'Most goalkeepers, if they told the truth, would have to admit that they are happiest when they are flying around at Anfield, being heroically defiant against superior odds, making dramatic saves and getting a clap from the Kop. Their side may lose 1–0 but they get a good Press – "If it had not been for some miraculous saves the score would have been six" – and they feel good.

'He's not like that. He's well pleased if he has nothing to do and the team win 1–0. There's no desperation for kudos. You find in him something that shines through in certain special performers. He won't dive for the newspapers because he thinks they are saying how good he is. He knows that, but he also knows what got him there and, unlike a lot of other stars, he doesn't think he has a licence to make less effort than he did in the early days. This bugger is as hard as ever on himself. He's hard on those around him too, but it starts with himself.

'Like anyone who is really brilliant, he doesn't always find it easy to see when he *is* at fault and, although I would never dream of licking any man's boots, I know that rushing in with blunt criticism, having a go at him in public, isn't usually the right approach. I trust him to be honest about himself, to hold his hand up before too long. More than once he has done that, literally, almost as soon as the ball was in the net.

'At Tottenham last season we lost six. We had such a raw team on the park that some of the young fellas were taking the opportunity to introduce themselves to their team-mates while the game was being restarted between goals. So he was having a rough time.

'But on at least one occasion he picked the ball out of the net and put his hand up right away as an admission that the goal was down to him. He was letting those young lads off the hook, with more than 25,000 spectators in the ground and Ray Clemence at the other end. It is not a small man who does that.'

When he was young at the game – a long time ago, considering that he started training at Leicester City when he was 11-years-old – Shilton was reluctant to let himself off the hook. Sometimes he wouldn't even come off the banister, from which he dangled at his parents' home (while his mother held his legs) to facilitate the stretching exercises that may have helped to increase his height to an unlikely 6 feet and to give him arms of abnormal and invaluable length.

With a muscular physique that tapers from wide shoulders to a narrow waist and appears even more powerful than his weight of 14 st. might indicate, he is well equipped to achieve the commanding presence that has meant so much over 17 seasons to Leicester, Stoke City, Nottingham Forest, Southampton, and, of course, in 55 appearances for England.

He is the schoolboy prodigy who has gone on being prodigious and, by and large, he has been appropriately rewarded with honours and money. 'I got married young and since an early age I have had a family to support', he says, 'but I'd have driven a pretty hard bargain anyway because if you want to be recognised as one of the top players in the country you have to be among the top earners.'

His transfer to Stoke from Leicester set a world record for a goalkeeper at the time but at £335,000 it still imposed a valuation on the importance of his position that Shilton, and a few more of us, find ludicrously low in relation to the sums handed over for some outfield players who couldn't trap a curling stone.

A truer measure of his worth was conveyed by the wages paid to him later at Nottingham Forest by Brian Clough ('Like anybody else who ever worked for Cloughie, I had my moments with him, but I admire him – he'd never let you down in a real crunch, he's a big man when it matters').

For their pay of around £100,000 a year, Forest drew a marvellous return. In his initial season with them, they won the First Division Championship for the first time in their history and Shilton conceded only 18 goals in 38 matches, the best figures of his career. When Forest won the European Cup in 1978–79 he yielded seven goals in nine matches, when they took it again the next season only five went past him.

In that 1980 Final in Madrid, against a blatantly more accomplished Hamburg team, he was easily the most vital figure on the field. Whether looming as an unnerving, athletic bulk in front of advancing forwards, soaring confidently for dangerous centres, exploding into reflex saves, making those brave, rigorously controlled sprawls at opponents' feet or exhorting, deploying and disciplining his defenders as no other goalkeeper can, he has tended to exert that kind of influence throughout his life in football.

During a long, relaxed conversation at a pavement café in Budapest last week – a few hours before he went out for an evening made even more relaxed for him by England's (and notably Hoddle's) excellence against an abysmal Hungarian team – the overwhelming impression was of a man who brings genuine substance to his work. 'I am not afraid of making mistakes, I am not really afraid of anything' Peter Shilton said. 'I've made mistakes in everything, in football and in life, and I've taken stick for them. I've been on the floor. You've just got to pick yourself up and get back in there. For me, that means getting on with proving I'm the best at what I do.'

Barring a late intervention from Mongolia, most of us are ready to agree.

16 October 1983   *Hugh McIlvanney*

John Gale interviewed Billy Wright before the game in which he won his hundredth cap, and Bobby Charlton's goal beat Scotland.

England's Billy Wright

Mr Billy Wright, who – barring accidents – will get his hundredth international cap next Saturday when he captains England against Scotland at Wembley, had an afternoon off last week in his top-floor flat in a red-brick house in Wolverhampton within sight of the tall pylons of the Molineux floodlights.

He was wearing a fawn sweater and relaxed clothes, but admitted, as he sat in a purple armchair opposite the television set, that life had been hectic lately, mainly because of the Press. Yet he was calm, helpful and straight-forward. He produced a scrapbook, showed his records (from opera to Sophie Tucker, with a good deal of Mantovani in between), and talked about his rug-making: 'I go so mad at it. I want to see the finished product.' His present task is a cream rug with a large rose-pattern. His fair hair was receding a little; few men can have more smile-lines round the eyes.

He said it was quite true his football career nearly ended almost before it had begun: Major Buckley, manager of Wolverhampton Wanderers when Billy joined as a boy in 1938, told him shortly afterwards that he was too small for a footballer, and advised him to try something else. But at the last moment Buckley relented and kept him on.

In his early days with Wolves, Billy played in every position except goal. Finally he settled down at left-half – although his first appearance for England was at right-half in January, 1946, against Belgium. Since then, he's missed only three internationals for England: an astounding record, unlikely to be equalled. The most remarkable thing about his play has been his consistency.

He was first chosen to captain England in October, 1948, against Ireland, and heard about it by chance on a bus when he was coming home after playing for England against Denmark. Playing for England and, particularly, captaining England, he regards as a great honour: 'honour' is a word he uses often, and with great sincerity.

Wright is well known for saying very little to his team on the field. 'I love to be in the game and doing a lot of work,' he explains. 'I do shout occasionally when it's needed. But I'd rather do my work. If they see the captain bawling all the while and not doing anything to help the team, they've got good cause to grieve.' This has always been Wright's philosophy.

But reliability and a good example have not been his only qualities as captain. He has a great football sense and the ability to 'read the game'. His mental awareness seldom allows him to be deceived by new tactics – particularly by Continental sides.

The most troublesome centre-forward he's played against in England is Nat Lofthouse: 'We've had some tussles. Then, going abroad, there's big John Charles. And, deep-lying centre-forwards, Di Stefano of Real Madrid, and Kopa of Real Madrid and France. Wonderful ball players.'

He thinks the Hungarian side of 1954, which beat England so thoroughly at Wembley, were the best team he ever played against; they were probably the best team ever.

He will never forget the Hungarians against Uruguay in the semi-final of the World Cup in Switzerland in 1954. 'It was played in pouring rain before 63,000 people, and you got wonderful football the whole time.'

Perhaps his most exciting moment was when England beat Austria, then the leading Continental team, 3–2 in Vienna in 1952. Lofthouse scored the winning goal just before the end, and British soldiers ran on to the field and carried off the England players. Other memorable moments were when Wolves beat Leicester City to win the Cup at Wembley in 1949, and when they beat Honved and Spartak under the floodlights at Molineux. There was also last year's lunch at Buckingham Palace. 'It was marvellous,' said Wright. 'A wonderful lunch. I enjoyed it remarkably well.'

Bad moments? 'I think the worst was when the United States beat us in the World Cup in Brazil in 1950. We had all the play but couldn't take our chances. When we came home people said: "How did the United States beat you? They don't play soccer, do they?" It took some living down.'

Last year Wright married Joy, one of the Beverley Sisters. Their baby is due on the same day as his hundredth cap. 'I feel so well towards Joy,' he says. 'She's done so much in coming into my life. We've had a wonderful year. I want to be a good husband – and now a good father.'

Billy Wright is 35. How long can he continue playing in the exacting position of centre-half? He says he enjoys it as much as ever at present – including the training. He'll stop as soon as it gets hard or his play deteriorates. Perhaps in two or three years.

And then? Well, it will be something to do with soccer, which has been his life and has given him his chances – unlike some players, he has never had a trade or business to fall back on. 'I'd like to keep my knowledge in the game.'

5 April 1959   *John Gale*

Ron Greenwood once commented that it helped his understanding as a manager that as a player he had been one of those who had to look at the team sheet to see whether he was playing while the stars only looked to see when the bus was leaving. Some of the great entertainers of the game have also had that problem of wondering if they would make the team. Len Shackleton's individualism and acid comments left him titled the clown prince of soccer with fewer caps than his great talent deserved. Another undervalued player of immense skill who had difficulty even holding a place in the fine Spurs side was Tommy Harmer. This is a fine tribute to the little man. It appeared anonymously but is in fact one of Brian Glanville's favourite pieces as he captured the essence of this 'Familiar Sprite'.

'A Familiar Sprite'

One of the greatest reproaches against league football is that it leaves no room for the artist. Points must be won, Cup-ties hurdled, relegation survived. This being so, it is inevitable that functionalism should triumph at the expense of the unorthodox – and of such a player as Tommy Harmer, of Tottenham Hotspur, who has just come back triumphantly into the league side, after being dropped for four games.

Harmer, the familiar sprite of London football, is over thirty now. He has never played for England and it seems unlikely that he ever will: less a commentary on his merits than on the real value of an international cap.

165

He is almost unknown outside this country – though Fussball Klub Austria of Vienna once paid him the significant compliment of trying to sign him – and it has taken him six years to win a regular place in the Tottenham side. When he asked for a transfer, Cardiff City alone made an offer, during the eighteen months in which he was 'for sale'. It has all been a strange anticlimax to one of the most spectacular British post-war débuts.

This was made at White Hart Lane on a sunny September afternoon in 1951. Tottenham were playing Bolton, Baily was not available, and they included at inside-left a tiny, fragile Tom Thumb figure, chapped and hollow cheeked, wearing shorts which were far too long; the living refutation of theories that football is a game for athletes.

Within a few minutes, the crowd was laughing and exclaiming like a delighted ogre; Harmer's Cockney impertinence and extraordinary ball control had won him a place in its favour which, through all his vicissitudes, he has never lost.

George Orwell must have been wrong when he said that if 'Jack the Giant-Killer' were written today, it would be called 'Giant the Jack-Killer'. The whole fascination of Harmer's performance lay in the fact that, through sheer skill, he was making bigger men look foolish. Sometimes the space available to him was so confined that it seemed physique must prevail; yet again and again he would extricate himself with a shuffle, a quick wriggle of the hips, a mock kick at the ball, or even a backheel while it was still in the air.

All the time his expression was as tense and preoccupied as when he came on to the field; an indication that these things were being done, not for a laugh, but because they were integrally part of Harmer's game.

If he has a Cockney self-assurance, it is reserved for the football field. He remembers old friends and has never, even when he most needed it, consciously looked for publicity. He is serious, conscientious, yet despite an astonishing natural grasp of position and tactics, remains an utterly instinctive player, with little to say about the game. One could not imagine his teaching it.

Harmer was born in the East End of London; an area which sings its own praises less vocally than the North-East, but rivals it as a footballers' spawning ground. He developed his control by juggling with a tennis ball, and carried it with him everywhere, long after Spurs had made him a professional. They discovered him as an amateur, apprenticing him to Finchley, but it was in Army football that he began to make a name.

That Spurs should be his mentors was ironic, for his style was for many years the antithesis of their own. Harmer is, above all, a midfield player. He can dribble superbly when he wants to, moving at a deceptive jog-trot, a straight-backed series of stops and starts, sudden swerves, abrupt changes of direction, the ball moved coolly aside with the outside of the right foot, or pulled back with the sole of the boot.

But he prefers to hold the ball, then move it, with an infinite series of subtle passes; a through pass to his own winger or centre-forward, a cross-field pass to the opposite flank, a 'square ball' to the wing-half. Tottenham, in 1951, under Arthur Rowe's managership, were the supreme exponents of 'push and run', and Harmer liked to kick the ball, rather than push it, while expecting other people to do the running.

Not until the advent of Danny Blanchflower, Ireland's captain and right-half, and the passing of Ramsey, Baily, Medley and Burgess, the arch-priest of push-and-run, was he able to come into his own, after years of frustration, and criticism.

He has been accused of being a clown, ineffectual except on hard grounds, reluctant to fight for the ball. But to call him a clown monstrously ignores his constructive genius; he has never been merely a static entertainer.

If he does not play a heroic part in defence, then neither does Haynes, England's *chef d'orchestre*, and Harmer has the excuse of extreme fragility. As for his partiality to dry grounds, this is a myth. Like any ball player, he is most at home on a holding ground; effective in any conditions but thick mud.

In Blanchflower, whose flair equals his own, Harmer found an ideal complement. Together, they have provided some bewitching duets. Talking to him one feels that he has sadly come to terms with ambition; it is a stricture on the modern game that he should have been forced to do so.

12 October 1958   *Brian Glanville*

Julie Welch met a key member of Ron Greenwood's old guard as England qualified for the World Cup finals in Spain in 1982.

The Pride of Dad's Army

It is just as well for a match that has already assumed the proportions of a national anxiety neurosis that one of the most important members of the

England squad intends to shape up to it with the sick tension of a shire-horse delving into a nosebag.

'Trevor Brooking,' his manager John Lyall once said in tones of huge affection, 'is a big old lump really.'

The twice scoring pride of Dad's Army, the England side who beat Hungary 3–1 in Budapest in June, Brooking has a legendary equanimity of temperament that might be as crucial on Wednesday as his more tangible gifts. 'It sounds silly,' he says, 'but we really have to imagine that we're just on three points for a win as usual. Obviously, whoever's selected will give as much as they can, but we mustn't try for the extra touch or anything out of the ordinary. It's essential to treat it as just another game and forget about the magnitude of it all.'

The magnitude of it all must be difficult to overlook when Brooking has rarely been able to walk down the road all week without being reminded of the impending confrontation. 'People really are rooting for us. Everywhere I go, car windows wind down and people shout "good luck." I know a lot of people think that Ron's going to go for the old guard on Wednesday; if so, I just hope we're up to it.'

Interestingly, at an age when most players are beginning to creak at the joints a bit, the 33-year-old Brooking has produced some of the best football of his distinguished career. He regards his second goal against Hungary, hit with such sweet force that it lodged in the stanchion, as the most notable shot he has ever struck. These days, too, his game has a bite to it – 'It was Don Revie who suggested that I added more aggression to my game. He said I had a tendency to drift along with play instead of shaping it the way I wanted it, and I must accept that I could have been more assertive. I've also been helped by John Lyall, who was an aggressive player himself. Since he became manager of West Ham, our training has been far more competitive. He pairs people up for possession work and I've noticed that someone who fancies a quiet morning gets teamed up with one of the grafters, and your pride is at stake then, so in a subtle way he makes sure that everyone works.'

Brooking is delighted, naturally, that Ron Greenwood has brought three other West Ham players, Alvin Martin, Paul Goddard and Alan Devonshire, into the England squad. Devonshire's selection pleases him particularly. 'He really deserved it and I think he might finish up as England's left-side flank player. He's got the ability to take the ball past defenders and get in a winger's cross and he can perform in midfield as well. In Ron's earliest days as England manager we played with two wingers and we had a very successful spell, so it was interesting that Tony Morley has been brought in along with Alan. Perhaps we're getting back to a more flexible system.

'I'm sure, too, that Glenn Hoddle will get more games to try and confirm his standing. The problem has been that we haven't had the kind of matches in which opportunity is there to try people out. The matches we have played have tended to be too important to take risks. So that's probably why I'm still here. Last summer I played four internationals in which younger ones were tried out. Maybe if those matches had gone well, they would have stayed in.'

From his own point of view the unfamiliarity of another player can be an inhibition. 'Understanding is the main thing – knowing how a player shapes up to a ball. When you don't know him you tend to give that little extra look to see what he's up to so you are in the odd situation of taking more time to do things instead of less, at the highest level.

'So the main thing is to get this game out of the way, celebrate, and then see what we come up with in the next few months. It's been very difficult for Ron; you can ask ten people in the street and nobody would come up with the same side. Even if we win on Wednesday, that won't change for a while. I can't think of anyone in the team who will be able to say, "Right, that's it, I'll keep the summer free." '

15 November 1981   *Julie Welch*

Ronald Atkin reported on a man who typifies the courage and strength of the traditional British centre-forward.

Gray – the Man Who Makes Defences Turn Pale

At the end of a game in which he had scored one of Everton's goals and manufactured the other two, got himself booked for a retaliatory swing and inflicted considerable physical and mental distress on Bayern Munich, Andy Gray was the only player on either side to seek out the trio of Swedish officials and offer each a hearty handshake.

The referee, Erik Fredriksson, and his linesmen may have been a mite bemused but such is the style of the man. Gray regards the opening whistle as a factory hooter, the signal to go to work on the opposition. Any aggro or unpleasantness is set aside as soon as the shift ends.

The comment of Bayern's coach, Udo Lattek, that Gray is more suited to rugby union was cheerfully dismissed by the 29-year-old Glaswegian as 'sour grapes'. Though Gray himself did not choose to make the point, it was also a highly inappropriate remark coming from the man who once trained Barcelona to a pitch of ferocity which could comfortably have seen off the likes of London Welsh.

Anyway, as the fifty thousand who jammed Goodison last Wednesday will bear witness, it was Bayern who started the kicking. 'We were quite surprised at their physical attitude,' said Gray. 'They made it known early doors that was the way it was going to be and just tried to break up the rhythm of the game by conceding free kicks. So it was a matter of looking after yourself and they cried a little bit when they were on the receiving end.'

Bayern are by no means the first team to be reduced to tears by Everton this season. The club have looked positively ironclad as they forge towards the holy grail of league championship, FA Cup and European Cup Winners Cup, and since they began that stupendous unbeaten run on Boxing Day no one has contributed more than Andy Gray.

The Manchester United manager, Ron Atkinson, recently paid tribute to Gray as 'the most dangerous centre-forward in the First Division, brave, aggressive and as effective as he ever was with Aston Villa'.

Atkinson further revealed he had seriously considered signing Gray in 1983 when his contract at Wolves came to an end 'but I was put off by his record of injuries'.

He may yet regret that decision when United and Everton contest the Cup Final on 18 May. In three Cup visits to Wembley Gray has still to troop off a loser and in two of them (Wolves v Forest, League Cup 1980, and Everton v Watford, FA Cup 1984) he scored crucial goals.

Neither of those goals was a Charlton rocket or the culmination of a Best dribble, rather the result of a willingness to get into areas where bruises are the most common thing on offer.

Gray admits readily, 'I am not the most gifted of players. I realised that very early. But there are other ways you can make up for lack of skill and my competitiveness is one of the ways I make up.'

He added: 'When someone puts a tag on you it tends to stick' and in Gray's case the description 'competitive' is usually uttered in the same breath as his name. Another label is 'injury-prone' and this one (the very same which ended Ron Atkinson's interest) Gray disputes.

'I have had three operations on my right knee, and that's basically it. Touch wood, I have never broken any bones. I have never even had a pulled muscle, just a few sprains and strains. I have played close to 400 games in England since I came down from Dundee United and that's not bad.'

Aston Villa were his first league club, but his successes there were not repeated when he moved across the Midlands to Wolverhampton for £1·5 million, and at the expiration of his contract Howard Kendall stepped in to sign the 'injury-prone, competitive' Gray.

Ironically, it was injury which cost Gray his place in the Everton team earlier this season. He was hurt at Newcastle in mid-September, missed eight games and then couldn't get back because Graeme Sharp and Adrian Heath formed such an effective partnership it produced 22 goals in 19 games while the fit-again Gray fidgeted on the subs' bench.

Having lost his place through injury Gray retained it because of the misfortune which removed Heath from Everton's line-up for the season at the beginning of December.

Wearing the number eight shirt, Gray was competitive as ever but went nine games without scoring. Then Sharp was hurt, Gray donned the number nine and scored twice against Leicester. 'So the boss told me to keep wearing number nine and it has worked well. I've kept on scoring and Sharpie has been among the goals in the number eight shirt.'

The partnership of the two Scots who room together and golf together (10 goals in 14 games for Gray, eight in 12 for Sharp) drew Jock Stein, the international manager, to Goodison on Wednesday. Gray is delighted to think he might add to his 19 caps 'but whether I will do is a different matter'.

He is quick to pay tribute to the reason for Stein's attendance. 'Without a shadow of a doubt this is the best team I have ever played in. We had a magnificent team at Villa in 1977, probably as good as Everton going forward. But Everton have a much better defence, the best back four and goalkeeper they have had for many, many years. I am just thankful I have had the opportunity to play in such a great side.

'It's also wonderful what success has done for the supporters. You see blue-and-white scarves by the thousand. The fans have come out of the cupboard and are walking around with heads held high. The past 15 years they have suffered a lot of ribbing from Liverpool's supporters. Now they can get their own back. It's nice to hear a few jokes about Liverpool for a change.'

Gray is looking forward to the demands of playing Manchester United at Wembley only four days after the Cup Winners' Cup in Rotterdam against Rapid Vienna, who have progressed to the final after being eliminated by Celtic in a rough house and then re-admitted on appeal.

'I don't go round smacking people when there is no reason for it but if there's going to be a confrontation in that final I am not one to shirk it,' he said. The referee can expect a handshake, too.

29 April 1985   *Ronald Atkin*

*In 1981 Hugh McIlvanney was captivated by a young player who was
to be the outstanding success of the 1986 World Championship Finals in
which he steered his Argentinian side to the trophy. For English fans it
was no doubt upsetting that on the way to final victory he swept aside a
worthy England team not just with one magical goal, but with another
unfairly punched into the net. There was further annoyance when he
spoke of the 'hand of God' doing the fouling. But on this day there was
a win at Wembley to savour as well as Maradona's skill.*

A Marvel Called Maradona

These are days when Ron Greenwood has no reason to feel like borrowing
one of Don Revie's surplus yashmaks. The England manager can afford to
be seen and to be seen to be smiling. His players are a winning lot in both
important senses of the word.

Tuesday night at Wembley was further proof that they are capable of
beating talented opposition with positive exciting football. The victory
over Argentina was memorable not as a justification for nationalist
preening but as a celebration of some of the pleasures the old, ill-used but
stubbornly beautiful game can still give.

Anyone who did not enjoy the skill, fluency and competitive surge of
that match should acknowledge that his taste in sport is, to say the least,
idiosyncratic. He should try watching ludo tournaments or, if his condition is really extreme, professional wrestling.

The supreme thrill of the evening was, as had been promised by the
advance publicity, the brilliance of Diego Maradona. At 19, he might have
been inhibited by the weight of the eulogies that preceded him but in his
case youth works in the opposite way: it persuades him that outrageous
virtuosity can be a commonplace in his work. That conviction informed
and illuminated Pele's play until the end of his career and it is to be hoped
that the same inspired optimism will stay with Maradona.

Comparisons with the greatest Brazilian are already distressingly rife.
Cesar Menotti the tall, thin, long-haired and appealingly lugubrious man
whose management did much to win the 1978 World Cup for Argentina
and will surely make them a major threat in 1982, succinctly exposed
the stupidity and unfairness of such blethering. Emphasising his composure by smoking only one cigarette at a time, Menotti said after
Tuesday's match: 'Maradona is a young player who is already among the
best in the world. But when talking of Pele we must first talk about 1,500

goals, three world championships, and 21 championships with his club. However, if anyone can fill the place of Pele in football perhaps it will be Maradona.' The statistics of the tribute to Pele, as filtered through a translator, did not sound altogether accurate but the basic point was unquestionable.

Equally unlikely to be challenged is the belief that, barring serious injury, Maradona will be one of the most exciting and influential figures of the World Cup in Spain. He has the control, acceleration, imagination and muscular persistence to destroy defences single-handed. His exceptionally powerful thighs (so powerful that for him excessive thickening around the hips may be the biggest threat to longevity in the game) gives the explosive strength to launch himself dramatically through the air, providing a range of movement astonishing in a short, stocky man, and help him to withstand the strain of sudden, wrenching changes of direction. He is the kind of ballplayer who gives the impression of having in Dave Sexton's phrase 'a crotch of cast iron'.

Defenders who mean to dispossess him could do with carrying guns. When he spun to make his most spectacular break towards goal, midway through the first half, four England men were rendered helpless by the swift, subtle manoeuvrings of his left foot. He favours that foot most of the time but as a well-balanced runner who can play off both feet. He is, all in all, something to behold but preferably from the sidelines, not from the standpoint of an opponent.

The thought of teaming Maradona in Spain with some of the vigorous survivors of the national side that succeeded two years ago, and with other impressive young men like Diaz, Simon and Barbas, will prevent Cesar Menotti from becoming too gloomy about the way ahead. If he took a nagging worry away from Wembley it would concern the panic spread through his defence by England's intelligent use of high balls across goal and the generally erratic form of Fillol, a goalkeeper who was as vital as Kempes in the winning of the World Cup.

The result itself should not depress Menotti unduly. In football, the championship of the world cannot be won or lost outside a self-contained competition played every four years. To beat Argentina on Tuesday evening and imagine you had usurped the status the country's footballers earned in 1978 would be as realistic as knocking out Sugar Ray Leonard's brother and claiming the world welterweight title. Ron Greenwood's mind does not accommodate such folly.

Greenwood will be happy to see what was achieved in midweek as a quality performance against quality opposition, as confirmation that the long-held principles he brought to his present job can be effectively implemented by the players currently at his disposal and as a profoundly encouraging omen for the European Championships in Italy next month.

18 May 1981   *Hugh McIlvanney*

One of the most enduring and endearing players of recent years has been West Ham's John Bond, who played the game with courage, versatility, and humour as Clement Freud acknowledged in this 1959 report.

Exoneration of John Bond

West Ham   4   Bolton Wanderers   3

The West Ham mud-pitch was looking particularly attractive, the sunshine showing up a seasonal undertone of green to welcome the first day of spring and prove once again that famous Bolton saying of 'Where there's muck there's grass.'

Injuries forced both sides to field three reserves, and West Ham further excelled in this end-of-season improvisation by switching John Bond from right-back to centre-forward.

In defence Bond positions himself impeccably, his deceptive turn of speed, tenacity and humour combining with great natural footballing ability.

It was fascinating to see him in attack; the smile remained on his face but he emerged as a debonair, elegant dandy with a touch here, a deflection there, yet an utter lack of that devotion to duty that so distinguished himself as a full-back.

In the second half he scored twice and a husky man behind me said: 'He's exonerated, that's what he is, exonerated.'

This seems unimportant. Bond is an infinitely better back than he is a forward, and the West Ham defence pathetically weak without him.

 But his presence at centre did give the home side an immensely individual forward line, with newcomer Obeney showing signs of great promise and scoring the first goal by bringing down a difficult ball and steering it past Hopkinson.

Both defences must have felt that their future lay in attack, and the game became a duel between attackers and goalkeepers. A quick look at the score will show you that the goalkeepers lost. Time and again a full-back's clearance would find a forward out on his own.

Stevens equalised for Bolton before Bond and Dick restored West Ham's lead; more mistakes in defence, and Bolton were back in the game with the Parry goal, only to let the Londoners restore a two-goal lead. This time Bond, 30 yards out with no one to pass to, took a kick at goal and surprised Hopkinson, us and – let's face it – himself by seeing the ball end up in the net.

Playing now as if they were six goals up, the West Ham defence gathered on the half-way line, and when Hill reduced their lead with a simple goal they were as unperturbed as when Lofthouse failed to equalise from a chance that should never have been his to miss.

22 March 1959   *Clement Freud*

In advance of Wimbledon's surprise win in the 1988 FA Cup Final Frank McGhee watched Vinny Jones enhance his reputation as a hard man – and as scorer of important goals.

Vin-triolic

Wimbledon 3   Tottenham Hotspur 0

The naïve may believe that the growing reputation as a hard man of one of Wimbledon's goalscorers, Vinny Jones, was further enhanced by the caution and the yellow card he received in the first half. In fact that reputation is a little less deserved than would at first appear.

Most of the authentically evil players in the game are, and always have been, swift, skilful, secret and silent. Jones is about as discreet as a scream in a cathedral.

Until yesterday he had made himself notorious for verbal threats directed at Kenny Dalglish ('I'll tear his ear off and spit in the hole'); and physical intimidation of Paul Gascoigne (he was pictured trying to steal the Newcastle man's jockstrap and its contents without first removing his victim's shorts).

Yesterday his targets were less obvious because Jones seldom managed to get near enough to any of the vastly more creative Spurs players to cause them any discomfort.

He made up for it in the 38th minute when referee Ward booked him for a blatantly illegal scything slash from behind at the legs of Clive Allen.

Since Jones had been the most vehement of the Wimbledon protestors two minutes earlier when an unnecessary foul by the same Allen saw full-back Goodyear stretchered off to hospital and out of the FA Cup semi-final with a suspected broken leg, the referee was perhaps entitled to wonder whether the vengeance was deliberate.

It was typical of Wimbledon that adversity brought the best out of them in the second half, when they were even more dominating than Tottenham had been earlier.

It was very much in keeping with the run of play when they went in front through Jones in the 62nd. He got behind the Spurs defence when a Thorn free-kick was flicked on by Cork and steered it effortlessly into the net and it was no surprise to see Wimbledon wrap up the game in the 81st minute when Fashanu got his head to a Gibson cross. Wise added a third in the last seconds.

Scorers: Wimbledon: Jones (62 min), Fashanu (81), Wise (89).

Wimbledon: Beasant; Goodyear (Sub: Scales, 36), Phelan, Jones, Young, Thorn, Gibson, Cork, Fashanu, Sanchez, Wise.

Tottenham Hotspur: Mimms; Statham, Thomas, Fenwick, Fairclough, Mabbutt, C. Allen, P. Allen, Ardiles (Sub: Hodge 69), Samway, Walsh.

Referee: A. W. Ward (London).

20 March 1988 *Frank McGhee*

As any centre-half or goalkeeper who faced him will tell you, Jimmy Greaves was the most lethal goalscorer in the British game. His first game with Spurs in 1961 was typical. The tag of being the first £100,000 player, the vast expectations, the problems of fitting into a new team were shrugged aside as he ran out to enjoy the game as usual and to pick up three goals as well. He expressed himself so well on the field that my own and Danny Blanchflower's view of him that day may be tribute enough to this truly great player.

Greaves Gives Value
For All That Money

Tottenham 5   Blackpool 2

'Well, here we go again,' said Greaves cheerfully as he disappeared towards the dressing-room. How right he was, and how the crowd enjoyed it as, with his sure sense of occasion, he took three goals in his stride. Forty minutes seemed to many spectators a long time to wait before Greaves hooked the ball high into the roof of the net, but then the hats, scarves and hands were waving wildly in the air.

Perhaps the strangest thing in the strange Greaves saga has been that as the most expensive English professional he has re-stated the amateur view that there is more to soccer than money.

From the start he played with the infectious enjoyment that so soon communicates itself. From the moment he ran through the encircling photographers, giving a hitch to shorts that always look baggy on his slight frame, he was completely at home in the Spurs side.

Blackpool have a strong, hard-tackling defence, but Crawford kindly gave Greaves plenty of room in midfield, scorning to mark him closely and venturing upfield as if determined to treat him as an ordinary player.

But, as has long been clear, Greaves is no ordinary player, and he was soon exercising his special flair of materialising in the right place at the right time. Three times a desperate foot foiled him as he was poised to run the ball home.

Then, at last, Mackay's long throw was headed on by Medwin, and Greaves leapt high to hook the ball left-footed over Waiters.

Before the excitement had died Blanchflower slipped a free kick to Mackay, and as his lob floated to the far post Greaves, slipping backwards, headed it into the narrow gap that Waiters had left with the sure touch of a Joe Davis pocketing the red.

Just to rub in what Chelsea have missed, on the stroke of half-time Allen took Blanchflower's pass to pivot daintily past Gratrix and drive the ball low into the net.

But Blackpool are no mean side, and they were not to be easily shaken off. They answered Spurs' sweeping moves with two equally graceful, equally effective. Horne slid the ball to Parry, whose pass inside the back left Charnley free to dribble round Brown and score.

Then Horne himself went racing free down the left and as he pulled the ball back across goal, Norman trying to intercept, turned it in.

But Mackay and Blanchflower hustled Tottenham back into attack before they could brood on these setbacks and so Greaves settled the issue, jumping high to head in Allen's swinging corner.

In spite of the crowded area Greaves and Allen kept wriggling through, their swift movement and clever control miraculously dividing the solid wall of defenders.

Waiters, his green jersey growing steadily blacker, kept them at bay till Allen sent Greaves through the centre and himself moved up to run the ball in as it bounced gently off a post.

It was a perfect end to a happy homecoming, the perfect answer to whether Greaves was worth all that fuss and money.

Spurs. – Brown; Baker, Henry; Blanchflower, Norman, Mackay; Medwin, White, Allen, Greaves, Jones.

Blackpool. – Waiters; Armfield, Martin; Crawford, Gratrix, Durie; Hill, Peterson, Charnley, Parry, Horne.

17 December 1961   *Tony Pawson*

Danny Blanchflower added his own comments after the match on playing with Greaves:

He really is a Spur

The newspapers and radio's Sport's Report were talking in terms of 60,000 at White Hart Lane for Jimmy Greaves' debut with Spurs, but I *knew* it wouldn't be that.

You wouldn't get that the Saturday before Christmas if Santa Claus himself were playing. There was bound to be more than usual because it was a thrilling affair, this marriage of Greaves and Tottenham.

I had expected some excitement and anticipation in the dressing-room but little was evident. Jimmy has been training with us for over a fortnight and he's like a piece of the furniture now.

I thought about him as I watched him across the dressing-room. . . . He is only a boy in his early twenties and already his experience of the game is vast and his ability to score goals renowned.

I wondered if he would score. It wouldn't have bothered me if he hadn't, because we usually beat Blackpool at home and I felt sure of that. The boy himself was calm. It didn't seem to bother him that thousands outside were expecting him to score goals.

From the start, everyone on the ground (except the Blackpool players) was looking for him to score. There was a gasp of anticipation when he got the ball, even in positions not usually thought of as dangerous. But in the early stages, when he was in likely positions to get through, it didn't work out for him and I began to think he might not score at all.

We were forcing the game, but our play was ragged and not convincing. I was struggling to find my true rhythm and my attentions gradually slipped away from Jimmy.

Suddenly he scored; and a couple of minutes later he got another. Through slackness in the second half, we lost two of our three goals advantage. Then there was Jimmy again heading in one from a corner kick almost under the Blackpool goalkeeper's jersey.

His ability to score goals is amazing. Even we who had expected it of him were startled.

'He's like a magnet near the goal,' John White said.

He will add further to a talented team at Tottenham and we will be more formidable than ever. It will take a little time for all of us to improve our understanding with him. What subtle alterations to the rhythm of the team and what small changes may affect our collective style remain to be seen.

But the possibilities ahead are exciting.

17 December 1961   *Danny Blanchflower*

CHAPTER 5

The Supporting Cast

There was a time, before the great Herbert Chapman bestrode the game, when all the limelight was on the players and the manager was a peripheral figure. Now it is the managers, particularly the fast-talking, quotable ones, who attract most of the publicity and get credited with supernatural powers or messianic attributes.

Whatever the general impression the manager has little effect during play itself with all that shouting and waving of arms serving a useful purpose only in the release of his own nervous tension. At the highest level the game is so quick it has to be a matter of instinct rather than intelligence, and only a manager's final sentence of instruction is likely to remain in the mind.

So perhaps there was wisdom in the very short briefing I received before my first First Division game with a Charlton side with whom I had never practised and among whom I had met only the three Kent cricketers in the team. Instead of the massive instruction I expected before taking the field against the League leaders at White Hart Lane the only comment was, 'Take a tot of whisky for your nerves and kick your corners to the far post.'

The first was very welcome; the second turned by accident into a tactical master-stroke. After twenty minutes we were two down and I was exhausted with fruitless running. Came a corner on a quagmire of a ground and with the leather football now saturated with mud and water. Trying too hard to loft that canonball to the far post I succeeded only in slicing it diagonally backwards along the ground. While I and twenty other players stared aghast Kiernan hit it into the net.

After victory in the final minutes our manager, Jimmy Seed, explained to the press that the game had turned on a cleverly planned and well executed dead-ball ploy. So I never do take those post-match managerial lectures too seriously. But the whole cast of managers, coaches, directors and referees have a significant contribution to make to the game. From many rich characters among the managers my first

*selection has to be one who made such an impact on our Pegasus team
as well as nearly taking West Bromwich Albion to the double:*

Buckingham of the Albion

Football management has a rich diversity of characters ranging from the
rugged and explosive Cullis, with his motto 'There is no substitute for hard
work', to the shrewd and placid Busby. But in so exacting and insecure a
profession, with its high turnover, managers tend to divide into the
forceful, the determined or the harassed. Outside the general pattern is Vic
Buckingham, manager of West Bromwich Albion's attractive team which
for months has been lying second to the Wolves at the top of the First
Division.

A gay and successful individualist, his enthusiasm for the game is at once
apparent in his lively comment and expressive gesture. Born in Kent and
educated at Bromley Grammar School, he had at first no soccer ambitions,
being more promising at cricket, but at 16 he was a good enough footballer
to play in the grammar schools match between London and Glasgow and
attract the notice of a Tottenham scout. Spurs at once offered to engage him
but it was two years before he could be convinced that soccer was a
worthwhile career.

In 1933, at the age of 18, he played his first game for the club with which
he was to stay for 18 years. He began as a left-half but soon moved to left-
back. The change was shrewdly judged for he might well have had
difficulty in keeping his place had he tried to compete for the half-back
position against Ron Burgess whom he early recognised as an outstanding
player.

The same forethought went into the development of a career interrupted
by the war. Despite playing in two war-time internationals he realised that
at 30 he was past his peak and with a limited future as a player. So he started
to spend his summers abroad coaching in Norway, Sweden and Germany.
By 1947 he was chief FA coach for Middlesex and by the following year
was more active for Tottenham as a coach than a player.

In 1950 he was loaned as temporary unpaid coach to Pegasus – giving
them such time as he could spare from his other duties and guiding them to
their first victory in the Amateur Cup. Despite the fee he could have
commanded it was typical that he should come for the enjoyment and the
experience.

Certainly it was useful experience, for his method is to discuss and persuade rather than assert, and a team of undergraduates, each with his own theory of the game, is not the easiest to convince. But if Buckingham said that wingers should come back, there might be argument but there was never any doubt that they would and that they would understand the reason. If things went wrong there were no tirades at half-time, just the puzzled query: 'Why aren't you doing so and so? You agreed it was the best method.' A most effective approach.

After Pegasus he went as manager to Bradford Park Avenue and then five years ago was appointed to West Bromwich Albion. In his first full season with the club they came as near to achieving the double as any team in recent years and they have continued to do well since. As a player he had relied more on intelligence than on physical skill and perhaps for this reason much of his coaching is devoted to making his players more perceptive and quicker, in thought and action.

Buckingham has a flexible approach to tactics. He starts from the assumption that any First Division player must have mastered the basic principles and skills of the game and can use his own initiative to improve on them. Most managers would say that it is an elementary mistake for backs to stand square since there should always be diagonal covering to prevent two men being beaten by one pass. Buckingham, however, will simply tell his backs to stand square when they want to but only if they are quick enough in anticipation and movement not to be caught.

Since he encourages intiative his team tactics are naturally based on fitting the style to the player rather than moulding the players to a pre-determined pattern. Just as he had seen Tottenham develop a style to suit Clay and Grimsdell and change it for a later era so has he always based Albion's style on the abilities of Allen and Barlow and other key players.

Buckingham's training methods are in line with his tactical thought. There are no preconceived plans and the schedule may be altered by the needs of the moment or the dictates of the weather. But always there is a full morning's training with many of the First Team doing two more afternoons as well and with the week's programme leading up to Saturday's match. Apart from the practice of the normal skills there is unusual emphasis on weight training to build up stamina and on gymnastics to improve balance and movement. With the aid of a physical training instructor, the Olympic weightlifter Bill Watson, Albion have devised a series of exercises which are achieving excellent results.

Another reason for his success is his clear knowledge of the limitations of his job. Where managers were once regarded as of little account the modern trend is to over-emphasise their influence. Buckingham is shrewd enough to know that a manager is only as good as his team and that his main function is to get the best out of them. His flair is for saying the right thing in the right way at the right time.

One of my own most vivid memories is the way he stilled nervous speculation before Pegasus' Amateur Cup Final with advice which seems to sum up the best approach to every important match. There were just four points he made:—

'Don't worry about what the other team are going to do, make them worry about what you are doing.

'Whether you are playing well or badly all of you must want the ball and look for it.

'Don't worry about who was meant to have marked whom but just remember that if you are the nearest player then you go for the opponent with the ball.

'And finally, win or lose, cup final or friendly, enjoy the game.'

It is his own enjoyment of the game that Buckingham imparts to his players and which makes him the most relaxed and entertaining of managers.

12 January 1958   *Tony Pawson*

In the fifties The Observer *ran a series on 'Our Masters of Sport'. This began with my look at the style and methods of England's leading coach and manager, Walter Winterbottom. His erudite comments on peripheral vision occasionally floated over the heads of Jimmy Greaves and Co., but his record was one of which several subsequent managers would have been proud. He also took over as manager of our Great Britain Olympic team in Helsinki in 1952. As the only selected right-winger in the party I was a little surprised to be left out by him in favour of someone who had never played in the forward line. However, I like to think he was just saving us amateurs from humiliation. If we had survived another round we might have come up against Puskas and that outstanding Hungarian side which went on to thrash the full England team at Wembley after winning those Olympics.*

England's Soccer Manager

As the Football Association's Director of Coaching and as Manager of the national team Walter Winterbottom has had the main responsibility for the development of English soccer over the past 11 years.

Tall and dark, with a slightly donnish air, he looks what he is – a mixture of teacher and athlete. Soccer and teaching indeed have been the twin threads of his life.

Born in Oldham, he went to the Grammar School there before going on to train as a teacher. After two years at Chester Training College he went for a final year to Carnegie Physical Training College, and was then promptly appointed to their staff. Already he was a soccer player of high class, and for several seasons before the war he was a member of Manchester United's team as centre-half or wing-half.

During the war he came to the Air Ministry as a Wing Commander in charge of physical training and while in London he was a guest player for a year with Chelsea. Abruptly his playing career was ended by an attack of spondylitis, an illness which damaged his spine. The Middlesex Hospital cured him so effectively that no trace is apparent in his bearing and it has not hindered his active coaching.

In 1946, at the age of 33, he was appointed the first Director of Coaching. There was little on which to build, and the present organisation is, therefore, a clear reflection of his own views and policy.

There were two main premises on which he based his coaching system. The first was that the vital teaching should be done in the schools, and the second that with our winter weather there were only limited periods suitable for outdoor coaching.

Instead of relying on a small body of expert coaches he concentrated from the first on having available a large number of part-timers who could be used for concerted action over a wide field. These 300 or more coaches are deployed through the County Associations who are best placed to know the needs of their area and who allocate them as necessary, subject only to a limit on the number of visits a coach may pay to a particular school or youth club.

Such visits excite interest and plant ideas, but solid results can come only from more continuous training. The natural corollary therefore was the training of a number of schoolmasters to become proficient coaches. This has been done successfully on a large scale. In Durham, for instance, where no outside help is accepted in the schools, over 30 teachers have the full coaching certificate and over 200 have taken the training course.

It is characteristic of Winterbottom that he should insist on exacting tests for these certificates since they set the standard for the whole scheme. The examination for the full certificate is in four parts, a practical coaching test, a test of football ability and two written papers, one on coaching theory and one on the laws of the game. . . .

The most interesting developments in which he has assisted have been in coaching method itself. At the time of his appointment coaching consisted mainly of the demonstration and routine practice of certain skills. The first improvement he introduced was pressure training – the sustained practice of one particular skill, such as volleying for goal, without respite or interval. This helped to make the execution instinctive as with practices for 'grooving' the stroke at cricket, and to show how a player reacted as he tired.

But the next step was the vital one – the attempt to teach a skill in the context of actual play. This is a difficulty which does not arise in cricket where the challenge is in the main an individual one between bowler and batsman. But in a true team game like soccer the exercise of a skill is always modified and conditioned by the movements not only of the opposition but of one's own players.

Like all good coaches Winterbottom has the conviction which inspires confidence and the enthusiasm which excites interest. In expounding a coaching or tactical problem he is a fluent and easy talker with a polished professional delivery, concentrating on being clear rather than concise.

He is, perhaps, best know to the public as England's team manager, and his personality fits him ideally for this work. Here his responsibility is as much for selection, tactics and welfare as for coaching, since the team can rarely get together for practice. Despite the recent improvement the opportunities for training are so limited that there is little chance to concentrate on more than ensuring pre-match fitness, developing under-standing of each others' play and making minor adjustments rather than radical alterations of style.

As regards selection, Winterbottom is responsible in conjunction with the chairman of the Selection Committee and one other member for choosing the team to submit to the full committee. This allows considera-tion of the proposed team as a whole instead of the old system of voting on individual positions. And since tactics must always be designed to suit the players chosen it has allowed for the development of a consistent policy. Clearly Winterbottom favours a balance of craft and thrust in the forward line and the inclusion of one attacking inside to act on occasion as a second centre-forward. The selection of Kevan is an example of this since he is a player who fits the plan rather than the best player in the position.

Winterbottom views a side's tactical plan like the opening gambit in a chess game. It sets the pattern of play, but the decisive factor will be the individual reaction to the unexpected opportunities and dangers as the play develops.

For this reason he has been a keen student of detailed play as well as broad principles. He has taken a lead in utilising a system of analysing games designed to reveal trends and to give a searching review of what each player does when he is not in possession.

For most spectators and critics the one important point is how a player uses the ball. But since he will be fortunate if he is in possession or challenging for a ball more than three or four minutes out of the 90 it is of equal importance how he helps to shape the game by his movements without the ball.

It is because of his attention to this kind of detail that Winterbottom is a sound and successful manager. In a game where fame tends to be transient he has long had an established reputation at home and abroad.

When his work began in 1946 it was hampered by the general complacency born of past success. After the shocks of defeat by America in the World Cup and of Hungary's overwhelming victories, excessive complacency turned, as so often, to excessive criticism. This has been answered by England's record over the past few seasons – 15 successive international matches without defeat.

For that Winterbottom deserves his share of credit as well as for the system which has helped to maintain a good general level of play in the country.

20 October 1957   *Tony Pawson*

Barry Norman took a look at a manager who was stronger on producing winning sides than quotable comment, and on another whose losing streak as manager never inhibited the confident flow of words. First, Arsenal's Bertie Mee.

Mee, the Man Who Has to Finish First

Bertie Mee was rather disappointed when his own football career came to a premature end. Not that it had been much of a career, really. He was an outside-left with Derby County before the war, in the days when teams marched boldly forward in the famous 2–3–5 formation and outside-lefts were nippy little blokes like Bertie Mee.

He'd had his dreams of glory, naturally, but these were all frustrated soon after the war when injury put him out of the game. 'It was a great disappointment, certainly,' he says now. 'But I hope I'm a realist as well as an optimist. The fact is, I was no good – not good enough anyway. I would have played league football at a low level but I'd never have made a First Division player and I like to be first in whatever I do.'

This, actually, is quite an assertive statement, coming from Bertie Mee. As a rule he delivers his remarks in a precise, formal manner as if handing down the tablets or, more likely, as if everything he says is likely to be taken down and used at some later date to embarrass him. Not a suspicious man perhaps, but certainly a cautious one.

Still, it could be that, as manager of Arsenal, he feels he *is* number one or, as he would put it, first and, if so, it's a tenable theory.

Since he became manager in 1966, somewhat to his own surprise (he had, after all, joined the club only in 1960 as a physiotherapist), Arsenal have won the Fairs Cup and done the double and been runners-up in both the League and F A Cups. Other managers may claim comparable records, but Mr Mee is possibly alone in feeling confident enough to proffer advice to Brian Clough.

'Every club suffers a let-down after winning the League,' he said. 'I faced this the season after we'd done the double. I bought Alan Ball at Christmas, but it was too late. The problems, really, were in the first three months.

'The thing is: when you're young and you've done it all, what do you do for an encore? If you're Jack Nicklaus or Lee Trevino you go on and do it again. It's easy enough, perhaps, for one man to capture that sort of drive, but how do you instil it into 11 men?'

It's on this subject that he has been advising Mr Clough. His own solution, he said, had been to drop people ruthlessly from his team and make them fight for their places. He has also bought new players, for example, the £200,000 Jeff Blockley.

Tentatively, I put forward the theory that it was only fairy gold anyway – that the same £250,000 or so went wearily from one club to another in exchange for one player or another; a great fat wad of greasy notes.

Mr Mee agreed that, broadly speaking, this was so, but nevertheless prices were absurd. He himself, of course, was not responsible for that situation, but . . . 'I can't afford to stand aside and watch. I have a wife and children to support.

'The game has reached a stage where success or failure is measured by the result of each match. If you lose it's a real crisis for three or four days, or until your next win. There's no comfort in failure at all. You have to win and keep on winning – the spectators demand it.'

The double team of 1970–71, of course, did exactly that, but it was still criticised for being dour, hard and unattractive. Did such criticism hurt? Mr Mee said it didn't and, clearly, neither wild horses nor even wild Charlie Georges would force him to say otherwise.

'These days,' he said, 'a manager has a number of priorities – 1, you don't lose; 2, you start to win; 3, you don't lose away. Now, 15 years ago, that was enough to win the League championship. Today it's not. Today you have to win everything at home and two out of three away.'

I said that, with this kind of pressure, it was a wonder that he still enjoyed his football, and he said that, on the whole, he didn't. 'I enjoy it when we're not playing or when there's ten minutes to go and we're leading 5–0. Otherwise I don't enjoy it at all. The pressures are tremendous and they're reflected in the high cost of players. It's a panic measure by some clubs to pay over the odds in an attempt to achieve success – like Malcolm Allison buying Rodney Marsh last season and Brian Clough paying a high price for David Nish.

'I suppose I could be accused of the same thing by buying Ball and now Blockley. But I bought Blockley as cover for Frank McLintock, who is 32, and because I don't want a situation such as Leeds have where they're desperately trying to find a centre-half because Jackie Charlton is waning.'

This pressure, though – was it greater at Arsenal than at any other club? On account of the traditions? Yes, he thought possibly it was. Arsenal, after all, was the number one club; always had been.

'I can't imagine any more attractive job in football than the one I have here,' he said. Even so, surely it was inhibiting to have that bust of Arsenal's first great manager, Herbert Chapman, glowering at him every time he walked into the stadium.

Mr Mee, caught off guard perhaps, permitted his eyebrows to rise fractionally in surprise. 'Herbert who?' he said. 'Bust? What bust? Where is it? I've never seen it.' For a moment I was fool enough to believe him but, of course, he was really making a joke. Mr Mee doesn't make many jokes and when he lets one slip he doesn't telegraph its coming.

'Naturally,' he said, 'I can't concern myself with what Herbert Chapman did. The past is dead; it's only tomorrow that counts, although I think I can say with due modesty that, bearing in mind what had happened over the previous 12 years or so, the success ratio since I took over has been quite high.'

Indeed it has, so was there anything left for him to achieve? 'Yes,' he said. 'I should like to win the Euroean Cup, something that no other manager has done.'

Well, hang on, I said. I mean, Matt Busby and Jock Stein. . . . Mr Mee regarded me across his desk with mild contempt. 'I meant, of course, something that no other *Arsenal* manager has done,' he said.

15 October 1972   *Barry Norman*

Then Barry Norman talked with Malcolm Allison.

It's All in Players' State of Mind

In the long run, said Malcolm Allison, the answer might well lie in psycho-analysis. He waited, with a defensive grin, for the laugh.

Psycho-analysis, I said, not laughing (and indeed it would take a bigger and braver man than I to laugh at Malcolm Allison), for his footballers? Exactly, he said. Brazil had psychiatrists attached to their football squad so why not Manchester City?

After all, there he was with potentially the finest bunch of players in the land, trained to a hair, almost indecently fit, erupting with skill and yet they were pretty damn nearly bottom of the league.

'It's not ability they've lost,' he said. 'It's confidence and what do you do about that? Ask advice? No. You get plenty of advice offered but you don't go seeking it. If any manager knew the answer he'd win everything every year.

'There's nothing physically wrong, you see. Players these days are stronger, run faster and jump higher than ever before. But we're not nearly so professional at sorting out the mental side of the game. We don't use psychiatrists. We should, though, and eventually we will. It'll come, I'm sure of that. As a matter of fact I've been thinking about it seriously for a couple of years.'

We eyed each other solemnly across his office. 'Yeah,' he said. 'You can imagine the gags, can't you? "Here, look what old Mal's got there – right bunch of nut cases."

'It's a matter of convincing the players that a psychiatrist could find out why they're playing badly, why they're not happy in their work. And they

189

aren't happy at the moment: they're bloody miserable. They don't like losing any more than I do.'

Meanwhile, and until the climate is right for the club psychiatrist to be appointed, failure brings other problems in its wake. New rumours spring up every day – Lee's going, Doyle's going. The football gossip columns hint at a berserk and panic-stricken Allison booting his entire squad out of Maine Road. Untrue, he said, all of it.

'I'm a person who makes quick decisions and one of those decisions was that I wouldn't sell any player until I could replace him with a better one and where do I find better players than the mob I've got? God, it's an unbelievable game, football.

'I can tell the exact minute when they're going to start playing badly. They play the first half, they're putting it together, playing great – and then the whistle goes and in the dressing-room everything's gone. It all falls apart – and there's not a thing you can do about it.

'I can talk to them, sure. I do. I talk to them individually, I talk to them in groups. I tell 'em I believe in them – but until they start believing in themselves again they're not going to get the results.'

Wasn't it possible, though, to trace failure back to its source; to pinpoint the moment when things started going wrong? He looked at me with justifiable scorn. Blimey, hadn't he tried that?

Well, then, how about Rodney Marsh? City were top of the league when he joined them; two weeks ago they were practically bottom. Was he perhaps the wrong kind of player for this team?

'No,' said Allison, 'that's nonsense. You can't blame anything on Rodney Marsh. It may be that because he came here with a reputation as an artist, a brilliant ball player, the others felt they ought to show the crowds that they can play a bit, too. That might have upset the rhythm a little but it's hardly Marsh's fault, is it?

'I bought him because he's got more skill than anybody else in English football, he can score goals and he's just got that thing. He affects people – like Bestie, Cassius Clay or Tom Jones. I don't know what it is but he's got it. Besides, I like his originality. He's got the sort of footballing brain that can spot the other team's pattern of play and know just where and how to break it up.'

He prowled about the office in his track suit, a naturally worried but still philosophical man. The situation was serious but not desperate, or desperate but not serious depending on the level of his optimism.

He said: 'Just before the season started I went and looked at the stadium. It was great. The pitch looked great, the stands looked great. The players were confident, the spirit was good. I thought, "Christ, what a season we're going to have."

'I was proud. I looked at all these things and I thought, "It's there. It's all there."' A long, rueful pause, 'And it *is* all there.

'Losing a few games doesn't change anything really. It just puts you in your place, makes you realise you're not infallible. You see, my players were over-confident. That's what started the whole thing.

'Even when they were getting beat, they were still over-confident, up to a certain time. I remember Arsenal had the same trouble the year after they'd done the double. We went down to Highbury and won and Bertie Mee said to me, "What do I do, Mal?" and I said, "I don't know, Bertie. You just work." That's all we can do here – just work. I always reckon I'm luckier when I work harder.

'But we've had bad patches before – just after we got promoted, then when I got suspended and the team didn't win in 12 matches and again after we won the championship. Anyway, this season's only a quarter of the way through.

'Not that anybody likes the present situation. The players say they can't go into a pub, can't talk to the next-door neighbour. They're ashamed to go into town and it's no consolation that Manchester United are doing just as badly.

'There's no comfort in that. I mean, I can't go and swop worries with Frank O'Farrell. I can't talk to any managers. All they could advise me on is tactical things and I'm not bothered about them. It's the players' state of mind that causes all the trouble and maybe I haven't worked hard enough on that.

'And yet, in a way, I quite like this situation. I get a certain pleasure out of being down and knowing that I've got to get this right and that right.

'That's what I'm here for. It's what my job's all about.' A helluva job, I said. 'Yeah,' he said. 'Sometimes you think, "I don't need all these pressures; I'd like it a bit easier," and then you think you'd like to go and work at a smaller club, maybe abroad, and have a quieter life.'

He stared wistfully out at the car park and then he said: 'Ah, but what the hell! If you've made a bit of a name for yourself they'd expect things of you wherever you went. There'd still be pressure. So, finally, I reckon I'm better off where I am.'

29 October 1972   *Barry Norman*

Once Jimmy Greaves was bought for £100,000 extraordinary sums soon began to be paid for very ordinary players. In October 1972 Barry

Norman quizzed Bert Head of Crystal Palace on his outlay of over quarter of a million pounds.

Waiting for a Pay-off at Bert's Palace

Crystal Palace   0   Norwich City   2

If Bert Head were playing Monopoly, someone remarked with more wit than charity, he'd buy the Old Kent Road instead of Mayfair. Not true at all. He started the week by trying to buy Mayfair (assuming Ted MacDougall at £220,000 can be so described), but Frank O'Farrell landed there first.

Mr Head may have finished up with a package deal of three lesser properties at £280,000 the lot, but it would still be unkind to liken them to the Old Kent Road, begging Millwall's pardon, of course.

As it happened, only one of the new Palace acquisitions, Iain Phillip (£110,000 from Dundee) was on display, since Paddy Mulligan (£75,000 from Chelsea) was poorly with a sore throat and Charlie Cooke (£85,000 from Chelsea) was ineligible. Thus Mr. Head was in the frustrating position of a gambler limited to putting only a third of his stake on the table. 'Don't equate today's result with the £280,000,' he said afterwards. 'It's not fair.'

Palace had been played on to the pitch with much canned music – though not, oddly enough, 'Hey, Big Spender' – and the record of having failed to score in their last six matches.

This distinguished run they stretched to seven without any trouble at all. A flick over the bar early on by Craven, an optimistic thump by Hughes, an even more optimistic scissors kick by Craven again and two or three uninhibited long-range drives by Hinshelwood were about the best they could muster.

Yes, said Mr Head later, you could say Palace were still in the market for another player. A striker? 'Call him what you like,' said Mr Head. 'Some bugger who puts the goals in, anyway.'

Norwich, actually, were quite well equipped with buggers like that. Bone scored the first after 12 minutes, a corner and a scene of total chaos in the Palace penalty area. Fifteen minutes later Paddon got the second, amid similar panic, with a header.

Meanwhile, Phillip – neat but not gaudy – was dividing his attentions between Bone and Cross and doing quite well. His colleagues treated him with polite reserve, as though they hadn't been formally introduced yet, and rarely gave him the ball. He shouldn't feel too slighted by that, however, since they rarely gave it to one another either. 'Phillip?' said Mr Head. 'He'll be all right once he's settled down and sharpened up. The lads were a bit disjointed today. They'd lost confidence, don't believe in themselves any more.'

On the whole, though, he was encouraged by the thought of the players he'd signed. 'Not a bad week's work,' he said. 'Of course, I'm still a bit sore about MacDougall, but he's gone so there's no point in talking about him, is there?'

True. But it was a lot of money he'd spent nevertheless. Didn't it worry him, gambling all that on three players? 'It's the way prices go, isn't it?' he said. 'Of course they're ridiculous – a £100,000 transfer is nothing these days. It's like bananas – they used to be two-a-penny, but they're not any more. No, I'm not worried, though. You back your fancy, that's all. It's the occupational hazard of being a manager. The day I lose any sleep through worry is the day I pack it in.'

On the field Norwich had skated the first half and eased up a little in the second when, to do them credit, Palace did look somewhat more business-like. Even so, just before the end the slow handclapping started, somebody waved a banner saying 'Head Must Go' and Bone came off, being in the elegant phrase of his manager, 'knackered'.

So once again Palace are in their familiar position near the bottom of the league. 'Well,' said Mr Head, 'we're in the process of building traditions here. I didn't buy these players on a short-term basis, just to get us out of trouble. If you're spending that much money you have to think long-term. You have to think of getting into Europe, otherwise it takes years to get the money back.'

In any case, he said, though he's invested £750,000 in players in the last four years he has got most of it back by selling others. 'Anyway, look at it this way: if I spend half a million pounds this season which I might, it'll seem an awful lot. But I may not spend any more for another five years. You have to judge it, not week by week, but over a length of time.'

He was not, then, feeling in any way desperate? 'We're never desperate here, mate,' he said. 'We're never desperate here.'

1 October 1972   *Barry Norman*

———————————————

*To an outsider gifted only with commonsense rather than the arcane
wisdom of managers it was the expensive purchase of the unpredictable*

Rodney Marsh which transformed Manchester City from a team on course for winning the League to one struggling to stay in the First Division. Jimmy Hill once pointed to a managerial failing of compounding error by keeping in the side a high-priced import who does not fit in, but whose fee has to be justified. Allison, in fact, had made himself victim of that transfer madness of which Arthur Hopcraft wrote.

Why They've Gone
Football Crazy

It was a valuable coincidence of the preposterous that Mr Ken Grimes should receive a piece of paper enriching him by half a million pounds last week at roughly the moment when Rodney Marsh was saying he was 'worth' the £200,000 Manchester City have paid Queen's Park Rangers for him. Perhaps the best way of seeing the exchange of a large sum of money properly in perspective is to compare it with another.

Where money is concerned there comes a point when figures can have only their own, private, sense or nonsense; like the dawn chorus or the applause during 'Come Dancing'. What does Flash Rod mean by 'worth'?

For one thing, he means that Manchester City, in the insistent will of Malcolm Allison, have decided that it exists. For another, that Rangers know when a player's selling price has reached its peak and must decline inevitably (and imminently in Marsh's case, since he is already 27). For a third, players must know it, too.

Marsh will get £10,000 for his signature, and it seems unlikely that he will earn more than this sum a year in Manchester. Such an income invites complaints of excess and absurdity from some quarters, as do six-figure transfer fees.

But Mr Grimes' massive good fortune on the football pools surely answers the objections, if only with a sort of overkill of the ridiculous. Why attempt to justify the costliness of good players when there is such wealth in parasitical business of guessing results; at any rate, in moral terms?

Of course, in economic ones the trafficking in footballers has reached bizarre proportions which are about as defensible as Muhammad Ali's reputation as a poet. And *of course*, the level of transfer fees has alarming implications for the survival of half the clubs in the English League. Also, *of course*, there is little evidence in the attendances at half the League's weekly matches that the country much cares about that.

The transfer market, in which more than £5 million have changed hands this season, reflects with a suitably dazing image the anxiety and the joylessness of so much of professional football.

The game has always been instructive as a comment on some wider social attitudes; certainly more so than any other sport and probably more than any other public entertainment, including television (so diffuse), because it focuses so pertinently on direct, personal competition.

Football poses questions: like, is winning important? Or, what *kind* of winner is admirable? Or, when are rewards enough?

In this context the transfer market has developed into a sort of state-of-the-game index. All kinds of pressures act on it, and not all of them spring from factors which are directly connected with a club's problems in the League table. The personalities of managers, often complex, seem sometimes to interact all of a sudden to create a collective disenchantment with their own players and a frantic acquisitiveness for one another's.

Any manager can talk with smug vindictiveness about the worst buys made by others. One has heard some managers, having just bought expensively, uttering in stricken disbelief at their own stupidity.

It seems not to be a matter of a manager making an error of judgment, but more of having suffered some kind of aberration: like a bank manager who breaks out on a wild, weekend bender, or a housewife suddenly ordering a shop window full of furniture.

The word 'tension' has been overworked in discussion of modern football, but there is no denying that the condition is vitally significant in the game. Managers suffer from it day to day, as can be seen in their faces and heard in their voices, as commonly as their players get bruises.

A look at the list of transfer deals of the last eight months suggests not much objective logic in the trading, but much more impulse, hope, whim, desperation, on the part of the buyers. Who is surprised? Football lives in an agitated society.

12 March 1972   *Arthur Hopcraft*

There are crazy transfers, but also transfers which can help make a great side or a great player. Cliff Jones' transfer in 1957 launched him on a fine career, and he was an essential piece in the jigsaw of putting together that outstanding Spurs side. John Morgan reported at the time.

Sale

In Swansea's maritime and only flat suburb, the sea running at one end of the street, the world's oldest passenger railway at the other, Cliff Jones, Swansea Town's international outside-left, is wearing the price on his head in the manner born. The managers of seven First Division clubs are in pursuit of him, making bids, talking turkey. Do Swansea want £35,000 down? Or £10,000 and three sturdy backs or half-backs to keep them out of the Third Division?

'It's a little bit unsettling,' says Jones. 'It puts you off your game knowing all those people are in the stand weighing you up. I'll be glad when it's all over.'

Stephen, his 18-month-old son, kicks a miniature football powerfully with either foot and cries 'goal'. There are 200 oranges in the house, a present from the Israel team against whom the Welsh outside-left had scored a goal on Wednesday. The gramophone record being played is by Frank Sinatra, for whom all present have a great affection. 'Look Down, Look Down That Lonesome Road Before You Travel On', sang Sinatra.

Cliff Jones, who was 23 this week, has been playing League football for six seasons. At the moment he is doing his National Service in the Royal Horse Artillery but is a qualified ship's plumber. He is a frail, small man, slightly bow-legged and with fair hair and a sensitive cast of feature. His cheekbones are high, his nose aquiline. His accent naturally enough is pure Swansea.

Although extremely amiable, he is not talkative – at least not about football except that as long as he can remember he always wanted to be a footballer, indeed always has been one. About films and pop singers he is far more articulate. On the field of play he has never been known to foul anyone. That morning he had been chasing a mouse around the back of the house but did not kill it. 'It was so small.'

There are good judges of the game who think that once Jones moves away from Swansea Town into a kind of football which offers more space and less desperate concentration on him he may well develop into a player as good as Stanley Matthews.

9 February 1958   *W. John Morgan*

Jones was the most expensive of five top-class players Spurs had soon acquired and gradually the new design began to work with an effectiveness which even surprised the manager as Bob Ferrier reported:

The Spurs Enigma

'At West Ham the other night, Maurice Norman upended a chap on the penalty line. The referee decided it was just outside the box, I couldn't have complained if he had said "penalty". He didn't. We smothered the West Ham free-kick, broke fast, and before you knew it had the ball in their net. So instead of being 1–1, the game went to 2–0 for Spurs. Now how d'ye explain that?'

Tottenham Hotspur finished 18th in the First Division last April after stammering and bumbling their way through a miserable season. Now they are top of the heap and Bill Nicholson, a dour, intensive Yorkshireman who keeps a tight cork on his temperament, was seeking and not finding the solution to this sweet mystery of football.

Nicholson is a manager of the Winterbottom school, a rationalist who puts his faith in the percentages, who likes to analyse facts and figures and his own library of experience; a man who has an implicit belief in the therapeutic value of hard work for despondent footballers.

He said: 'The coming of Brown, Mackay and Marchi has made a great change. Given more character to the club. Marchi has always been very popular here. I've told him that he is too good a player *not* to be in the team, but that it is necessary for the good of the club at the moment. He has played three matches for me, in three different positions, and each time given me a fine game.

'Of course, we have been lucky. We caught Newcastle United and Manchester United when they played badly, and got five goals against each of them. On the other hand, we scored one goal at Old Trafford and we must have made 20 passes non-stop from our penalty area until we hit the scoring shot. The crowd was cheering before we got into their half of the field.

'And Mackay has tremendous enthusiasm for the game, a driver, forces the others to play harder. I see a lot of my own play in his game – except that he has more skill than I ever had.'

This Tottenham rally may well have had its origin in Russia where, in a summer tour, the team played well and won two of three matches.

Nicholson believes this carried over into pre-season training, in which the players 'seemed happier and showed more concentration'. What is not resolved is whether victory brings happiness or happiness brings victory.

Mackay's success has won him most of the current Spurs' publicity, and that in turn may have made Blanchflower's game crisper, for Danny relishes his place in the sun. And the old saw that 'when wing-halves play well the team plays well' probably still holds true.

Like so many other players, Mackay is a boy deeply in love with his football without being highly expressive about it. He says, 'The longer you go on without losing, the more confidence you get. The more confidence you get, the better you play.'

Blanchflower, Irish and impish and arch, has a word for most things most of the time. On television during the week, when asked if he knew where Spurs would finish this season, he replied, 'Of course – at White Hart Lane.' But even he can talk only of luck, and confidence.

Danny Blanchflower, indeed, represents the paradox within the mystery. The Spurs of 1959 are distinctly different from the great Spurs of 1950. Then, the team was rigidly classical, with one firm philosophical thread running through it, from Ditchburn and Ramsey at the beginning to Baily and Medley at the end. Now, classical has given way to romantic. If the point is not laboured, there was more skill in the old, there may be more talent in the new.

And Blanchflower, Harmer and to some extent Cliff Jones are the romantics, the emotionalists, the instinctive players in a team on which Nicholson seeks to impose a 'common denominator'. This will be a team in which such men will sacrifice their instincts and do the simple, obvious thing more often, and in which the others will do the simple obvious thing as well as they know how.

The present Spurs are a free-running Spurs for whom Blanchflower and Harmer perforce have to regulate the pace and decide on the direction. Harmer, by instinct and habit, wants to hold the ball, to finesse, to jockey until he gets the defensive dispositions exactly as he wants them. Only then will he rip off his passes. His only qualification for this is pure, abstract skill with the ball. Spurned by England, abandoned and reinstated by Spurs a dozen times, he wears now a puzzled, resigned, long-suffering look which makes his high skill and accuracy more poignant.

Cliff Jones, from what must have been an aimless prep school at Swansea, is plunged right into a harsh undergraduate life at White Hart Lane. He streams past almost any full-back with crackling speed and facility. And he is so often so astonished that he promptly falls over the ball, or forgets to finish the movement.

All these players have made compromises with their instinctive games, yet form remains the enigma which Tottenham, no less than any other club, cannot unravel. Why should the same men play badly one season, well the next, badly one week, superbly the next. It may have something to do with the digestive tract, but this intangible form, is what makes football magical and mysterious.

And as they find their way through this forest, Spurs, in a First Division which is rather less than distinguished, may find themselves first out of the trees next April.

20 September 1959   *Bob Ferrier*

Matt Busby has inspired deep respect whether as man or manager. This 1958 sporting profile was a tribute to him as he recovered from the crash:

'The Boss' of United

Everyone loves a fairy story, but fairy stories have no place in modern life. Yet the story of Manchester United since the tragic air crash in Munich on 6 February so resembled one that sentiment at first spilled over.

But there has been a reaction in the last few weeks, perhaps because we are embarrassed as sentiment turns to sentimentality and perhaps because we feel that by reacting against United we are compensating for our previous enthusiasm.

The facts are simple. Within three months of the air crash that killed eight of their first team and three of their officials, United are playing in the Cup Final at Wembley next Saturday.

Some people say that they have had extraordinary luck, but luck comes only to those who are capable of using it. Others say that their opponents have been at a disadvantage faced with such a weight of public feeling for United to win; but this was true only of the first two or three games at Old Trafford when the roar made that at Hampden Park sound like the applause for a Sunday afternoon string quartet. Footballers who have played against United say that United's only advantage was their own spirit.

199

To whom should the credit go? Many things make up a successful organisation, but in the last analysis it is the man at the top who creates the atmosphere for everyone else to work in. And at United it is Matt Busby who has created the atmosphere. However talented the players, however able the administrators, coaches and trainers, it is finally apparent that Matt Busby is, as the players call him, 'The Boss'.

 He has four qualities which have made him an outstanding manager: patience; ability to choose able deputies (and not to be afraid that their ability will outshine his own); quiet industrious efficiency; and an air of being indestructible.

When Busby was lying unconscious in Munich someone who knew him said: 'It is inconceivable that he should die – he is not the dying sort.' He had a hard upbringing. He was born in 1910 in a mining village in Lanarkshire, the eldest of four children. His father was killed in the 1914–18 war so that his mother had to take a job at the pit top to provide for her family. Later she decided to emigrate to America, but during the six-month delay for visas, Busby signed professional forms for Manchester City, in February, 1928.

At this time he was an inside-forward; but he was a failure in the position for two seasons, so much so that he dreaded going back to Manchester for the start of a new season. In the autumn of 1930 he couldn't find a place in either the first or reserve teams and made only intermittent appearances for the Central League team.

The turning-point in his career came when an amateur player who was having a trial failed to appear for a third team mid-week game. Twenty minutes before the kick-off Busby was told he was playing – at right-half. Within ten days he was in the first team and he never lost his position in the half-back line.

With this background it is not surprising that if you ask anyone at the club about him he is likely to speak first of his human qualities: his readiness with a helping hand in a player's domestic problem; the unexpectedly gentle word after you have played your worst game; the sense of general partnership in an enterprise given to the ground staff or the newest of 'the lads'.

So long as a player puts pride in United in first place, Busby's friendship and his efforts with someone who has struck a bad spell are unsparing. If there is talent there, he will persist just as Manchester City once persisted with him. His apparently boundless patience in this respect has paid every time. Critics have been confounded and there have been brilliant players like Whelan, Jackie Blanchflower, Viollet, and Charlton, all helped through lengthy bad spells, to show as reward.

The players know the United code backwards. It is a simple one. 'Keep playing football and the goals will come.' Busby never tires of repeating it – even or especially during a tough game when things are looking desperate. In some ways – in appearance for instance – he is like the headmaster whose only precept is that good breeding can meet any situation on the field.

How easily does he carry the responsibilities of a world-famous team? The compact figure, with a boxer's balance about the stance, the steady eyes, the pipe-smoking – all suggest the relaxed man. With the normal tensions of the crowded United season it would be uncanny if the appearances were all true. During a match the pipe is put away, cigarettes are chain smoked and the trilby hat comes a little farther forward over the eyes at each alarm.

In public, after a defeat, Busby is immaculately good-mannered with the stiffest of upper lips. In private, though, he is said to have wept at big disappointments and United's last failure at Wembley was one of the biggest.

Considering that he is the highest paid manager in English football – with a salary of upwards of £3,000 a year – his family life, which he greatly prizes, is on the quiet and modest side. His wife, Jean, a Scotswoman, his daughter, Sheena (married to Don Gibson, a Sheffield Wednesday player), and his young son, Sandy (a player with Blackburn Rovers), are all keen United fans, but they 'try not to talk about it all the time'.

Off duty – if one can say that he ever is – Matt Busby shows a pressing need for relaxation as though to dissolve some understandable inner restlessness. He likes to keep on the move, to get out and about – to the pictures, 'no matter what's on', a light theatre show, an evening with friends.

He enjoys a day at the races (where characteristically he bets on the darker horses), an unworried game of golf (handicap 'about 12'), watching boxing or Lancashire cricket. He admires style in every sporting field.

But these are distractions compared with the life's task of urging United on to more heroic efforts. And the players know it: a desire to please 'the boss' and to speed his recovery will inspire them as much as anything at Wembley on Saturday.

27 April 1958

John Arlott wrote of Alf Ramsey as he was in the process of taking Ipswich straight from Third Division to First Division Championship.

Rescuer of Wasted Talent

The only flaw in the general delight at the success of Ipswich Town – and its manager, Alf Ramsey – is that it has proved everyone outside Ipswich, and some inside it, so *very* wrong.

As a player (right-back for Southampton, Tottenham Hotspur and England), Alf Ramsey was a delight to the critics. They could dilate on his poise, tactical sense and ability to create attack out of defence. Then, they were right about him. As a manager, he has routed them all.

When he took over Ipswich in the Third Division in 1955–56, he was told, with helpful intent, that he would have to build a fresh side or stay down. He made hardly a change of playing strength, but went out on to the practice pitch with his men, changed their football and steered them to an unlucky third place in his first season, to promotion in the next.

Then, in the kindliest possible way, he was advised that he must buy extensively – indeed, expensively – even to stay up (the club's previous elevation in 1952 had lasted only one season). But, gathering strength unobtrusively, on shoestring fees or none at all, Ipswich won promotion to Division One last season.

Now, it was said, there could be no flukes, even Alf Ramsey would *have* to buy; the side simply was not strong enough to stay in the First Division. He did not buy (the average Ipswich gate of 1960–61 was little over 15,000: bare running money). In any case, 'These chaps I've got are great triers, learning and improving all the time.' This morning they stand among the leaders of the First Division.

His side has an average age of 29. But then the theory of youth in football has never worried Alf Ramsey. He was already a mature-looking solid-teddy-bear-shaped man when, as a private in the DCLI, he first played as a 'guest' for Southampton in war-time football. He was almost 30 before he first played for England.

Rarely among managers, he remains – overtly at least – as he was on the field, cool to the point of blandness. He can watch his side lose without a shout, an anguished gesture or even the slightest nibble at his nails.

Football satisfies a hunger in him, so that he seems to prefer solving its problems the hard way. During Ipswich's first two seasons in the Second Division, their deficiency in finishing-power was pointed out to him scores of times each scoreless week. He replied that he was waiting for Phillips to return to full fitness. He waited two seasons – but last season Phillips' goal-scoring was a major factor in winning promotion.

Only two of the present Ipswich first team players were there when Ramsey took over five years ago. Phillips was one. The other was

Elsworthy – then a strong but slow inside-forward – whom Ramsey turned into one of the most consistent wing-half-backs in the country. For the rest, he relied upon his ability to detect talent that other managers had examined, but missed.

His second goal-scorer, Crawford, was little esteemed by Portsmouth, even when they were struggling against relegation and Ramsey took him for a quarter the fee Crawford would command now. Stephenson – with Burnley and Leicester City – and Leadbetter, with Chelsea and Brighton, never made good their glimpses of promise as inside forwards but Ramsey made them, in their different ways, two highly effective wingers.

In defence, Bailey and Carberry were two early and economical 'buys' while Compton, fitfully brilliant as a Chelsea half-back, was taught to direct his prodigal energy by a manager who was a master in the position. Baxter was a centre-half until Ramsey 'released' him to employ his mobility at wing-half. Above all, Nelson, lacking in constructive ability as a West Ham wing-half, was guided to become the model defensive centre-half. As one local wit put it, 'If Alf Ramsey put a number 9 shirt on the groundsman, he would probably do the hat-trick.'

Ramsey has always had a rare ability to live his own life exactly as he wished, without seeming to be aloof. As one of his old team-mates put it, 'Alf was always a solid chap; on the field he was in with you; but off the field he always reserved the right to come in and go out when he wanted.'

He was always a dedicated player: he never smoked – still does not: he would take a beer for companionship's sake but showed no undue enthusiasm for it. He has an interest in horse-racing and dog-racing, but has never committed himself beyond interest. In clubs where golf was part of training routine, he played amiably enough, and played well but was never enthusiastic enough to play alone.

Talent wastage in first-class football usually arises from a manager demanding that his players play to his ideal – even though it is foreign to their style and outside their powers. One day, perhaps, the sense and simplicity of Ramsey's philosophy will be recognised by all managers. Then Mr Ramsey will have to think of a fresh idea. He is quite capable of it.

5 November 1961   *John Arlott*

Peter Corrigan enjoyed the success of an England team under Joe Mercer as kindly caretaker manager. Joe prepared the way for the equally sensitive and sensible Ron Greenwood's appointment.

Uncle Joe's
Champagne Tour

We in this particular representative group of English football abroad this week have so far managed to keep our riot to ourselves but any more England performances like that in Leipzig on Wednesday could cause all Heaven to be let loose among those who perpetrated or supported the dismissal of Sir Alf Ramsey.

The Football Association should not be begrudged their pleasure (although they are still one or two decisive steps away from vindication) that the exciting adventure shown against Argentina should have been followed by the spirited and skilled rattling of East Germany's pre-World Cup composure.

But the removal of Ramsey's ball-and-chain atmosphere on England's tours might well have sent some straight up to the clouds. With a team like Yugoslavia awaiting on Wednesday euphoria is a travelling companion to be suspected.

Sir Andrew Stephen, president of the FA, was anxious to explain the reasons for the riddance of Ramsey on the first day out and grasped at the promising display on Wednesday as a practical demonstration. 'Our action was intended to bring hope of a new future. No matter how far we have to go the Leipzig performance gives us more hope than any since 1966.'

To that hope the FA now want to fasten a pattern of planning to develop the English football style at all levels under the new manager's direction. Such an earnest dream deserves not to be summarily dismissed, but neither does it merit acceptance without any sign of realistic application.

The new manager will need to adopt much of Ramsey's intense concentration on the senior team and its disciplined behaviour on and off the field, otherwise we shall return to that state of erratic performance in which odd moments of magical play are a hope only of a future of odd moments of magical play. Success in international football demands a much more secure base than that.

It was significant that in the criticism of Ramsey permitted by the extrovert performance in Leipzig none came from the players. Perhaps they sense that what we are experiencing is no more than a pleasant interlude between dynasties. If so they are reacting well to it and Wednesday's performance has helped to make this an enjoyable trip, with the only discord coming when England arrived here to find that their hotel had been condemned as unsafe and they had been packed, two or three to a room, into the hotel allocated to the Press.

Not until the party arrived in the centre of Sofia was it discovered that

Stainless memories of a maestro. Finney finds time to reflect at his beloved Deepdale.

Peter Shilton, the perfectionist, exhorts his defenders to reach his own high standards.

Handing it out. There were boos for the £1,000 a minute man but Maradona still had his moments as the Football League XI beat the Rest of the World team (1987).

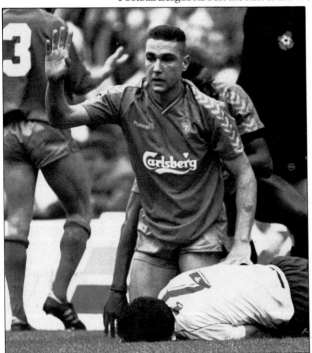

Hard man Vinney Jones puts up a hand in contrition after a tackle (1988).

Julie Welch sits behind Steve Coppell to get a dug-out view of his Crystal Palace team losing to Wimbledon (1984).

The old fox and his cubs. Jack Charlton fires up his young hopefuls Kelly (left) and Sheridan.

The enthusiasm of soccer! A happy young fan exults in Forest's success.

the Press had been thrown out to make room for them. There followed angry confrontation, the summoning of a British Embassy official, three bottles each of Polish beer on the house, a night in an inferior hotel, the early departure of a party of American tourists and now we are one big happy family again.

With Joe Mercer around it would be difficult for the atmosphere to be anything but chummy and he, more than anyone, deserved to see England beat East Germany. I would not recomment that his relaxed approach to training and off-field discipline should become a permanent feature of the English abroad but he has rightly judged this to be correct for this particular period.

Someone bought him champagne on Wednesday night and the cork popped with such force it hit the ceiling and rebounded into the company. 'Christ, we've hit the post again,' he said, and once more engaged a tirade against those large, square slabs of East German wood which England struck five times in that encouraging display of attacking.

Mercer is looking for a little more stability against Bulgaria tonight and he urged his players to be more patient when the opposition have the ball. If he has a concern it is that in both the Argentine and East German games England's failing was a lack of composure in the last half-hour. But he lives on that first hour when England made the most of a poor defensive display by East Germany. It was then we saw the hope in this basically young, talented and eager side. Dobson, Worthington, Brooking and Watson are the newcomers whose urgency complements so well the more mature artistry of Bell and Channon.

'When I was at Manchester City I used to say to Francis Lee, "Why can't you play for me like you play for England?" And I would ask Bell, "Why can't you play for England like you play for me?" But these last four games have been wonderful for him – I thought he was our best player in Leipzig.'

In the general guessing that still drags on about who will be the next manager Mercer cannot be overlooked. Indeed, I understand Mercer has already been asked if he would consider extending his caretaker period. Mercer will not give exact details before discussing the position with Coventry but he seems keen at the success so far achieved. If things go right during the rest of the tour he could be with us for a while yet.

Even in the face of the happy smiles of the men responsible for equipping England with a new leadership it is too soon to say if a good team is about to happen on this journey.

2 June 1974   *Peter Corrigan*

In 1973 this was my contribution to an Observer *Soccer Management investigation:*

We Liked Billy But Walked All Over Him

According to Joe Mercer, a man not altogether without experience in the matter, eternal optimism is the quality most needed by a football manager. Of the 92 who will approach the coming League season in England with hopes high, fewer than 20 can possibly see their team win either promotion or a major title or cup. The rest can expect only hard work and heartache.

The football manager's lot is certainly not a happy one. More than 800 have parted company with English League clubs since the war, making three years the average life expectancy.

The casualty rate is even higher for Scotland's national team. Since their first part-time manager in 1954 there have been 10 appointments in 19 years. The most predictable departure was Andy Beattie's after he sent the Scottish FA a pleasant little note informing them he would be watching his new club, Nottingham Forest, in preference to seeing Scotland play Wales. The most harrowing failure was Bobby Brown's when he was hooted into oblivion at Wembley in 1971 as 30,000 infuriated Scots made him the focus of their misery for humiliating defeat by England.

The most surprising failure was the formidable Jock Stein's when a weaker Polish team prevented Scotland qualifying for the World Cup finals in 1966 by beating them at Hampden Park. 'Most roads are paved with good intentions, but this was littered with obstacles,' was Stein's caustic comment. Certainly the Scottish firing squad has been perennially at the ready until the ebullient Tommy Docherty gave *them* the bullet, quitting in the midst of their current World Cup preparations.

It is rare even for the most successful manager's career to have a happy ending. Herbert Chapman stage-managed this best, by dying suddenly in the 1932 season at the height of his fame and with Arsenal still top of the League. More characteristic are the two father figures – Stanley Cullis and Matt Busby. Cullis's ferocious will to win made Wolves the only side to match Manchester United's achievements, but once they faltered he was dismissed, without a word of thanks for past service. And Busby's remarkable reputation has been shadowed at the last by controversy over the Best affair, over the shabby treatment of Frank O'Farrell, his successor, over the crudeness with which United clawed their way to safety last season. Currently no English manager has a better record of results than

Don Revie, of Leeds, or England's Sir Alf Ramsey, yet such is the antipathy to them that they have only to lose one crucial game to be submerged in abuse.

Why, then, do people take the job? As well ask youngsters why they aim for the wearing world of the pop star. The distant glitter of fame and riches is less important than continuing involvement with the one thing that excites them. For with the rarest exceptions football managers have all been professional players of ability, totally absorbed in soccer. The heartache and the cut-throat competition of the glory game is nothing new to them. This is a business in which half the apprentices fail to make the grade and most players are permanently insecure. They have had to accept the manager dropping them without notice if he thought it would benefit the club's results, so they understand the same thing happening to the manager.

Ron Greenwood, of West Ham, turns the experience to his advantage. 'The great performers only looked at the notice board to see when the bus was leaving. I always had to look to see if I was in the side. That gives me a better insight into the feelings of the average footballer.'

Billy Wright and his Arsenal successor Bertie Mee give the perfect illustration that playing ability bears no necessary relation to management skill. Wright had been England's most capped player but it was a relief for him when he was finally asked to resign as Arsenal's manager after a match at Highbury had drawn fewer than 5,000 spectators. Bertie Mee, the physiotherapist who had played a little for Derby County, then took Arsenal to the double.

Billy Wright was too easy going with his players, as Terry Neill noted. 'We all liked him but professional footballers are hard competitors by nature. Give them the chance and they will walk all over you. That's what we did to Billy.' Where Wright was weakest Mee is strongest, proving man management and organisation more important than playing reputation.

There is no apprenticeship for a manager, so the job always holds surprises. Even the meticulous Mee was taken aback by two aspects. 'I had studied it at such close quarters that I was confident I knew all about it when they offered me a year's trial. What I hadn't appreciated was how disjointed the work is. I liked to deal with problems in an orderly way but as soon as you concentrate on one you are interrupted by the Press, or a call from Gigi Peronace in Rome, or a query about travel or tickets or an injury to a player.

'If the club's doing well you can take it in your stride but the distractions are hard to bear when you are already depressed by results. And I hadn't realised the importance of humour. It was Jimmy Robertson who finally said to me, "I can't work with you, boss. You are too serious." Football *is* a serious business but I realise now it has to be leavened with enjoyment.'

Dave Mackay, captain of Hearts, of Tottenham, of Derby, and now manager of Nottingham Forest, thought he knew it all from working so closely with managers. 'What I hadn't appreciated was the strain of watching. As a player I was keyed up but never nervous. As a manager I can't sit still. I want to make all the tackles myself. It's giving me a permanent twitch.

'Then the plans are always being upset. Friday morning everything is fine. Then John Robertson, my best player, is three-quarters of an hour late for training. To maintain discipline I have to drop him and that means reorganising the team and the tactics. Next week it's three men down with flu.'

For the new manager the lack of preparation is made more critical by the demands for quick results. Bobby Robson looks back without anger from his established position at Ipswich to his initial insecurity at Fulham. 'They had known me long enough as a player to be able to judge what they were getting. But within a few months they had lost confidence in me because there was no immediate success. My mistake was one I won't repeat. I took advice from administrators on football matters instead of trusting my own judgment.'

Joe Mercer, now general manager at Coventry, had the point made more forcefully to him in the days when the club boards were apt to want to select teams and dictate playing policy. Harry Storer, the most outspoken manager of the time, told him: 'If you try taking the chairman's advice on football in order to keep your job, you'll lose it quick enough on your results.'

'The higher you start the harder you fall' is the maxim about the managers that Noel Cantwell endorses after his abrupt demotion from Coventry to Peterborough at the bottom of the Fourth Division. 'I walked off the field one Saturday and was manager of a First Division club the next Tuesday. In retrospect that was as ridiculous as the office clerk taking over as managing director without training.'

In their approach to football management the Charlton brothers have shown an impressive perception of the likely problems. Jack hesitated over Middlesbrough's offer till he had resolved his doubts about the change in life style. 'As a player I've enjoyed the freedom and the vast amount of leisure time. Am I ready now to devote myself to the job with the single-mindedness it demands?'

Bobby Charlton, so experienced as a footballer and the new manager of Preston North End, has recognised this is only part qualification by going on the PFA's first football management course at St Helens College of Technology. In introducing the course Derek Dougan commented: 'We have long felt the need for such a course, which is specifically aimed at the professional footballer entering management. The emphasis is on the problems that beset the manager in his early years, problems which in the past have produced unhappy consequences. Many of the hundreds of managers dismissed since the war have suffered from lack of preparation. Any improvement in the training of managers must also be a gain for the players.'

Soccer, so professional in its outlook, has been remarkably amateurish in its selection and induction of managers.

12 August 1973   *Tony Pawson*

In his 'World of Sport' column in September 1971, J. L. Manning looked at the help Clifford Lloyd was giving to players in trouble.

This Week Will Be Quite a Trial

For a full-back who played it hard in League matches for 13 years without caution or sending-off, Clifford Lloyd has a lot of time for footballers in trouble.

This is very necessary these days. Lloyd is secretary of the Professional Footballers' Association. Behind the headlines of the George Best acquittal – the *Sun*'s SWEET FA won the prize – is the case of Ernest Machin of Coventry City. It is well up the legal pipeline.

This law suit by the PFA on Machin's behalf could have a bearing on the whole system of FA discipline. This is among the few in sport which do not permit legal representation of either party to a complaint. There is no limit of punishment, and costs may have to be paid on a scale unknown to players when considering whether or not to ask for personal hearings.

Lloyd says: 'Footballers have less chance of justice before an FA commission than you and I have in a court of law.' Perhaps, but I would settle for what happened to Best. 'But,' said Lloyd, 'that wasn't luck, it was merit.'

Best must pay the costs of the hearing, despite his acquittal. Quaintly, these include match fees of referee Burtenshaw and his two linesmen who gave evidence. Attendance at a hearing, rules the FA, is part of the game. So that is £42.50 for officiating at Stamford Bridge, and the Great Western Hotel, Paddington. There is travel and subsistence as well for all witnesses, of whom Best called two. 'The trouble is,' says Lloyd, 'you don't know how far witnesses are coming or going.'

Lloyd goes to Crewe for his most telling argument against the season's purge. The Fourth Division's Alexandra won £30,000 second prize in the Ford Sporting League last season with only three cautions. They are building a new grandstand. This season so far: one sending-off and five cautions. 'But we're not pulling down the stand,' says secretary Tagg. 'It'll be a tribute to our previous achievement: one sending-off in 1954 and another in 1961.'

Crewe Alexandra's motto is the same as Clifford Lloyd's, *semper contendo.*

19 September 1971   *J. L. Manning*

In 1960 Bob Ferrier saw Danny Blanchflower as more than a great player. He was also a spokesman for all players, but one with an independent and irreverent view on many aspects of the game he served so well.

Impish Spokesman

With his flat, heel-down stride, Danny Blanchflower, captain of the Northern Ireland football team, walked wearily off the darkening Wembley field last week, his team beaten 2–1 by England. Blanchflower is a contemplative person, and this was probably a melancholy moment for him.

The end of an 'empire' is tinged with melancholy, and this match may well have marked the end of a time of heady greatness for the Irish.

In the past two years they beat England at Wembley, qualified against Portugal, Italy and all the odds for the World Cup final tournament, and in Sweden, against the best of the rest of the world, reached the last eight.

The more removed we are in time from that remarkable success, the more incredible it seems. Blanchflower has written an astonishing book, in which he talks of beating Czechoslovakia to enter the last eight in the World Cup: 'In the end we won 2–1. I shall never forget the sight of our little band of officials and supporters dancing madly in the grandstands. It was the greatest night of our lives.'

Of the final match against France, '. . . our trail of glory had come to a sad ending. Up in the stands our officials and supporters, loyal to the end, sang "When Irish Eyes Are Smiling" . . . We did not really win anything–
. . . but as the Cinderella of the soccer world, we caused quite a stir at the ball.'

Now the great achievement, and its lingering aura, fades as the light faded for the Irish at Wembley.

Blanchflower is a warm, kind person with a copywriter's dream of a smile and a great love and sympathy for footballers, in all their finite variety. At a time when players are not considered to have opinions and are frowned on by authority when they express those they do have, Blanch-flower, by virtue of a lively intelligence and a facile tongue, has become the impish spokesman of the species.

At Wembley two years ago he greeted Billy Wright in mid-field with 'Best of luck, Billy, and I hope you lose by six.' His comment on all the talk of 'tactical plans' in football was, 'The Irish team has a new plan – we're going to equalise before the other side scores.' On television he once told the president of the Football League that he thought the players' contract 'diabolical'.

Danny is Irish, an emotionalist and a romantic, and his judgments spurn the coldness of intellect and rationalism. He is an intuitive person. Like Jung, he does not have to 'believe'. He 'knows'. Thus he can be dogmatic. But quote himself against himself and he says simply, 'A man can change his mind, can't he?'

He justifies his extreme, sometimes outrageous, even ridiculous remarks as being necessary to call sharper attention to what he sincerely believes are evils in the game. 'Authority should represent us, not dominate us, and I believe our football authority is a bad one. I have ample proof of this. How can footballers respect a contract which the Football Association and Football League have publicly confessed is invalid in law?'

But Blanchflower in essence conducts a love-hate relationship with the game, relishing deeply the battle on the field, detesting lustily the tendentious power of the establishment off the field. He believes it has far too much unchecked power over the player and his life in a profession which, certainly at the top, is prosperous. To have his intelligence insulted in this way irks him.

211

As many critics and writers do, possibly in self-justification, he rationalises the game on the field into life itself, as twenty-two little ants working out their patterns of destiny on an acre or so of green, each of them using contrasting methods to reach the same end – victory, a victory rendered meaningless with every following week. He delights in the players themselves, variously cunning, cowardly, staunch, subtle, obvious, forthright, introverted, domineering, petulant.

He says, 'I don't believe in idols – I believe in human beings. I admire the warmth and humanity of Matt Busby. He creates a purpose in life, instead of searching for a purpose.' Then again, 'Peter Doherty was the greatest personality I ever saw on a football field. Zest, enthusiasm, a huge keenness for the battle – that was Doherty.'

Captaincy, at a time when many people discredit it? 'Inevitable. A matter of evolution. In any group a leader is thrown up. Without it, you have mob rule.'

He sees an *élite*, a super-league of more quality, less quantity at the top, as our soccer salvation, with greater financial incentives and the right to negotiate his own contract for the player.

A true guide to his approach to life is perhaps in one of his favourite sporting tales, of Walter Hagan scoring 84 in an Open Championship and saying, 'No, I didn't win – but they'll remember Hagan's 84 long after they've forgotten who won.'

Danny Blanchflower has an opinion about everything and claims there is no such thing as having a 'wrong opinion'. He believes in believing, right or wrong, and passionately, too, and the only man he cannot tolerate is the man who doesn't believe in anything.

And football is such a big game – such a very big game – that it should never be afraid of opinions, not even Danny Blanchflower's.

Bob Ferrier

In 1984 The Observer *took a look at the managerial situation in an article by Peter Ball and then required three of us to report our Saturday game with an eye on how the various managers affected their teams. John Dougray, Peter Ball and myself made these comments on how the personality of six managers was reflected in their teams' play.*

Mal's Walk-on

Hughes v. Allison

Rotherham Utd   1   Middlesbrough   1

'We've had more interest shown in the club in the past week than we've had in the past five years,' said the new chairman of Middlesbrough, Mr Mike McCullagh, when asked about the impact of Malcolm Allison's arrival as manager.

Allison, who knows a thing or two about publicity, went walkabout in Middlesbrough's town centre at the beginning of last week to talk to the locals. Though his side were unluckily knocked out of the Milk Cup by Burnley last Tuesday night, the first 10,000-plus gate of the season was recorded at Ayresome Park.

Yesterday, Allison – who has made headlines for the past 20 years in England, Turkey, the United States and Portugal – brought his team to Rotherham, where the manager is Emlyn Hughes. At 35, Hughes is 20 years younger than Allison, but he also knows how to exploit the popular media's hunger for football gimmicks.

Known as 'Crazy Horse' at Liverpool, where he won four championship medals, he obligingly donned Red Indian costume and war paint for the photographers after it was announced that Rotherham would meet Liverpool at Anfield in the third round of the Milk Cup.

Like most coaches and managers, Allison suffers the frustration of having to watch from the sidelines. But Hughes is still playing for Rotherham, orchestrating tactics from the back.

Allison says that the most important lesson he has learned in football is patience. 'If you teach with patience, the results will come.' Such a laid-back philosophy seems curiously at odds with a coaching and managerial career which has spanned at least seven clubs in three continents.

But, for the moment, Allison is with Middlesbrough, and for a club which was heading for a black hole of obscurity and failure, there is now a ray of hope.

Under Hughes, Rotherham's home gates have risen to more than 9,000, which is better than Middlesbrough's so far this season.

After an early United flurry, Middlesbrough took the lead with only five minutes gone. Bell, a 17-year-old who had been turned away at the main entrance by a commissionaire who mistook him for a young gatecrasher, turned the ball inside to Otto, who scored with a cleanly-struck, left-foot drive from 20 yards. Rotherham came back strongly but Towner, McEwan and Fern all missed easy chances. In spite of Rotherham's profligacy in front of goal, Hughes stayed remarkably cool, content to sweep up behind his defensive colleagues.

Allison, however, was in the dug-out and showing signs of increasing anxiety. The photographers homed in on him to record his every twitch and grimace.

Middlesbrough's young substitute, Roberts, who had displaced the injured Mowbray shortly before the interval, was cautioned early in the second half for tripping Towner. Bolton, too, had been booked for fouling the winger, whose sinuous runs had been perplexing Middlesbrough.

Hankin, the Middlesbrough centre-forward, who has had more suspensions than some scaffolders, became the third Middlesbrough player to be booked, for arguing over a free-kick decision.

Altogether, there is a much more combative attitude among the players now Allison has inherited.

Hughes had a marvellous chance to save the match for Rotherham with 10 minutes left, after Brownlie had miskicked, but he sent the ball trundling wide of the far post. The referee, however, allowed three extra minutes for stoppages and, in a last-ditch attack, Moore scored for Rotherham to deny Allison and Middlesbrough their first away win of the season.

John Dougray

A Pair of Aces in Their Different Suits

Mullery v. Macdonald

Crystal Palace 1   Fulham 1

At the end of as exciting and good-spirited a match as one could hope to see, Alan Mullery and Malcolm Macdonald both announced that they had enjoyed the match although Mullery, with typical confident exaggeration, claimed that his side had hit the woodwork four times. In fact they did so twice. The claim, though, reflected Palace's dominance of the second half when for a long time their enthusiastic approach threatened to bring them a winner.

If Mullery had been at Palace in their fashionable period of the mid-Seventies he would undoubtedly have been a classic example of the manager as superstar. He has all the trappings, the smart suit, the cigar, the quick patter and even the shades, although these are a medical requirement rather than an affectation.

But after Brighton and Charlton he has arrived at Palace when the South London club are in straitened circumstances, and his natural bent as an operator on the transfer market has little opportunity for expression.

Yet the few changes he has been able to make, coupled with his undoubted ability as a motivator, has changed the team. Even in the midst of their struggles last season, Palace were a touch side, full of the little flicks and one-twos left over from the days of Terry Venables. Now they reflect Mullery's direct personality, full of drive and with the ball played early for his one buy, the big centre-forward Edwards, to get on the end of.

Edwards did so frequently yesterday to the considerable discomfort of the Fulham defence. An Edwards header at the near post set up Palace's equaliser for Hilaire, and both Edwards and his partner, Mabbutt, hit the woodwork with other airborne efforts.

But although Fulham survived shakily for long periods in the second half, survive they did. Not undeservedly so, for in spite of the absence of their leading scorer Gordon Davies, his replacement Dale Tempest and Robert Wilson, one of their excellent young midfield players, they gave every indication of the quality which had taken them to the top of the Second Division in their first year back at that level.

Unlike Palace's football, it was a style difficult to associate with Malcolm Macdonald, whose days as a head-down and crash centre-forward gave little evidence of such subtlety, even if his commitment to attack was reflected in the general air of unease shown by his defence.

Yet Macdonald's inherent astuteness has enabled him to be one of the first managers to become a paid director, and at the moment he is filling the role admirably.

Shrewdly spotting the wealth of young talent on the books when he took over he has nurtured it beautifully, and his free transfer acquisition of Houghton has been a masterstroke. On yesterday's evidence, the football manager has a big future – as the paid Chief Executive.

Peter Ball

Clough Plants a New Forest

Pleat v. Clough

Luton Town 0   Nottingham Forest 2

In a game of adventurous football and squandered chances Forest's firmer finishing gave them a comfortable margin over entertaining Luton. If teams do indeed reflect their managers' personality then it was no surprise that Forest should be more flamboyant, more decisive, and have the last word.

Like Forest's Brian Clough, Luton's David Pleat is an advocate of attacking football who pays more than lip-service to the concept. His team was always attractive to watch and, on another day, several of the openings created would have been put away by Walsh, Stein and Moss.

Clough is the apotheosis of the managerial myth, the club being more closely identified with him in the popular mind than with the team on the field. He has the first requirement of such cult figures, the ability to churn out quotable comments and be involved in controversial action. Unlike many of them, however, he also has the ability to build and maintain high standards in a team. On this performance it looks as if another formidable side is emerging from a transitional period.

The match was won by the nice timing with which his players moved up from deep positions and by their midfield control where Steve Hodge's youthful dynamism was effectively complemented by Bowyer's experience. As with any business executive, man management is the most important function of his and this is Clough's special forte. Bowyer might well be taken as his trademark. Bought by Forest for £40,000, he gave splendid service before being sold to Sunderland for £250,000. When they could not get that value from him, Clough bought him back for £45,000 last season to give further sterling performances.

It was Bowyer, seconds before half-time, who ended the sequence of near misses. Racing unexpectedly into space, he hit a ferocious drive which soared up off the bar for Birtles to head sideways and Wallace to volley home.

The Luton side had been reorganised following Stephen's abrupt transfer demand. Managers face more problems than usual in this era of economic squeeze and freedom of contract, but Pleat is one of the rare breed who takes a realistic view that the manager is paid to make the best use of existing resources not solve every problem by resort to the cheque-book.

There was much for Pleat to appreciate in the approach play of Hill, whose sinuous dribbling and neat passing made Luton the dominant team of the first half. But the vital pass, the simple shots, went sadly astray.

Robertson settled the issue, lobbing the ball across for Gunn to hit an angled shot which dipped over Findlay into the far corner.

Tony Pawson

On 4 October 1981 Hugh McIlvanney paid tribute to the memory of one of football's great managers and characters, that pugnacious romantic, Bill Shankly.

Shanks for the Memory

Opponents of Liverpool Football Club would be rash to assume that they have done with Bill Shankly. Once Bill's ashes have been scattered on the pitch at Anfield any visiting forward who is setting himself to score an important goal is liable to find suddenly that he has something in his eye.

Certainly Shanks would want us to believe in the possibility. Even after the results were in the paper, showing a scoreline against his men, he always refused to give defeat houseroom. Maybe we should follow his example and regard his death as just an ugly rumour.

To those who knew him well his loss is about as sore as any could be. But there is some easing of the grief in the knowledge that few men ever had such a capacity for warming and delighting their fellows without being physically in their company. For many of us he really will always be there.

Most of the thousand and one Shankly anecdotes, the tales of his doings and his utterances, are distorted and diminished in the telling, but he communicated such a strong sense of himself that enough of what was unique and marvellous about him is bound to survive. Nearly everyone connected with British football has tried at one time or another to impersonate the accent and the mannerism he brought out of the south Ayrshire coalfield as a teenager and guarded against even the tiniest erosion through half a century in England.

217

Few of the impersonators get within touching distance of the reality but nobody minds. The Shankly legend is the living, genuine article and the smallest fragment of it can spread laughter in any group of football people.

Clearly, however, he needed far more than earthy, utterly original wit to make the impact he did. His unshakable attachment to the ordinary supporters of football ('I'm a people's man – only the people matter') was a big help but his real strength was, perhaps, drawn from something even more unusual.

With his drill-sergeant's hairstyle, his boxer's stance and his staccato, hard-man's delivery he did not fit everybody's idea of a romantic. But that's what he was an out-and-out, 22 carat example of the species. His secret was that he sensed deep down that the only practical approach to sport is the romantic one. How else could a manager persuade grown men that they could find glory in a boy's game. Shankly did that and more.

Looking into the faces of some of his outstanding former players in the last few days, men like Ian St John and Ronnie Yeats and Kevin Keegan, we could see how much they felt they owed to the Boss. He gave them more than a share in trophies, nothing less than a wonderful dream.

He fed it into their spirits by many means; by humour, dedicated example and that romanticism that insisted on talking defeats away as if they were fleeting embarrassments that a malevolent and dishonest fate had inflicted on his teams without regard to their true worth. His performances in that line were like those of a witch doctor, full of blind faith and incantations. They worked so well that his players never allowed defeat to become a habit.

Of course, he had learned plenty about the nuts and bolts of the game in his long career as a player with Carlisle, Preston (where he developed a bottomless admiration for Tommy – never Tom – Finney) and Scotland, and his management years at Carlisle, Grimsby, Workington, Huddersfield (where he had a brief memorable alliance with the young Denis Law) and from 1959 at Liverpool.

His Liverpool won the Second Division championship in 1962 by eight points and by the time he retired prematurely in 1974 they had taken the League title three times, the FA Cup twice and the UEFA Cup once. It is no diminution of the splendid manager who succeeded him, Bob Paisley, to say that Shankly left behind a foundation that contributed hugely to the subsequent domination of Europe by the club.

He also left behind a great deal of himself and the pathos of his self-precipitated conversion into a peripheral, haunting and sometimes embittered figure at Anfield was painful to his friends. But he was never reduced in the eyes of those who knew him best. No manager ever gave more to the spirit of a city or the folklore of a game than he did.

'Me havin' no education,' I once heard him say, 'I had to use my brains.' He used his heart, too. It was as big as a town.

4 October 1981   *Hugh McIlvanney*

Julie Welch had a manager's eye view in 1984 as she watched Wimbledon's Dave Bassett get the better of Crystal Palace's Steve Coppell.

Football Views
from the Dug-out

Wimbledon   3   Crystal Palace   2

I knew I was hooked when Alan Cork bodged up a shot and I kicked the air in sympathy. I was also suffering from Assistant Manager's Twitch, a nervous condition caused by having to stay in your seat when the lads are hanging on to a 3–2 lead with four minutes still to go.

Further up in the stands and around the ground they were probably already whistling shrilly to tell the ref it was time to blow, but from the dug-out all you could hear was a deep insistent moo. The crowd hardly existed for us, down there by the touchline, so close you could see the sweat drip off the centre half's nose, hearing the heart beat of the game.

'Come and watch a match from the bench,' Dave Bassett, Wimbledon's lovely manager, had said. How could you resist an invitation like that, the chance to pretend that you were really part of it, not just stuck in a press box being sarkily detached about it all? What was it like, did they exchange priceless nuggets of tactical information, did they throw things at the other manager or have nervous breakdowns out there? It was 11.15 on a crisp Sunday morning at Plough Lane, and I was about to find out.

The fixture was against Crystal Palace – local derby, good crowd and spiced up by the fact that Dave Bassett once agreed to go there as manager, then 24 hours later changed his mind. 'It was crazy,' he said, 'I knew I didn't want to go.' So he stayed with Wimbledon and carried on turning it into one of the most incredible football stories ever – a club which 10 years ago was in the Southern League, which gets small gates and doesn't have much money, yet is now in the Second Division playing against the likes of Manchester City, Wolves and Leeds United. And has done it all, what's more, without losing one bit of its charm and warmth.

I was tucked in beside Alan Gillett, the assistant manager and Sid Neale, the kit man. Steve Coppell of Crystal Palace sat just across the gangway and at half-time I moved behind him to hear the voice of the opposition. Dave Bassett was watching from the stands. He had probably decided to give his ears a rest. At school, we used to have this games mistress called Coolo who hounded you in lacrosse by baying, 'Come along, you twerp, put a little more oomph into it.' They were bellowing much the same message from the dug-out, only not in words which you are allowed to print in a family newspaper.

They have an entirely different lexicon too. I now know why managers talk in clichés on the television, it's because the rest of us just wouldn't comprehend the idioms of football. 'Do your work, do your work,' Alan Gillett was screeching. 'John, do 50–50. Go on son, get the bits.'

Steve Coppell was quieter but no less esoteric! 'Tuck in, Davy, tuck in,' he piped up. 'Tuck in, Phil.'

You knew they were absolutely dying to be out there, Coppell chewing gum at 5,000 revs a minute, Gillett sitting on the edge of his seat, his toes the only part of his feet which touched the ground. The Wimbledon bench were ferociously tense, one down through a ninth minute penalty, a shot that found Palace's net disallowed, two players booked, one from each side. Just before half-time, Wimbledon should have scored but didn't. Gillett was bent double. 'We got Stevie hitting free kicks at the smallest front player. Would you believe it, hitting free kicks to Gagey? Gagey! Gagey! You can do no better than get it in first time! Get it in first time, right?' Gagey's reply was inaudible.

Half-time came and went and Gillett and Coppell exchanged pleasantries about Manchester and the weather. No enmity there, they were all in the same boat. Then, with Palace still leading, midway through the second half Dave Bassett came rushing down. He had been agonising for 10 minutes whether to put on Andy Sayer for Steve Galliers. 'You can often get egg on your face with substitutions,' he said. But Galliers came off, getting a maternal pat on the head from Gillett, and Sayer only went on and equalised.

Two more goals followed in quick succession for Wimbledon, then, with four minutes to go, Palace got one back. 'Ffff,' muttered Gillett, slapping the side of the seat. Bassett was in there by now, shouting hoarse gibberish. 'Get Cassius in! Get Cassius! Hodges! Get in the mixer!' And I guess he did, because Wimbledon won 3–2.

Afterwards I asked Bassett whether the players can actually hear what you're saying. He said they can, some of the time. 'Depends on the noise. And whether they want to hear or not.' He also said that sitting in the dug-out made him really pent up because he wanted to be out there running about. 'That's why I enjoyed being a player better than a manager.' Mind you, I think I'd put up with all the problems of management if I could sit in the dug-out every game.

11 November 1984   *Julie Welch*

Hugh McIlvanney wrote this tribute to Jock Stein after he died of a heart attack at the end of a World Cup qualifying match between Wales and Scotland.

Hero Worshipped by his People

The larcenous nature of death, its habit of breaking in on us when we are least prepared and stealing the irreplaceable, has seldom been more sickeningly experienced than at Ninian Park in Cardiff on Tuesday night.

Those of us who crowded sweatily into the small entrance hall of the main stand to wait for word of Jock Stein's condition will always remember the long half hour in which the understandable vagueness of reports filtering from the dressing room area lulled us into believing that Jock was going to make it through yet another crisis. The raw dread that had been spread among us by his collapse on the touchline at the end of the Wales-Scotland World Cup match gave way to the more bearable gloom of acknowledging that the career of one of the greatest managers football has known would have to be ended by immediate retirement.

Then – off in a corner of that confused room – Mike England, the manager of Wales and a deeply concerned first-hand witness of what had been happening to Stein, was heard to say that he was still 'very, very poorly'. There was no mistaking the true meaning of those words and suddenly the sense of relief that had been infiltrating our anxieties was exposed as baseless. We felt almost guilty about having allowed ourselves

221

to be comforted by rumours. Then, abruptly, we knew for sure that the Big Man was dead and for some of us it was indeed as if our spirits, our very lives, had been burglarised.

Of all the reactions to Stein's death, none meant more than that of the thousands of Scotland's travelling supporters who learned of it haphazardly but with eerie swiftness as they got ready to celebrate a ragged draw against Wales that should guarantee their team a passage to the World Cup Finals in Mexico next summer. They are, given half an excuse, the most raucously exuberant fans in the game but as midnight neared in Cardiff on Tuesday they wandered through the streets in subdued clusters, sustaining the unforced atmosphere of mourning that pervaded the hundreds who waited silently in the darkness outside Ninian Park after the last hope of reviving the stricken man inside had been abandoned.

There is no doubt that the Scots have a highly developed capacity for the elegiac mood, especially when there is a bottle about, but what was to be encountered in South Wales last week was no cheap example of the genre. When travel-soiled units of the tartan expeditionary force interrupted their morose drinking to propose toasts to the lost leader, anybody cynical enough to see such behaviour as just another maudlin ritual doesn't know much about the way the power of Jock Stein's nature communicated itself to millions of ordinary people.

His achievements in football were monumental but they can only partially explain his impact upon and relevance to so many lives. Perhaps he was profoundly cherished simply because he was a true working class hero – and that is a species which is disappearing almost as fast in industrial Scotland as elsewhere, if only because the values that governed its creation are being relentlessly eroded day by day. Even the common misery of unemployment has not halted the fragmentation of a sense of community that once seemed indestructible.

In an age when, if I may quote a line from my brother William's latest novel, it is as if 'every man and his family were a private company', Stein was the unpretentious embodiment of that older, better code that was until not so long ago the compensatory inheritance of all who were born of the labouring poor. No one was ever likely to mistake him for a saint, or even for a repository of bland altruism. He could look after himself and his own in the market place or anywhere else, but there was never the remotest danger that he would be contaminated by the materialism that engulfs so many of those who find prosperity through sport or other forms of entertainment.

These days it is hard to avoid having the eardrums battered by some unlikely pillar of the New Right who – having persuaded himself that a largely fortuitous ability to kick a football or volley a tennis ball or belt out a pop song or tell a few jokes more acceptably than the next man is actually evidence of his own splendid mastery of his fate – insists that the dole queues would fade away overnight if people got off their arses, got on their bikes and showed the enterprise that has carried him to what he imagines is glory. Stein's whole life was a repudiation of such garbage.

He was utterly Scottish, utterly Lanarkshire in fact, but his was the kind of loyalty to his roots that made his principles universal.

His father was a miner who was a miner's son and Stein himself worked underground until turning belatedly to full-time professional football at the age of 27. During a long, incalculably rewarding friendship with him, I heard him say many memorable things and some of the most vivid were inevitably about the game he loved and the great practitioners of it, but he was most moved and most moving when he talked of that earlier phase of his working experience.

There was a dynamic, combative quality to most of his conversation (mischievous wind-up was a favourite mode and, though he did not drink alcohol, he occasionally dipped his barbs in curare) but when the subject was mining and miners a tone of wistful reverie invaded his voice.

'I went down the pit when I was 16 (at first I was working with ponies – it was still that era) and when I left 11 years later I knew that wherever I went, whatever work I did, I'd never be alongside better men. They didn't just get their own work done and go away. They all stayed around until every man had finished what he had to do and everything was cleared up. Of course, in the bad or dangerous times that was even more true. It was a place where phoneys and cheats couldn't survive for long.

'Down there for eight hours you're away from God's fresh air and sunshine and there's nothing that can compensate for that. There's nothing as dark as the darkness down a pit, the blackness that closes in on you if your lamp goes out. You'd think you would see some kind of shapes but you can see nothing, nothing but the inside of your head. I think everybody should go down the pit at least once to learn what darkness is.'

Phoneys and cheats did not flourish in his company during four decades of involvement with senior football. As a player he was shrewd, well organised and strong rather than 2oustandingly gifted, though he made a fundamental contribution to the rich streak of prize-winning enjoyed by the Celtic team he joined unexpectedly for a fee of £1,200 after modest seasons with Albion Rovers and a motley troupe of non-League men at Llanelli in South Wales. He became an influential captain of Celtic and when his playing career was ended by an injury to his right ankle that left him with a noticeable limp for the rest of his days, it was clear that he would make a manager.

His old employers were certain to be impressed by his successful introduction to the trade in charge of Dunfermline, for he gave that humble club the Scottish Cup by beating Celtic in the final tie, and after a further rehearsal period with Hibernian he went back to Parkhead as manager in 1964. It was a genuinely historic return, perhaps the most significant single happening in the entire story of Scottish football.

All of Stein's family associations, centred on the Lanarkshire villages of Blantyre and Burnbank, were vehemently Protestant but he had never hesitated for a second over first identifying himself with a club traditionally seen as carrying the banner for the Catholic minority in Glasgow (and throughout Scotland) and when he emerged as Celtic's first non-Catholic manager he became a living, eloquent rebuke to the generations of bigotry surrounding the Rangers–Celtic rivalry.

Under him, Celtic dominated the whole range of Scottish domestic competitions to a degree that stamped him, in his context, as the supreme achiever among the world's football managers. Nine League championships in a row is in itself a record no one can ever hope to equal but it was the triumphant lifting of the European Cup in Lisbon in 1967, a feat that had previously proved beyond the most powerful British clubs, that set him totally apart in the annals of the sport. That other legendary Scot Bill Shankly got it just about right when he held out a fellow miner's hand to Stein after the brilliant defeat of Inter-Milan and said in his coal-cutter voice: 'John – you're immortal.'

Celtic in Lisbon performed with irresistible verve, representing perfectly Stein's ideal of blending athletic speed and competitiveness with imagination, delicacy of touch at close quarters and exhilarating surges of virtuosity. Of course, when all Stein's technical assets had been assessed – the vast tactical awareness that owed nothing to coaching courses, the precise judgment of his own and opposing players, the encyclopaedic retention of detail, the emphasis on the positive while eradicating the foolhardy – the essence of his gifts as a manager was seen to reside in something more basic and more subtle: in his capacity to make men do for him more than they would have been able to do for themselves.

Stein's allegiance to Celtic withstood more than one attempt to coax him to switch dramatically to the manager's chair at Rangers and it was sad that when his connection with Parkhead was eventually severed in 1978 he should leave with a justified feeling of grievance about how he had ultimately been treated. By that time he had survived a warning of skirmish with heart trouble and a car crash that almost killed him in the summer of 1975. Many men would have throttled down there and then but he had been a compulsive worker around football most of his life and when the manager's job at Leeds United was offered he decided, at the age of 55, to move south.

However, two months later he received the call millions of admirers believed he should have had years before and was given control of the Scotland team. He took them to the World Cup finals in Spain in 1982 (the Soviet Union kept them out of the last 12 on goal difference) and after a match last Tuesday notable for its tensions and controversies, never for its quality, he had the result required to open a way to the Finals of 1986. But suddenly the strains that have been mounting mercilessly over the years, strains whose ravages the obsessive in him insisted on belittling, proved too much for a system weakened by that earlier illness and, most crucially, by the desperate car crash of 10 years ago.

The pain of his death from a heart attack dug deepest into his wife Jean and into Rae and George, the attractive, strong-minded daughter and son of whom he was so proud. But there were many others in many places who felt last week that they did not have to go down a pit to know what real darkness was.

15 September 1985   *Hugh McIlvanney*

In March 1988 Peter Corrigan talked with Jack Charlton, whose Irish team was to make such an impact in the Finals of the European Nations Championship.

Jack Among Giants

The first shots have been fired in the build-up to the European Championships. Holland winged England's feeling of well-being at Wembley, the Soviet Union had a four-goal burst against Greece who had drawn in Holland during the qualifying stages – already the finals in June are giving off the whiff of great battles to come.

But when the manoeuvres began in mid-week there would have been no more heartening sight than the Republic of Ireland team to play Romania in Dublin being announced by Jack Charlton, reading the names from the back of a Carroll's cigarette packet.

Charlton's presence, not to mention that of Ireland, among the elite of European football has yet to enjoy its full impact but it will – and the first testimonies may well come from a small squad of Dutch reporters who ignored Wembley to make a close study of the man whose arrival among the top eight international managers in Europe has been unorthodox to say the least.

The scene at that team announcement was a good starting point. Charlton couldn't make out one of the names on his fag packet and had to be prompted by a press man. Then he referred to Romania as Bulgaria. 'Do they really think I don't know the difference?' he asked indignantly the following morning when British newspapers reported his slip of the tongue. The Irish reporters had ignored it completely. His flights away from strictly accurate nomenclature have become a protected species over there, and so they should because it is a fault common to many successful managers.

The decision to bring in the tall, gruff and ready northern Englishman was as inspired as it was courageous. Ireland have been repaid by their first-ever qualification for a major international tournament and, following the 2–0 defeat of Romania, the only run of six consecutive victories in their history.

They may also have initiated a trend we shall see developing over the next few years. The Welsh attempt to obtain the services of Brian Clough had its foundations dug by the precedent of Charlton.

In addition to the obvious difficulties in gaining acceptance in his new international role, Charlton has had to live down the image of a man reluctant to be dragged away from fishing and shooting. That was the point at which the Dutch decided to open their questioning. He told them they could have half an hour. They said they would prefer four or five hours. 'I can tell you everything I know in half an hour,' he insisted. They began by asking: 'Why are you a maniac about hunting?'

'A maniac?' he repeated with commendable control. 'All I do is stand by a river dangling a worm in the water. Some men play golf as a relaxation. I fish and do a bit of shooting.'

There were many more penetrating questions to follow but, alas, he ushered his interrogators out of earshot where, no doubt, he brought them round with that raw, persuasive eloquence that is the basis of his success. Not only has he had to talk his squad into match-winning form, he has had to persuade some of them to become Irish in the first place. The benefits of dual qualification have enabled countries like Ireland to make up for the ravages of emigration, which is fair enough. Liverpool stars Ray Houghton and John Aldridge became footballing Irishmen in Charlton's first match two years ago while they were still with Oxford United. Unfortunately, neither could make it on Wednesday and with Brady, Lawrenson, Whelan and McGrath also ruled out through injury the Irish were severely depleted.

'The trouble with losing players of this quality,' said Charlton, 'is that it upsets the balance of the side and you can never hope to recover that balance with different players. Things were going great until these recent setbacks. I thought we made the most of a difficult game and more players have gained valuable experience but any of our future opponents watching it would have learned nothing about how we're going to shape up in the Finals.' . . .

Charlton reckons it takes 12 matches to become an international player and there are only four preparatory matches between now and their opening game against England in Stuttgart on 12 June. 'It is wrong to think of a job like this as part-time. Apart from preparing for 10 matches a year you have to watch each of them play for their clubs as often as possible and then have a chat to them. Changing club attitudes to the demands of international games, showing how and where to apply their techniques in a different manner, is very difficult. And the make-up of the Football League will never allow proper preparations. If they cut down the number of club games players are expected to play you would see a vast improvement in all the international teams who take the bulk of their players from the League, including England.

'But although it is frustrating I enjoy it very much. You don't get involved in all the admin that a club manager is bogged down with. You are just thinking all the time and that's why Brian Clough would do well as an international manager because he is such a great thinker on the game. Whether he could have done it part-time is another matter.'

What about the British club managers abroad, like John Toshack and Howard Kendall in Spain? 'British managers used to go abroad because they couldn't get jobs here. Since Terry Venables they are going because they are in demand. Who knows where it could end?'

It would be ironic if the Football League, that great sapper of strength and guile from generations of players, were to provide a greater management influence on world football. One of the fascinations of the European Championships is that for the first time two English managers will be parading their ideas. If the Irish can maintain their romantic assault on those previously unassailable heights, who knows what they could have started?

27 March 1988   *Peter Corrigan*

Directors were a target for Danny Blanchflower in 1958 with Chappie D'Amato defending the Fulham Board's approach. Then in 1985 Julie Welch interviewed Robert Maxwell as the 'Lord of the Manor' began to spread his influence far beyond Oxford's Manor Road ground.

The Directors' Obsession with Success

Why do so many football managers fall by the wayside? Why is it that so many others are willing to replace them? Where stands the manager in football to-day?

There is some innate, instinctive feeling that blinds a man to calculated reason and drives him to the challenge of a football manager's chair. It might be the call of the hunter that lies dormant in every man; or the unfounded conviction that tempts the gambler to favour a long shot, with the implicit faith that providence will desert the natural laws of chance and bring home the unpredictable – just for him. And it's got something to do with what made Adam take the apple and bite off more than he could chew.

A manager is appointed to a club by its board of directors. This directorate usually consists of five men, or more, adventurers from varied ports in the world of commerce, who, by some means or other, control the limited shareholding of the club.

The directors do not democratically represent the wonderful public institution that a big football club really is. They are not voted into authority by the many followers and paying customers who foster the club. They have no special knowledge or charm that selects them as leaders to advance the common cause. They have merely bought the legal source of the club's authority.

The Laws of Association drastically limit dividends, so being a football director is no business venture for them. They simply covet the social prestige and the personal satisfaction of being celebrated men of sport.

The more successful their team is, the more celebrated they will be. So their obsession is not for sport; but for success – continual, permanent, enduring success. And as football is their hobby, not their business, it only makes them more impatient and less understanding in their search for a winning way.

When they appoint a manager they will have little tolerance whilst that man methodically builds a sure and solid foundation. They merely want some magician who will immediately produce everlasting success. But as they have no special knowledge of the game, they have no clear image of the qualities essential in such a magician. If they knew the tricks, they would not need the magician. In their ignorance, they are more than likely to choose the wrong man for the manager's job.

As the directors do not democratically represent the followers of the club, their choice of manager holds no link of faith with the club's public. Unless the manager quickly produces results he will have little affection from any quarter, and his chances of succeeding immediately are slim.

The competitive nature of the business limits his chances right away. There are twenty-two teams in the League, and only one team can win it. One manager will be a success, while twenty-one will be failures – some bigger than others.

Successful teams do not appoint managers. Why should they? So the man who accepts a managerial position must face the reality that he has inherited an unsuccessful team. He may be optimistic about the situation and feel: 'That as the team is unsuccessful things can't get much worse.' That may be so. But how is he to make them better?

If the team is not successful then it is not good enough. If anything simple can be done to make it good, why hasn't it been done? Perhaps, at the beginning, he feels that he will have some new ideas that will improve the team. He will be very fortunate indeed if he finds the bad players capable enough to carry out good ideas. And he will be very brilliant if he has ideas that will make a bad team good.

He could develop his own young players but that takes time, and his directors and public are impatient for success. And it is a difficult thing to develop young players, properly, in a bad team. Furthermore, the good youngsters will prefer to join the more successful teams.

As a last resort, he can enter the transfer market and buy the players he needs but the club he manages may not have the wealth to afford such frivolities. If they have, where can he buy the players he wants? Presumably he wants good players and value for money. He will soon find that other clubs are seldom willing to sell their good players, so that ventures into the transfer market can be a very precarious proposition.

While the manager has all these difficulties to consider, he must also manage the day-to-day affairs of the club. The managing of people in any walk of life is difficult enough; but to keep a bunch of virile young men, who are continually in competitive conflict and are subject to the injustices of an outdated and ridiculous system of contract, in a happy state of being, calls for the touch of a genius.

Sometimes a man can rise above all this. A few men have the magic wand to smooth out the impossibilities and attain success. These men are much envied. Their directors may not like them getting the 'lion's share' of the glory. Other managers do not like them, because they are failures by comparison, and often their own players feel that they are not so important as they would appear.

So when the great man falters, everyone is eager to condemn him before he regains his step. And everyone heaves a sigh of relief when he is 'pushed' and falls by the wayside.

Another manager has been sacrificed to the idol of quick results by a board of directors who know little about the game.

22 February 1958   *Danny Blanchflower*

We Are Never in a Hurry for Success

I must answer Danny Blanchflower's article of last Sunday in *The Observer*, in which he so strongly criticised the directors of football clubs. All professional football clubs bar one in the First, Second, Third South and Third North Divisions are limited liability companies and as such are subject to ordinary company law, as is any other business.

There is a board of directors with chairman, vice-chairman, a certain number of directors and shareholders according to the articles of association. Our primary function is to run the business matters of the club in a proper manner and endeavour to make a profit or at least keep the company solvent. The only difference between ordinary business company directors and those of a professional football club is that we give our time and business knowledge to the company without any remuneration whatsoever.

Our function in the building-up of a successful football club is to engage a manager who will be responsible for the fostering of very young players through delegating his authority to coaches and trainers engaged by the directors and to be responsible for the form of the senior or first team.

Of domestic matters I can only speak or write with knowledge of my own club, Fulham. We as a board, and I include our secretary and general manager, Frank Osborne, and our manager, Dugald Livingstone, are never in a hurry for success. We know through experience that this comes slowly by building-up from the fourth, third and second teams.

Our present brilliant team is a magnificent example of this. Johnny Haynes, our captain, and surely the greatest genius in Association Football to-day, Roy Dwight, Trevor Chamberlain, Elio Macedo, George Cohen, Joe Stapleton, Eric Lampe and Arthur Stevens all graduated from our junior side – and this was not achieved in a hurry.

No, the directors and the managements of clubs are not in a hurry for success. It is a small section of unthinking spectators with which most clubs are cursed who are the ones to blame. The champions of to-day can be the relegated of to-morrow and the relegated of this season can be the champions of the next. That is the spice of the game.

If the team is successful the players and manager are praised, and rightly so. The directors are not noticed – we don't mind, for we are all genuine and enthusiastic supporters and just as happy as the man on the terraces. If a team is going through a bad spell the directors are noticed and the manager comes in for a lot of criticism. But managers are often experienced players themselves and know before they take their job that they are liable to be blamed for out-of-form play just as they were blamed when they were players.

We on the board at Fulham do not in any way interfere in the selection of the teams. We have always allowed our managers a fair period of time to prove their capabilities and if they are unsuccessful it surely is in their own interest that they are advised or allowed to leave and start in with another club. Directors of my club do know the game. I have played soccer for my local club, West Kensington FC, and have played in Italy, Austria, Holland, Belgium and Germany.

I was a supporter on the terraces for 18 years before I was invited to join the board. My co-director Jack Walsh lives in Fulham, as I do, and was also a supporter of the club for very many years and travelled to away matches long before he was asked to join the board.

The same is true of Tommy Trinder, also a director, who went to school in Fulham and was a supporter for 20 years before joining the board. The two sons of our chairman, Mr C. Dean, also played soccer and one of them sustained a serious injury that put him out of the game as a player.

Danny Blanchflower accuses us of seeking social prestige, but do I and Tommy Trinder get our prestige from the football club? Jack Walsh and the Dean family are successful business men and their knowledge is of the utmost value to a board of directors. We are all just Fulham supporters.

Danny says that we directors are not elected in a democratic manner. I am not sure what he means. What board of directors of any company is so elected? We have shareholders and they can have their say at the annual general meeting and can yell 'no confidence' in the board if they want to. But our shareholders have never behaved in this way and our annual general meetings are very pleasant affairs.

If we were not elected in a 'democratic manner' at least we are very democratic at Fulham. Danny need only ask any supporter of Fulham or any member of the team to find that this is true.

The post of manager of a professional football club is fraught with anxiety but still they line up for this exciting and exacting job and in most clubs they are treated fairly and given the full backing of the directors. However, this is not always the case and I am certain that in many parts of the country you will find the type of football director of whom Danny Blanchflower so strongly disapproves.

9 March 1958   *Chappie D'Amato*

Soccer's Lord of the Manor

We had come to interview Robert Maxwell on the subject of football, but first there were the *Mirror* bingo-winners to be sorted out. High up in a sky-scraperette off Holborn, in a suite whose windows gave out on to rolling cream clouds, the chairman of Oxford United FC, Mirror Group Newspapers and Heaven knows what else had his massive frame stooped over the lucky readers, chatting to them in a rich, soothing voice while editors waited for his nod on the next day's stories.

The bingo winners, who were already each ensured of £5,000 worth of MGN generosity, were placing scraps of paper with their names on in a revolving drum to see who would be entitled to Go For A Million.

Maxwell, who may have his impish side, asked me to perform the draw. He then enquired politely if his readers would like a fanfare, signalled two liveried gentlemen to burst into sound, and accompanied the fortunate candidate to an inner sanctum to choose a box number that might bring undreamed-of fame and fortune. (Alas, it did not.)

The entire, lengthy ceremony was carried out by Maxwell with enormous enjoyment and zest, and indeed he had to be persuaded away, striding back to his office while the rich voice boomed over his shoulder, 'Nice people, aren't they. Simple. Straightforward.'

It was with a similar gusto that, once back at his desk, he told the following story: shortly before embarking on a journey to take 50 tonnes of food to Ethiopia he, plus numerous reporters and photographers, attended the Milk Cup tie between Oxford and Arsenal.

The flight was held up as long as possible, but in the end the party had to leave while the score was still 2–2. During the journey to the airport the draw became a victory for Oxford, news which did not bring unmitigated pleasure to the hearts of the largely London-based hacks.

'We arrived at 2 am at Addis Abbaba,' continued Maxwell. 'There on Ethiopian TV was the Oxford–Arsenal match. What strings I had pulled to get that night's game on there to rub salt into journalists' wounds!'

Maxwell said he became interested in football in early childhood – 'I have played since I was a toddler. Left wing, as you would expect. I was very fast. Still am.' For some years, after watching Arsenal in 1938 in his native Czechoslovakia, he cherished the ambition to play professionally and, in fact, counted himself as one of Arsenal's lifelong supporters until he bought Oxford.

'I would have bought Arsenal if it had come up before.' And now? 'Nope. I didn't buy Manchester United so why should I buy Arsenal? We'll thrash them all at the Manor.'

It was the cue to find out how things stood with Oxford City Council who, when Oxford gained promotion last week, found themselves the subject of some heavy broadsides from our hero re their failure to chip in with help for the tiny ground.

Maxwell grinned and fished some correspondence from the neat pile at his left elbow. It had the salient points outlined in yellow ink. 'There you are. The official letter. The Council have agreed to give us expedited planning permission and £250,000 towards improving the Manor Ground for next season.'

In prospect, also, is a multi-purpose stadium at Charwell, to seat 20–25,000, people and with leisure and shopping facilities. The club will be submitting for planning permission shortly, and in return the council has first option to buy the present site.

Maxwell lives within 400 yards of the Manor Ground, at Headington Hill Hall. His daughter Ghislaine is a director of Oxford ('We visited Burnley and the chairman was absolutely flabbergasted') and his son Ian is the chairman of Derby County ('He has a much better stadium.') There are five other children – 'I have been married for 40 years. It's a very expensive hobby.'

I asked him why he thought football was so important to people. 'Why do people like ballet?' he countered. 'I consider football is a great art to be enjoyed. It is universal, exciting, it demands great skill, tenacity and courage in adversity.' He added that his favourtie players were ones who tried, 'that are determined and committed and have fun playing football. Our players. I admire plenty of others, but I have got great pleasure seeing our team come up from nowhere.' At that his voice took on an almost defiant note. 'You don't come up from the 3rd to the 1st in two seasons by luck.'

Did he mix with the players? 'I see them. I treat them as friends and equals.' He also goes into the dressing room at half time, 'not to tell them how to play, but to learn and to listen'. I wondered if they might not be in awe of him. 'You must ask them that.'

He said that Jim Smith was in charge of the players but that he himself looked after the contracts. 'If Jim Smith wants to spend money he has to discuss it with me and if I say no, it's no.'

Football, he thought, had to be run as a business. 'If not it would need a national subsidy. But with the unemployment we have how can you justify national subsidies for circuses? That is why we're so concerned to get more money from TV because football needs more money.'

It was a topic to which he returned later, when the time came to say goodbye. We thanked him for a most enjoyable encounter, and meant it. 'Have you got in my comment about TV?' he said. 'It's very important. It's boiling up into a big story.'

When we left, he was back at his desk, waiting for his chief sportswriter to report back to him with the latest news.

5 May 1985   *Julie Welch*

David Hunn in 1972 talked with the League Cup Final referee, trying to find out why he was happy doing the job when the referee's lot is perceived as such an unhappy one.

Why the Ref is
Always a Bastard

Nobody loves a referee except a referee's wife. His ancestry, so one hears, is in considerable doubt. So is his honesty, his competence, and his consciousness. Fifty thousand people hate him one minute, the next another 50,000.

The only time he pleases everybody is when he stops a ball with the back of his neck. 'For Gawd's sake don't revive him,' yelled an anguished fan, when a trainer applied the magic sponge to a fallen referee. 'Bury the twit.'

Norman Burtenshaw chuckled as he recalled the incident. 'Ah,' he said, 'they don't mean it.' Yesterday at the Football League Cup Final he was cast as worm and monster, coward and braggart, cissy and sadist, all within 90 minutes, or possibly nine. All for £10.50. What sort of man chooses that for a hobby? Why does he do it?

His eyes flicker at the question, and he kneads his fingers for a moment: not because he can't answer, but because he knows you won't understand. 'It's the taking part,' he says, a shade uncertainly, 'the belonging.'

Not the power, the dominion, nor the glory? 'No. No, no. I hate using my authority against a player. I would much rather have a quick word, unobtrusively, than have to put a lad in the book. But if it has to happen, you do it.

'Then I often wonder if it's my fault: whether there was some little incident I should have spotted earlier. He got away with that, so now he goes a bit further. And if I had had a word first time, this might never have happened.'

Burtenshaw has bitten more often than most referees the bitter fruit of unwanted notoriety. It was he who was flattened by the crowd at Millwall in 1967, after they had lost to Aston Villa; he who booked the entire Benfica team; who sent off George Best for using foul language, an offence he finds truly offensive; and he who, in the run-up to the League championship last season, allowed a Leeds goal ('Three yards offside,' said the *Mail* man) that nearly cost Arsenal the title.

'I never make a mistake,' he says cheerfully. 'No referee ever makes a mistake – at the time. They can replay it in slow motion as often as they like and prove you wrong, but they can't prove you made a mistake. You didn't. You did what you thought was right, what you knew was right. And you must keep telling yourself how right you are. Allow a moment's doubt and you are lost.'

His life has been shaped to accommodate refereeing. For 19 years Burtenshaw was a GPO night telephonist, but the whistle and jack plug did not go well together. The Post Office, he says, was curiously reluctant to allow him special leave for overseas trips (he once got as far as London Airport en route for nine weeks in Zambia before they agreed to let him go) and anyway he sometimes had to spend most of his match fee on paying a substitute to do his shift.

Now he has a sweet shop on the fast-developing fringe of Great Yarmouth, within a mile or two of his birthplace and in the heart of the area in which he has spent his whole life. The shop suits him well. Three mornings a week, when the early rush is over, he goes down to the beach at Gorleston and runs for an hour and a half. Mid-week matches are no longer a problem, nor are overnight jobs – for which the League allows £6 for hotels and £4 a day for food.

He is a happy, kind, and humdrum man who seems to defy the thought

235

that there must be something odd about anyone who puts his shorts on every week to be insulted. He drives an orange Volkswagen and has all the doors of his neat bungalow painted different colours, but you couldn't referee a Sunday school match without a stroke of extrovertion. What is so disarming is the depth of his love of the job, of the game, and even of footballers.

'People try to make out there's a great gulf between the referee and the players. That's not so. Basically we get on very well together, though it wouldn't be a good idea to be too friendly. You can even book a lad and have him come up to you at the end and say, well, anyway, you had a good game, ref.

'As far as I am concerned each match starts with a clean slate. Nothing is carried over from the last time, there are no reputations, and no trouble-makers.' You do find, he said, that a man you sent off last time may not be too pleased to see you. He had Best again the other week and they didn't exchange a word. 'Mind you, if we met in the street I don't suppose he'd want to speak to me, but then I wouldn't particularly want to speak to him.'

A referee's deepest dread is of having a bad game, of that chill moment when he feels it slipping away from him and knows there is nothing he can do to hold it. On such a day Burtenshaw may come home, throw down his case in the hall, and say, like yesterday's drunk, 'That's it. I've finished. Never again.' A patient family lives through those times and waits for Saturday and the adrenalin to start pumping again.

'It always does, you see Spain v Russia or Workington v Hartlepool. With some you reach your peak more easily than with others, that's all. I have to be on edge, tensed up, before I can do the job properly. Wembley helps, of course, because of the atmosphere, but in any dressing room I'm jigging about, doing deep breathing, talking too much.

'I have to have new laces, rub embrocation in my legs. I don't know if it does any good, but I have to do it. Part of the ritual. And all the time those butterflies are flapping down there until I can hardly wait to get out. Just talking about it has done it, look, I'm almost trembling. I could go right out there and referee a heck of a match, I really could.'

Yesterday's game gave Burtenshaw a rare Wembley hat-trick, with the Amateur Cup Final in 1966, and the FA Cup Final last year. Next season he hits the League's arbitrary age barrier of 47 and must remove himself from the action. 'I don't know how I'll get on,' he says. 'I'm still fit, d'you see, and a better referee than I was 10 years ago. I just don't know how I'll get on without it.' And he shakes his head slowly at the carpet, momentarily shattered by the sadness of the thought.

That magnificent line of his flashes into mind, when he was dropped from the international list for a year: 'Well, Mr Burtenshaw,' the chirpy reporter asked, 'how do you feel?' 'As if my legs had been cut off.'

5 March 1972   *David Hunn*

As a former referee himself Denis Howell commended the stricter disciplinary code introduced in 1972 and requested stronger support for referees so that they be regarded as 'sole judges of fact' off the field as well as on.

Who Would Be a Referee?

The football season started on a note of high controversy about the new disciplinary code. It is a remarkable situation that it seems to be ending on a note of apprehension lest the real gains that it has brought to football should be lost because of a weakening of resolve by referees to see the new code through to the end.

Very few people in the game can now be found to dispute the benefits that firmer refereeing has brought both to the playing of the game and to its spectacle as a sport. The footballer has come back into his own, as that astute manager Tony Waddington of Stoke appreciated and as a result of which he telegraphed an invitation to George Eastham to return home at once.

Eastham is an interesting case. He likes to hold the ball, to work it across the field, and to split defences by an intelligent appreciation of the situation and an ability to pass the ball accurately. He now has the time to do all these things. He does not have to fear the clogger or the foul tackle from behind. Last season it would have been possible to find plenty of players with instructions to 'play him out of the game' and with little doubt as to the meaning of such instructions.

This season players soon learned that bringing down a player from behind, or deliberately impeding his progress by obstruction, or stopping him head-on by going over the top of the ball not only brought a foul but also a certain caution if not dismissal from the field.

237

It is interesting to note that Stoke City have won the Football League Cup and reached the last four in the F A Cup. Other footballing teams have also had a good season. Perhaps more important, tougher teams who have enjoyed success with regular consistency have now found themselves struggling. They are having to change their whole style of play and a good thing too.

The most important benefits that have emerged flow from the re-established authority of the referee.

In spite of some criticism the football authorities have made a special point of trying to end the so-called 'professional' foul. The attempt to stop a goal being scored by any means. Many critics find an inconsistency when the full-back is cautioned for punching the ball over the crossbar in order to save a certain goal when they believe more serious fouls do not automatically bring a caution. However, there can be little doubt that rarely can there be a more dishonest action than to prevent a goal in such a blatant manner.

The result of this crusade has been much to the liking of the spectators. Play has become more flowing and entertaining. Stoppages are less frequent. The players have got on with the game, and as a result attendances have gone up. Interestingly, hooliganism on the terraces also seems to have declined.

However, in recent weeks louts have begun to creep in. Some of the over-strenuous tackling now shows signs of re-emerging. Players who were automatically accepting referees' decisions a few weeks ago now appear readier to argue with him.

There may be one or two reasons for these late-season developments. The tremendous tensions produced by the promotion and relegation struggle appear to be more intense this year and are bound to be reflected in conduct on the field. Associated with this are the huge bonuses for which players are competing at this time of the year.

More important even than the tensions is the feeling of being 'let down' which many referees have towards F A disciplinary commissions. The laws of the game state quite clearly that the referee is the 'sole judge of fact' on the football field. Referees believe that this should mean that their decisions on the field are automatically accepted by the disciplinary authority. This has not happened. These tribunals feel it is right to conduct an inquiry into the facts which the referee has already established.

There has even been one case this season where an independent assessor (one of whom is now appointed by the Football League for every match in order to give an independent report on the referee) was called to give evidence in support of the referee but still the player's case was upheld. Since these inquiries are conducted in private it is difficult to pass judgment upon them. Perhaps it would help to restore confidence if their proceedings were public as is the case in most other fields where discipline is administered.

Then there is an inconsistency about punishments. In particular, the growing practice of some of these commissions in deciding that a caution was 'justified' but that 'it will not count in the total of three cautions which bring automatic suspension'. No referee can understand the illogicality of such thinking.

Overall the gains have outweighed the disadvantages. If the F A face up to the problems that their commissions are creating and the disciplinary committee can be made to face these realities by their colleagues on the referees committee, then these disputes can be ironed out. The Football League will undoubtedly strive to ensure that the application of their new code is persisted with next season and pursued throughout the whole of the season. They believe they have achieved a great deal but they know they can only maintain these improvements to the game by a policy of eternal vigilance.

16 April 1972   *Denis Howell*

CHAPTER 6

Occasional Pieces and Unusual Aspects

A variety of Observer *writers contributed articles on interesting or unusual facets of the game. Terry O'Neill interviewed Elizabeth Taylor for her views on the pressures of top football and why these had affected George Best.*

What I'd tell Best, by Mrs Burton

Next Saturday, if you find yourself sitting next to a black-haired beautiful woman with violet eyes who's giving Charlie George a volley, don't chat her up. She's married. Her name is Elizabeth Taylor.

Talk to her about football or rugby if you like – she finds them fascinating. 'I think they're terribly exciting games and I get totally caught up in the side I'm rooting for. I just abandon myself to the game and forget everything. I scream and yell, shout and bawl, I love the atmosphere of the crowds.'

She thinks football has poetry and beautiful movements, but feels she is not an authority on it. 'I'm still a novice. I prefer rugby,' she says. 'I can follow it easier because it's more like American football, which I grew up on.

'In rugby I enjoy the violence, except when they start biting one another's ears off. I can't stand watching a boxing match, though – I hate that type of violence, two men punching each other and blinding each other and sometimes killing each other for sport. It's like watching a cockfight.

'I was fascinated and felt rather sorry for George Best when he went through all his traumas. Fame came to him when he was *so* young. I've seen it happen to so many young people in the film business. The pressure one gets is enormous, and I wonder if the managers and, indeed, his critics, understand the pressure of the emotional strain he must have been going through.

'It's a hell of a thing for a lad from his background, of his educational standard, whose life was just football. To become an international name, to have girls chasing after him as if he was a pop star or something . . . it takes a miracle not to become confused.

'What would drive me mad is to have, say, the producer or director tell me where I was going to live. To treat him like a juvenile delinquent, it would seem to me, would just cause an inner rebellion. They say they can't mollycoddle him just because he's George Best; that he's a player, he's no different from anybody else.

'But they've made him different. They've made him a special kind of hero. He draws in the crowds and the management haven't minded, have they? So they should try to undersand his emotional problems a little better and not treat him like a 10-year-old. He might respond to that kind of treatment instead of being treated like an idiot kid who runs away from school and needs to have his fingers slapped.

'For some reason George Best ended up in the pop world, and I don't think he asked for it. I think he went along with it at a young age, unknowingly. I feel very sorry for him.

'At one point, when he was thinking of quitting and he didn't know where to go or who to look to, Richard and I almost sent him a letter to say, "If you feel like getting away from it all, would you like to come and stay with us, a couple of old pros in the art of getting away?"

'But we thought maybe he'd think we were nuts and it would be an imposition. He's obviously very vulnerable, and I think a lot of his bravado is covering up a deep shyness. Overnight stardom is a bloody difficult thing to cope with.'

The advice she would have given him was excellent. 'First of all, I would have told him that he's not alone and it's happened to a lot of people. It would seem to me that at the time he was going through a period of panic and he wanted to escape. But one thing you can't do is escape from yourself – you just have to sit down and accept yourself for what you really are, take stock of the people around you and decide who are your true friends and who are hangers-on, find out the con-artists, and listen to the people who are genuinely concerned, even though they may not agree with everything you think is right.

'God knows, Richard and I have been through some pressure, and we've survived. If he can "use" his problems, it will make him stronger. I hope

241

that he never becomes cynical and bitter and I hope that he never passes the buck and feels wronged, though I think he has been wronged by a lot of people. But that's part of learning to take it head on; don't flinch or run away from it. Some people grow up scarred, some don't.

'I just hope he hasn't been too badly hurt. He's trying, and people have got to give him every break he deserves. I think he's a genius player, and he's starting to play well again this season.

'I've been in the limelight, well, since I was 12, and I've never taken anything for granted. You have to realise you're no different from anybody else, because everyone is telling you that you are special and you're not. No one is special. We do special things, but underneath we're basically the same.

'The onslaught of fame can turn you inside out, and you don't have time to grow up with it and prepare for it. That's probably what put George Best out of his stride. That's what makes people behave like that and do things that are outrageous.'

I wondered if she thought women found him attractive on the field. 'I don't know *what* they would think. There's a time and place for everything,' she said, doing an impersonation of Dame Edith Evans, 'and it's not on the football field.'

I left thinking what a great combination Elizabeth Taylor would make as a manager in tandem with a man with the coaching ability of Malcolm Allison. After all, Clough has *his* Taylor (assistant manager Peter), so why shouldn't Allison? They wouldn't have to worry about the crowds falling off, either.

1 October 1972   *Terry O'Neill*

Michael Davie was intrigued by the aseptic atmosphere of Russian football as he watched Arsenal lose in Moscow in the fifties.

Arsenal in Moscow

'You may care to try some of this sucking pig.' – Mr Ralph Parker, formerly of *The Times*, and now the *Daily Worker*, resident correspondent in Moscow, offered, plump and beaming, a dish to the Arsenal inside-right.

From either side of two long buffet tables in the Hotel National, Red Square, the hands of Arsenal and Moscow Dynamo players, British journalists and unidentified Russians and their wives stretched out for smoked salmon or bottles of apple juice. The reception given last week by the Committee for Physical Culture and All Sports was in full swing.

When supper was over a small orchestra played 'Alexander's Ragtime Band'. Couples danced, the Arsenal players cautiously unwrapped presents of painted black lacquer boxes, ladies with Dynamo players examined the Arsenal ties and shields presented reciprocally, and Sir Stanley Rous, Secretary of the Football Association, demonstrated to a Russian some dinner-table balancing tricks.

Mr Parker circulated with a match programme gathering signatures for auction at a *Daily Worker* bazaar. 'I believe the newspapers in London are taking the line that yesterday's match was not a victory for the Dynamos but a victory for friendship,' he said.

Outside the hotel, across a great square glistening under rain, the Kremlin was unlit except for the constant dull glow of neon Red Stars on top of its towers.

Later, on the stairs of the same hotel, in clerical collar and dark suit, there was a Chinese clergyman.

It has been a bizarre week and it is hard for a reporter to know where to start. But any report should indicate the reaction of the Arsenal players to what one of them described as 'our mystery tour'.

The Arsenal have not been overawed. For instance, there was Lawton at Minsk. The first plane-load of players and journalists had waited an hour and a half for the other plane-load. We sat in the Hall of Intourist at the air terminal talking spasmodically to a youngish Russian who spoke English fluently, and to two Army officers.

'Where is your great Lawton?' they asked.

'In the other aircraft,' we replied. Then Lawton appeared, a tall man with gleaming neat black hair. Lawton described his experiences. 'I'm not kidding,' he said, 'we've been in five countries since Prague. We've been round Everest and I don't know how Tensing climbed it. We've been to Moscow twice but we couldn't get across the river. And we were in the salt mines! They gave us swords. You slice the salt this way and that into blocks, then you pick a block up and hold it above your head and stagger up a big ladder.'

The Russians were at first clearly surprised, but later all went well in the cause of Anglo-Soviet friendship. Then there was Lawton in Moscow. In the bus coming back from the Dynamo Stadium after the match, our agreeable interpreter told the team about a tour of the Kremlin the next day.

'May we visit the tomb of Lenin and Comrade Stalin?' someone asked. 'Unfortunately no.' The tomb was being repaired.

Lawton leaned over, '*You* can get us into the mausoleum!' he said. He put his arm round the Russian's shoulder. 'Round the back!'

Even before this visit, Lawton had a Russian reputation. An Englishman in Baku was puzzled lately by a worker who repeatedly asked: ''Ow is Lowton?' The small male group, their black caps on the backs of their heads, who waited to see the Arsenal arrive at the Dynamo Stadium for their initial practice recognised him, muttered his name, and pointed him out to one another.

Not only the Arsenal players but the whole English 'delegation' seemed to be welcome last week, and not only to their official hosts. The crowd at the match was varied, as if County Kerry had mingled with Drury Lane. Many of the uniforms were splendid. But, uniforms or not, people recognising an Englishman tried out one or two words of English.

One giant in uniform came up and said twice, 'English, English,' shook hands and then went away again, apparently very pleased. I sat among the crowd, not in the Press box, and when the Dynamos scored their fourth and fifth goals people in front turned round and consoled me.

Our section of the crowd did not whistle. But the whistling from the popular section was ear-splitting, especially at the end of the match. Occasionally people clapped. They very rarely shouted. There was much less *rapport* between the crowd and players than there is at, say, Highbury.

Once, at the beginning of the game, the Czechoslovak referee whistled for a foul and Tapscott, the Arsenal right-wing, threw up his hands in a gesture which at Highbury would have instantly brought him down a universal roar. Here, all that happened was that a Dynamo player patted him on the shoulder.

Compared with an English League game, Arsenal v Moscow Dynamos was curiously aseptic. Afterwards I went into the Dynamo dressing-room, an unsurprising room under the stands. There was a table in the middle covered with apples, grapes, glasses of tea, bottles of fruit juice and sweets. Russian cameramen had rigged strong lights. A small boy in a black cap gazed in devotion through the windows. Photographs were taken. But the Dynamo players seemed neither exhausted nor elated. Several of them were dressed before the Arsenal players down the passage had got into the bathroom.

There were two other notable things about the match. First, a record of Paul Robeson singing 'St Louis Blues' over the loud-speakers – the Russians apparently like jazz. Secondly, the smell Tolstoy wrote of the 'delicious acrid smell' of the Russian people. But the post-Revolutionary Russian does not smell acrid but sweet – the jammed crowd at the Dynamo

Stadium had a light, perfumed smell, almost like incense, almost like oil fuel. This is the smell you notice everywhere in Moscow. I am told that it is the smell of all Russia.

10 October 1953   *Michael Davie*

In another fifties Sporting Print Alan Ross took comfort from Joe Hulme's book on How to Play Soccer.

How to Play

There is always something both comforting and vaguely comic about books with titles like *How to Win at Chess*, or *How to Play Cricket* or hockey, or whatever you like. It conjures up visions of some fiendish and bespectacled intellectual, text-book in hand, word-perfect, advancing confidently on to the field and surveying with calm superciliousness the crude oafs around him.

He can, of course, carry it off by sheer cunning, on the Gamesmanship pattern; but more likely he will become a *divertissement* in the Charlie Chaplin manner. He will attempt, shall we say, a leg glance, most cultured of strokes, yet the ball, no reader of text-books, will hit the edge of his bat and pop ungracefully up towards the slips. Of course, it will be the text-book's fault.

Yet this divergence between the attempted and the actual is one of the most comforting things to the spectator; one of the most comic, too, for did not the great French philosopher Bergson, in his Study of Laughter, put forward the idea that what is funny about a fat man falling on a banana skin is his fond belief that, at the moment we see him sprawled on the ground, he is still walking pompously along.

In professionals, however, we do not care for too much deviation from the classic. We wish performances at Lord's or White Hart-lane or Thurston's or Twickenham to conform as nearly as possible to what the text-book has led us to hope for. When we are young they really seem to; and we rightly carry these memories of perfection with protected awe through life.

But, alas, the more we see of the best players at work (for work is what it is these days), the more do we grow aware of their fallibilities. It is nothing unusual to see a slip-catch dropped in a Test match, of the kind that would earn a small boy at his preparatory school a sharp cuff, or to see a corner-kick put behind the goal in a football international, a crime usually rewarded by expulsion amongst well-bred adolescents. Yet we learn to put up with these frailties, even enjoying them, for if we no longer look with awe, we give to our sporting heroes a more tolerant human interest.

This may seem a long way to get round to Mr Joe Hulme's *How to Play Soccer* (Eyre and Spottiswoode, 9s. 6d.); but the great virtue of his book, a rare one, is that he combines instruction with readability. When he explains a common fault, he remembers how X, playing for Chelsea or England, made just such a mistake. That is good for morale. So, too, is the way in which, going through every position in the field, he contrives to make each in turn seem the most important.

No student, of whatever grade, will in fact find *How to Play Soccer* without comfort, encouragement, or stern technical value. It may not enable the literary critic, the balletomane, or the ship's doctor, simply by digesting its lessons, to expect an immediate contract with Tottenham Hotspur; but it will at any rate greatly increase their pleasure, both aesthetically and tactically, if they should happen to watch them play.

16 November 1952   *Alan Ross*

In a 1956 Sporting Print Geoffrey Wagner took a look at Soccer in New York.

Soccer in New York

'Roll, booters, r-o-o-o-l-l-l!' The yellow sweatered cheer-leaders, half-a-dozen girls with hour-glass figures, leapt into the air, spread wide their short-skirted legs to the roar from the bleachers, and came down into a crouch on the turf.

I sat on the bench with the team, scratching my head. According to my time-keeper, the end of the third quarter was due to be blown and we were in the lead. Should I call my first line out and rest them for a last ten minutes' spurt. Or should I switch my men on defence?

'Hey, coach, what say we quit goofing,' said a husky full-back on my left. 'These guys are fast-breaking us in mid-field.'

'Yeh, send Johnny in, coach,' came a chorus as the ball swung in a curling lob dangerously close to our goal-line. So when it next went into touch I bowed to demos and waved my hand to the near-side umpire for the substitution. Johnny trotted out.

Notre Dame versus The Army? American football? Not at all. A routine association football game in upper New York State and I was acting as coach to one of the teams.

Flattered as I had been to be invited to coach the soccer team of the American university where I was teaching, on the basis of a mere year in the Oxford side, I soon found out I had a lot to learn about the mechanics of my new position. American soccer is played in four quarters. The teams usually consist of about twenty players, since substitutions are not only allowed, but actively encouraged. I never travelled away with fewer than eighteen men. Equally essential are a time-keeper, a first-aid man with a large kit including stiff restoratives for the team (no half-time lemons for them), and a well-fed cheering section. Two referees (umpires) are provided per game, one watching each half as in hockey, and at least four linesmen.

It is probably well-known that the world's favourite sport has never caught on much in America, despite all the publicity on its behalf (including a sponsored contest between dwarfs at the Yankee Stadium) by the United States Soccer Football Association. However, it does make an excellent sport on the college level chiefly for those athletic types not possessing enough 'brute strength and ignorance' to make the football team. There are now soccer teams in all the major colleges and universities in the country.

However, 'It's hard to interest American kids in a sport in which they can't use their hands.' No Englishman can help noticing the extreme facility with which young Americans take up basketball, in contrast to their clumsy attempts to play soccer (although the goalies are usually excellent). Indeed, I used constantly to exhort my teams to watch the enviably dexterous manner in which basketball players move into unmarked positions for the ball.

The other week I watched the final of the College Metropolitan Championship of New York between Hunter and City colleges. Each team played the roving centre-half game and, since the kicking ability was pretty good, it made for a pleasantly old-fashioned and open game, with quick switches in attack and defence. However, neither side as a whole had much ball control; both would have been beaten, in my opinion, by a strong public school eleven at the height of its season. Yet on either side there were one or two players as good as, say, the average Oxford University Centaur, and these, I learnt without surprise, were recent immigrants.

It was the same when I played for one (unforgettable) season for a mainly German side in the American League. The standard of this kind of soccer was reasonably high, the marking system European. There were certainly two defensive players in my own team who could have played in Third Division soccer in England. These men are usually professionals, devoted to the game, and receiving about 10 to 20 dollars per match. When joined in an all-American side they might make a tolerably formidable lot.

All in all, soccer is likely to remain a college sport in the States, where in winter semesters the booters now hold honourable place beside the hoopsters (basketball players), matmen (wrestlers), and others. It is certainly an admirable addition to any American college hygiene, or athletic department's curriculum. It tests a boy's courage in a way basketball, widely boosted chiefly because it is such a comfortable spectator sport, does not. And as regards personal courage, the American students I coached were brimful of it. It was true that they seemed noticeably more brittle than English boys, but I never saw a college boy funk a hard tackle; indeed, they chafed at the umpires who are now rapidly 'sissifying' soccer in the States by penalising players for the very slightest roughness.

As I watched Johnny trot out to take up the inside-left position among my tiring forwards, I could not help reflecting that though the idiom of the admonitions from the crowd might be different from those heard at Iffley Road, the spirit was the same – including that of the cigar-chewing gent who shouted out, as my player went into his first charge, 'Ring 'is chimes, Johnny boy!'

January 1956   *Geoffrey Wagner*

In May 1959 Clement Freud looked back at the ambience of his football reporting season.

248

Press-box Imprint

Another football season is over and until next August I shall miss the Press-boxes up and down the country, from Newcastle where you sit in a glass-built afterthought on the top of a stand better suited to assessing players' dandruff than football technique, to Yeovil where I was placed on a small wooden bench in the front of the stand, and the word 'Press' chalked on its seat travelled all the way back to London on mine.

During the last season I have been locked into most First Division grounds in England, for by the time that I finish 'phoning through my match report, I am invariably the only person left in the place; there was one exception, Chelsea, where greyhound racing takes over on Saturday evenings and I was able to have a bet on a dog called Chinar Wagtail while finishing my copy,

I shall miss the friendly man who dispenses whisky at Leicester's Filbert Street – not the one who bars my entry into the tea-room at West Bromwich before the match ('At half-time and after the match, them's my orders'), nor the one responsible for never getting me a seat in the Press-box at West Ham ('*The Observer*, what's that, a local rag?').

I shall think nostalgically of the Arsenal box where the front row receives the raindrops from the roof and is only to be entertained in fine weather; of a Midland club where a wildly inaccurate closed circuit broadcast to hospitals is made from the Press-stand by local benefactors throughout the game, and a pleasant woman dispenses barley-sugar to visiting journalists by way of compensation. The efficiency and hospitality of Manchester United, the discrimination at Nottingham Forest ('I'm so sorry, I thought you were Mr Hackett, you'll have to go into that little room over there').

Saturday mornings at Paddington, Euston or King's Cross, wondering who else is going to be on the train. British Railways restaurant cars . . . and the consoling thought that if, as the result of a meal, anything happens to you, the entire Tottenham Hotspur team at the next tables will have it happen to them, too. And then your colleagues, those dear, kindly, hard-bitten, sober men, who seldom seem to watch the game at crucial moments, such as when a goal is scored; and keep a mystic minute-by-minute record of the match ('I make that goal 23 minutes . . . I make it more like 28 . . . 26 . . . 25 . . .') and then those who burst into the Press-box trying to glean players' Christian names: 'Higgs took a corner' is only four words towards the 300 words required, while 'Peter George Henry Higgs took a corner' contributes seven towards that total.

After the match, in the Press-room, it is, for me, almost impossible not to listen to the others' reports being 'phoned through. As I write: 'Matthews's form must make him at the age of forty-three a serious contender for . . .' I hear a man shouting into a black plastic mouthpiece: 'Is the old maestro done question-mark, I say No full-point, does the old maestro let up question-mark, I say not on your nelly full-point.'

I remember that this is a man whose reports every Sunday are read by the numbers who read mine in two months and I recall my sub-editor, that hatchet-faced guardian of propriety, who on four occasions this year, when a match of mine had produced no score after forty-five minutes, has changed my 'At half-time the game's virginity was still intact' to 'There was no score at half-time.'

3 May 1959   *Clement Freud*

Chris Brasher organised an Observer *challenge to the old transfer arrangements and helped the players to win freedom from a system of contracts which was known by the authorities to be convenient, but illegal. After a heated debate between players and officials on 'Panorama', Brasher arranged for a Q C's opinion to be published. Its impact was such that the FA and League banded together to make instant reply. Brasher fired the first shot in this article.*

Wanted: A Guinea-Pig

Hardly was the ink dry on our article last week entitled 'Youth and Age in Open Conflict', before the young and the old clashed on 'Panorama' on Monday night.

The footballers represented by Mr Danny Blanchflower and Mr Jimmy Hill (Chairman of the Professional Footballers' Association) seem to have got the better of their argument with Mr Joe Richards (Chairman of the Football League) and Mr George Swindin, ex-Arsenal player and now that team's manager (who deftly sat on the fence). Certainly the Football League Secretary, Mr Alan Hardaker, thought that the footballers had won the argument judging by the petulant remarks which he issued on Wednesday.

Mr Hardaker said that the two players' harsh comments (on the League system of wages, players' contracts and transfers) were 'a poor return for the efforts towards improving the status of footballers during the past year'. Mr Hardaker went on: 'It was a pity that Mr Richards was not allowed an opportunity during the debate of replying more fully to these one-sided comments.'

We would like to remind Mr Hardaker that this was an open discussion and that no amount of protestation by him in support of his chairman will alter the impression of millions of viewers that the footballers have a very good case.

Mr Blanchflower referred to footballers as 'slaves' – a harsh word that is liable to make any discussion heated. We prefer to say that there are restrictive practices embodied in the Football Association Rules.

The chief source of disquiet is that a player's contract can be renewed or terminated annually at the option of the club; but the player, for his part, cannot terminate the contract. A player may refuse to play for the club to whom he is under contract; in that case the club may retain him on its books while at the same time denying him the right (should the club withhold its consent) to sign for any other club in Great Britain or abroad.

All the club is required to do is to pay the player a reduced retaining wage of £418 a year and have the approval of the Football Association that the contract offered to the player is a reasonable one.

After the Panorama argument some of the Press (notably the *Daily Express*) pooh-poohed the idea that players' conditions were contracts of slavery, arguing that they lived in the lap of luxury.

'But benevolence in operation, although it may mitigate the effect, cannot remove the evil of tyranny,' as Mr Justice Lloyd Jacob said recently in a case involving an employee's freedom of choice of employment.

Certainly the present footballer's contract, however benevolent in its cash payments, imposes oppressive conditions which restrict a footballer's freedom to follow his chosen profession.

What would happen if these conditions of employment were applied to the profession of Mr Desmond Hackett, the *Daily Express* columnist who protested that Messrs Hill and Blanchflower were talking rubbish?

Having signed a contract with his newspaper at an early age (at a salary fixed by an outside body and binding on all columnists, whatever their worth) he finds after some years that the *Express* are so pleased with him that they offer him a Christmas bonus. But if he, as a professional, accepted this money, both he and the newspaper would be suspended.

At a later stage he finds that he no longer agrees with their editorial policy, and decides that he would like to change newspapers. But now what happens?

The *Express*, unwilling to lose his services (as we are sure they would be),

251

put a high transfer fee on him: a higher fee than any other newspaper is prepared to pay.

If Mr Hackett persists with his disagreement his employers would be entitled to demote him to the reserves – whatever that might mean on that paper – and cut his salary. Alternatively they could prevent him from writing merely by paying him a retaining wage of £418 per year, or transfer him to some obscure Fourth Division newspaper. It can be a cold job writing for the *Orkney Beacon*, Mr Hackett.

It is not difficult to apply these conditions to one's own chosen profession and realise how unacceptable they are.

We believe that no amount of argument can produce a solution to the problem of these contracts. The footballers' only ally is the Law.

Twice in recent years footballers' contracts have been the subject of comment in the courts. In a case against Airdrieonians FC, a Sheriff in a Scottish court had some harsh things to say about the terms of the player's contract.

What is needed is a precise ruling by the High Court whether the contract is in fact valid for all footballers, and in particular for those footballers under the age of 21. The sooner a footballer offers himself as a guinea-pig to court proceedings the better for the whole game.

11 January 1959   *Christopher Brasher*

Following this, The Observer *commissioned and published a Q C's opinion with Arthur Drewry and Joe Richards responding for the F A and the League.*

Q C's Opinion on
Soccer Contracts

This column has constantly campaigned for a new deal in sport. Nowhere is this new deal more necessary than in Association Football – our national game. It was for this reason that we asked a prominent Queen's Counsel to give us his opinion on the legality of the standard contract which every professional footballer must sign in order to follow his chosen profession . . . and his opinion – reported on Page One – is that the contract is not legally enforceable.

We believe that the administrators themselves will be concerned at this and in particular with the concluding sentence of the opinion. 'In recent years the American courts have, to my knowledge, broken up restrictive practices in American football, baseball and boxing promotion. It seems to me that unless football administration is more equitably operated for all those concerned in the sport, it will be necessary to apply our type of antimonopoly legislation to fields of sports.'

We have taken this particular case as far as a newspaper can. Now it is up to the Professional Footballers' Association and the Football League and Association to work out a solution.

22 February 1959   *Christopher Brasher*

The F A and League Reply

From the Chairman of the Football Association and the President of the Football League

Sir, – In reply to the article 'Q C's Opinion on Soccer Contracts', which appeared in last Sunday's *Observer*, we, the undersigned, think your readers should know that the Football Association and the Football League have always understood that the agreement between a club and a professional footballer is not enforceable by law.

The effect of the written agreement of the professional player is to create a 'Contract of Service', or lay down the conditions of employment. The professional player is a 'workman' within the meaning of the Workmen's Compensation Acts, and in practice, professional clubs invariably insure against liabilities for injuries or loss of service in respect of professional players. The clubs in the Football League have decided on a basic maximum salary which has been raised from time to time (and is now £20 per week).

The fact that a professional in League football cannot be paid more than this agreed salary does not mean that he cannot play professional football elsewhere. If, however, he agrees to play in the Football League, then he agrees to accept the conditions of employment with a League club.

The rules of most clubs and leagues make provision for the payment of a 'benefit' to professional players after a certain period of service. This is not provided for in the player's contract of service; nor is the provident fund, by which a player is paid a sum equal to 8 per cent of his total earnings when he reaches the age of 35 and finishes his League football.

The Football Association and the Football League feel that they should bring to your notice the progress which has been made to safeguard the welfare of the players, namely:-

(a) the formation of a joint standing committee;

(b) the inception of the provident scheme;

(c) the increase in international players' fees and insurance cover; payment of television fees;

(d) the opportunities for many players – there are over 200 on the present panel – to earn extra money as Football Association coaches in this country and abroad;

(e) the organisation of vocational courses to fit players for careers and employment after their playing days are over.

It is also pointed out that the Football League has introduced certain regulations relating to Retention and Open-to-Transfer registration lists in order to prevent either the club or player being victimised; that players whose registrations are not placed on either of these two lists are free to sign for any other club; that registrations of players whose clubs refuse to re-engage them at wages as specified can be placed on the Open-to-Transfer list, and that it is open to any player whose registration is included therein to apply for a reduced transfer at any time.

The League transfer system is not an instrument of the buying and selling of players but is a plan to protect the weaker clubs, to stifle poaching and approaches, to create a working basis for clubs, to raise the status of the player and to ensure him receiving pay during the summer, thus giving the feeling of permanence to both club and player, which is most important where there is a staff of professional players and a team-building plan. Then, too, the League's provident scheme emphasises this feeling of permanence.

Any player who wishes to become a professional player is at liberty to refuse to sign the 'contract of service', but even if he does sign the contract, it can be terminated by mutual consent. Clubs are bound by this contract, but many players during the period of the contract have, of their own volition, left League football, to take up other occupation. Never has a club sought to compel such players to fulfil the full terms of the agreement.

ARTHUR DREWRY,
Chairman of the Football Association,

J. RICHARDS,
President of the Football League.

1 March 1959

The man who was shortly to be the first £100,000 player in British football was understandably concerned at being paid a mere thousand pounds a year. In discussion with Michael Moynihan, Jimmy Greaves gave the players' view, which fortunately prevailed enough for the threatened strike to be averted.

'What I want is Security'

A goal more problematical than any he is likely to face this season lies shadowily ahead for Jimmy Greaves, possibly the brightest young star of English soccer.

Recently he became the youngest 100-goal man in League history. Playing inside-forward for England, he scored eight goals in four games. Already one of the greatest crowd-pullers in the game, he is 21 next month.

'But I've got to look to the future. I'd be a fool if I didn't want to make as much money as I can while I can. Football's all I'm good at. What I want's a feeling of security for when I retire.'

Jimmy is talking in the spacious sitting-room of 'Chelsea', the pleasant semi-detached house in Hornchurch, Essex, which is home so long as he remains a member of the Football Club of that name.

He is standing goalie in front of a blazing log fire, warding off attempts by his two-year-old daughter Lynn to infiltrate between his legs. Irene, his pretty blonde wife and most critical fan, has half an eye on the telly.

'There are these reports that Bologna would pay £70,000 to Chelsea for me if the foreign-player ban ever came off,' says slim, 10-stone Jimmy, who is at present earning £20 a week for his scintillating performances at inside-right. 'One report said that would mean I'd collect a £20,000 signing-on fee. Mr Mears, the chairman, knows more about all that than I do. It's all right playing for Chelsea. But of course I'd like much better playing for a world-class club that paid real money.'

Lynn, sturdy and grimy-kneed, makes a dash for the french windows where Jimmy's Christmas present to his wife, a massive, nine-month-old St Bernard, is gazing in.

Jimmy, who was taught the rudiments of soccer at the age of four by his father, an underground train driver on the Central Line, has been to 19 countries. He is not blasé about it. And he shrugs off a reputation of being the life and soul of his party off-field, the ice-cold tactician on.

'One thing, I never get butterflies before a match,' Jimmy goes on. 'And after, if I've done well or badly, I always remember there's a next time. Smoking helps me relax. About ten a day, but they don't affect my fitness. I like the odd drink, too.'

Spectators as well as players have been dazzled by the speed with which Jimmy can trap a fast ball, swivel and kick. 'There are some things you can't get from practice. You might say you're born with them. I don't think about my movements when I'm playing.'

Jimmy was 'discovered' when a Dagenham schoolboy of twelve by scout Jimmy Thompson. After leaving school he worked a spell in a publishers. 'I could have got a job on *The Times* as a printer's apprentice. But I knew it had to be football.'

Football is very much part of his wife's life, too. She understands its finer points and gives praise sparingly.

Nowadays she contents herself with tennis, which they play together every Sunday at the local club. On Saturday nights Jimmy likes just to flop in front of the telly or to listen to Sinatra on the stereophonic player. And to play with Lynn.

Lynn is too young to mourn Jimmy, her baby brother, who died in his cot from a bronchial attack on 9 October. That was the day England beat Spain at Wembley, with Jimmy Greaves scoring the first goal in the first minute.

'Football's a profession like any other,' says Jimmy now, glancing across at the row of cups and badges under a large reproduction of the Mona Lisa. 'Except it doesn't last so long. What have I got – ten years? And then what? Of course, playing for England in the World Cup's my big ambition. But if any foreign club offered me a place so I could put good money aside I'd be a fool not to jump at it. I'll be loyal to any team that's loyal to me. Nobody wants to strike. But it's high time there was better pay and prospects all round.'

Lynn has trundled to the kitchen to help feed Bruno. The white kitten they found abandoned in the coal-shed frisks on the hearthrug. Firelight reflects from the Christmas tree baubles.

Even with that gap among the snapshot enlargements on the radiogram it is a cosy family circle. 'Chelsea' would be a perfect home – if only it were theirs.

8 January 1961   *Michael Moynihan*

The man who got Jimmy Greaves what he wanted was profiled in The Observer.

Jimmy Hill

The long wrangle in football has ended peacefully, with the players wringing more concessions from the Football League clubs than anyone would have thought possible. They have won freedom to negotiate wages, and have begun to unshackle the retain-and-transfer system. They have won because from their own ranks they produced a leader: Jimmy Hill, chairman of the Professional Footballers' Association.

In the last few weeks Jimmy Hill and his beard have become one of the most familiar sights on television. He has seemed a mild enough character despite the Tommy Trinder chin waggling up and down as he makes his points.

He has never thumped the table, never been vitriolic about his opponents, always insisted that the decisions rested with the players and not with him. Yet through a complicated series of negotiations he has never put a foot wrong.

At the age of thirty-two he has led a group of young sportsmen – average age about twenty-five – against a much older and smaller group of employers: the club chairmen must average well over fifty-five. He has had the impossible task of keeping all his 3,000 scattered Association members speaking unanimously and aware of exactly what terms they were being offered.

Individual and collective rebellions broke out here and there, but whenever Jimmy Hill appeared on the scene to relate the history of the negotiations and take the players point by point through the proposals, the rebellions died and the vote was virtually unanimous. If Hill could have met every one of his members personally, he would have been fighting for moderation.

He always wanted to be a professional footballer. When he won a scholarship from his elementary school in Balham at the age of eleven, he decided to go to the same grammar school as his boyhood hero, a previous captain of the school football team. He spent the war years sleeping in an Anderson shelter in the garden ('six of us regularly, sometimes even eight'); playing games whenever he could, soccer in the winter, cricket in the summer.

At school the ambition to be a professional footballer left him: 'It wasn't the sort of thing you do if you are a grammar school boy. You're destined for bigger things – a doctor, an accountant, an engineer, not a professional footballer.'

He matriculted, left school, and went into an insurance office, but left after a year. Then he joined a firm of stockbrokers and found it much more to his liking. 'You could either do the job or you couldn't, no messing around. I hate wasting time.'

He was called up, and it was while playing for his Army unit that he was spotted by Ted Drake, then manager of Reading, now manager of Chelsea, who offered him a trial for a professional job at Reading.

After his demob the stockbrokers said he could have his job back, but with the Labour Government in power things were pretty quiet and there didn't seem much future for him. Hill had lost a cartilage while in the Army, so he thought he'd go up to Reading and train with the team to get his knee fit.

He was looking around for a job in a desultory way, thinking vaguely of training as a teacher and playing for Reading as an amateur, when he realised that Drake wasn't going to offer him a job as a professional. 'I thought, "Blimey, he doesn't think I'm good enough." And that really riled me. I wanted to be a professional again.' Drake introduced him to Jack Gibbons, the new manager of Brentford, and Gibbons signed him for the 1949/50 season, when Hill was twenty-one, at £7 per week in winter and £6 in summer.

Gradually he built up a reputation as a wing-half until in March, 1952, he was transferred to Fulham in exchange for a player valued at £20,000, plus £5,000. So the twenty-three-year-old Hill, still earning under £15 a week, was valued at £25,000.

At Brentford, Hill had been the Players' Union representative (some years later the name was changed to the Professional Footballers' Association), mainly because he had had clerical experience and was interested in status and conditions. Within a few months of moving to Fulham he had taken over the same job there.

He is desperately envious of the ability of such players as Johnny Haynes and Stanley Matthews, and he has tried to make up for his lack of finesse and high skill by energy and enthusiasm. But he is a useful type of club player, as his record of 350 games in the First and Second Divisions suggests.

All spectators need a scapegoat for the failings of *their* team, and Hill, an outstanding sight with his tall figure, large head, beard and bustling energy, has been the scapegoat at Fulham. He has been at the receiving end of some classic exhortations. Once, with Hill at right-half and a player named George Cohen at right-back and in possession of the ball, Hill had called for it two or three times. Suddenly a voice shouted from the terraces: 'Georgie, the rabbi wants the ball. Give it 'im.'

The beard, as Hill admits, was grown because 'my face looks better with a beard than without, and nobody could possibly say otherwise'.

Strangely, he never felt lonely in his struggle, even when it seemed that he might have to lead the players into a strike with no money in the bank and not nearly as much public support as they have now. He saw it as a crusade. He has a passion for football and for making things better in football.

He has much in common with Sir Stanley Rous, the secretary of the Football Association, who had to stand aside in the argument. 'Sir Stanley's main responsibility,' says Hill, 'is to prosper football in this country. My job is to prosper professional football.

'But how can League football prosper, how can it look into the future, when it's controlled by men to whom it's a hobby or a pastime and who can only look into the future of their own particular club? When you add part-time thinking to that, and realise that there must be a two-thirds majority of all the clubs in favour of any change, then where do you get? It's no wonder that we've fallen behind the rest of the world.'

It's lucky for the sport that Hill isn't a better player. 'If I had had a chance of being selected for the England team, I couldn't in fairness to that ambition have argued so strongly for what I've believed in, and I couldn't have argued with the very people who are selectors.' That last remark is the reason so few innovations come from active sportsmen.

Hill was pressed to say what his plans would be when a settlement was reached. 'This assumes that overnight we will have a Utopia. That's nonsense. I have made it quite clear to the players at every stage that they have got to put all their energies and enthusiasm into improving the game.

'We've told the League that we'd back them up 100 per cent in disciplining anyone who behaves badly or infringes the system; that given a settlement we can believe in wholeheartedly, we'd be wholehearted about it. There's so much to do and to settle; spectator accommodation; the place of television; the size of the divisions and the League, to keep competition alive; how to inspire thought, better coaching, remedial treatment; better facilities.

'If we get these contracts right, we could forget all the arguing and get on with making it better and more prosperous.'

Sport makes and forgets names quickly. As a rule only geniuses survive. But it looks as if Jimmy Hill, the untrained and unpaid negotiator, will be remembered as the man who in three months has done more to improve the status of professional footballers than anyone else in the history of the game.

22 January 1961

Ultimately the players got fair contracts. But the way these arguments were conducted supported the view of J. P. W. Mallalieu that some players were more intelligent and constructive in argument than their 'masters'. He put this idea forward in reviewing books by Jimmy Hill and Danny Blanchflower.

Outstripping their Masters

There is much recent evidence that both in brains and education professional footballers have begun to outstrip their masters. Perhaps the most striking example was the contrast between the behaviour of the Professional Footballers' Association and that of the League Management Committee in their dispute over contracts earlier this year. The players were reasonable and convincing. The masters were neither.

Now two books just published offer further evidence. One of them – *Striking for Soccer* (Peter Davies, 18s.) is by Jimmy Hill, whose playing days have only just ended and who led the players in their long negotiations with the management. The book is mainly a factual account of these negotiations and as such is an interesting contribution to the history of industrial relations. It is also a sidelight on the social changes which have happened in the past twenty years, changes which appear to have passed football directors by. This is a book for the serious student of what is both an entertainment and a major industry.

The second book, Danny Blanchflower's autobiographical *The Double and After* (Nicholas Kaye, 15s.) is more for the amateur of life than it is for the professional student. Yet Blanchflower's message is much the same as Hill's. He gives his own experiences with directors who broke promises, with officials who, drunk themselves, pressed whisky on young players at daybreak, with directors who were so out of touch that one of them actually mistook a journalist for the star player in his own team, with a director who sent a player to eat in a hotel kitchen while he himself ate in the dining-room, and with directors who go behind the backs of managers.

He tells too of managers so rooted in traditional ideas that they refused to allow players to train with a football and sent them instead on long meaningless grinds round the track; and he tells of managers who were so weak they had no minds of their own but were blown this way and that by the directors or the players themselves.

The picture is all the more alarming because of the style Blanchflower uses to describe it. He seems to observe the jungle with bewilderment instead of bitterness. He writes as a wide-eyed babe in the wood rather than a reforming zealot. And his points slide home.

It is only when he comes to the sporting press that his pen becomes at all sharp. Hooligans . . . fiction writers . . . wide boys . . . beat the drummers . . . these are phrases he uses to describe some sports reporters. I look forward to reading his articles in *The Observer* partly because, if they at all resemble his book, they will be stimulating and delightfully written, and partly because I want to see how he can keep to the high standards he himself lays down for others.

15 January 1961   *J. P. W. Mallalieu*

---

13 December 1960 was the date originally set by Jimmy Hill and the Professional Footballers' Association for strike action over contracts and wages. By then Alan Hardaker, secretary of the League, was saying petulantly in public, 'Of course everything has to be legal now to satisfy The Observer.' *Having made his contribution to that debate, the busy Brasher had already got us all on another tack making up a grand design for soccer's future. This, too, aroused much interest and controversy as these thoughts on* The Observer *'Charter for Soccer' indicate.*

Last week *The Observer* **presented A Charter for Soccer. It advocated member clubs as opposed to company rule, a pyramid structure for the leagues, fuller control over the Football League by the Football Association and freedom for the player to negotiate his own contract. Here are some reactions.**

From Danny Blanchflower
(Spurs and Northern Ireland)
Sir, – When Moses descended the Mount with the Ten Commandments tucked under his arm he had reason to be proud of his new charter for civilisation. And later on, the boys who cornered old King what's-his-name down Runnymede way, to sweat out a few human rights, had excuse enough to feel pleased with their day's work.

Now – last Sunday to be exact – a bunch of *Observer* free thinkers have broken out in print with a new charter for soccer.

A big hand all round, fellows. It was good work, nobly done, and it sounded grand. But to tell the truth, it didn't turn up anything that hasn't been covered a dozen or more times, somewhere on the soccer front, this past decade. For all that, though, it still sounds a good charter. But the point is: so what? What difference will it make?

The source of the trouble is the player's contract and the restrictive practice of a maximum wage. Some time ago this paper sought counsel's advice, and published the opinion that the contract was legally void. In simple terms, I think it violates the spirit of human rights.

Some time ago the Professional Footballers' Association declared that they were in dispute with the League. The outcome was a series of meetings between the two, 'neath some white flag at the Ministry of Labour. Jimmy Hill and Joe Richards would emerge and be reported as smiling, saying, 'a happy meeting', 'no comment', or 'progressing satisfactorily'.

Joe Richards reported back to the League meeting and they voted to do nothing. It was obvious that the League had not taken a blind bit of notice of the players' desires. All that capering-about at the Ministry of Labour had been a complete waste of time.

What good will your charter, my charter, Moses' charter, anybody's charter do? The situation calls for clear thinking men in charge, men who can act and govern and improvise to meet the changing demands. The game now, more vitally than ever before, needs good administration. There is no evidence that we have got it.

Where's it all going to end? I don't know. But they are back at the Ministry of Labour again, 'neath the old white flag. The players are not going to mention 'strike'. The League have no new plan, no proposal.

Moses had a beard. So did John Brown's body (how did he get in?) and I'm sure the boys at Runnymede had. Jimmy Hill has a beard . . . that might be significant. But then he's a peacemaker, a middle-of-the-roader. So is Joe Richards. And they are both back at the Ministry of Labour holding friendly meetings, peacemaking.

There's one hell of a bottleneck in the middle of the road with all these peacemakers fighting it out.

You can keep your new, very good charter. I don't think it will make the slightest difference. Come to think of it . . . Moses isn't making out too well with his, and the boys at Runnymede didn't have such a good day.

From Arthur Rowe
Manager of Crystal Palace FC

Sir, – For many years we called the Continentals ballet dancers and decried their style of play. Lately it has been forcibly driven home to us that there is much to be said for the Continental style and some of our teams have adopted it. So why not, as you suggest, take a close look at the way they administer the game. We might have more to learn.

From Bill Slater
(Wolves and England)

Sir, – May I, as a player, congratulate you on your clear and sensible thinking. Your suggestion for membership clubs of the kind which exist in some parts of South America and Europe, and which cater for more than one activity, is particularly interesting, though I doubt whether it will have much support from League officials.

Particularly pleasant to a player are the thoughts that in such a club there might be full opportunity to welcome counsel and assistance from past performers, and that the club might grow strong and happy through a continuity of interest of this kind.

The development of a pyramid of leagues in this country, and the emergence ultimately of a Premier League, are surely inevitable. Also inevitable is the emergence widely throughout Europe of a European League. If this country is to contribute to this league it must begin to make preparations now. The confusion of priorities in football in this country at the moment is unbelievable.

You point out, as you have done so often in the past, that the restrictions inherent in the English League player's contract are the root cause of many problems in English football. May I stress that the players are not, as so many people imagine, campaigning specifically for a rise in pay.

The players are asking for a reasonable and adequate guaranteed minimum wage (they do not consider that a mature player having, say, a wife and two children can feel secure on a guaranteed wage of only £10), and the right, over and above that, to negotiate their own contract. They are also asking that a committee of appeal, if it is to adjudicate on problems fairly, should represent the players as well as the clubs.

Just what is it that the Football League fears an open contract will bring? It says an open contract will result in the best players finding their way to a small number of top clubs. Personally, I don't believe that this will happen to nearly the extent which the League says it will. English players have a basic sense of loyalty, I am sure, but are given precious little chance of demonstrating it at the moment. And, anyway, would it be such a catastrophe if a number of really top clubs did emerge, and if there occurred some concentration of talent at the top?

An open contract would see the end of the maximum wage – and some clubs who wanted to and were able to pay their players more would do so.

But many players would, of course, continue to be paid at approximately the same rate. To suggest that the players can take more from the game than is in it is ridiculous. An open contract would probably mean a pruning of playing staff at the top level and more part-time professionalism at the lower level – both of them sensible developments.

The players do not have a monopoly on the game, any more than the clubs, and I cannot see why the clubs could not protect their interests via a negotiated contract just as the players would hope to protect theirs.

From Jimmy Hill
(Fulham and Chairman of PFA)

Sir, – I liked the ideas you outlined in your Charter for Soccer – of membership clubs which are genuine sports centres for the whole community, of better facilities for spectators, of a Premier League – but the practical difficulties are enormous. You can build new stadia in Ipswich, say, or at Peterborough where they are working along these lines; but where will you find the room to expand near the centre of London? And how will you get the League clubs to agree? At present everyone is looking at football through the keyhole of his particular board-room. I don't want to discourage any constructive plans, but I think it will be years before they can be put into effect. Meanwhile, we must try to gain our immediate objectives: fair conditions of employment, and a recognition by the League that the welfare of football is more truly the business of the players than it is of the management.

The present state of the game has arisen out of the system: that system must be changed. We cannot go on having part-time thinking about what should be a full-time job.

22 November 1960

So the MPs Said

Mr Philip Goodhart (*Con., Beckenham*). – 'Professional football . . . is the most important section of our national sporting industry, but a section that is inefficiently organised, semi-bankrupt and only too often a thoroughly bad employer. There should, I think, be a certain mutual sympathy between Members of Parliament and professional football players. We both suffer from acute insecurity of employment. Both are only too likely to suffer from premature retirement. . . .

'Here is a serious difference. In the House of Commons we can alter our conditions and pay by agreeing among ourselves, but football players are bound to their employers by contractual conditions which would have been rejected with a snort of contempt by any intelligent young apprentice in the Middle Ages. . . .'

Mr Peter Thomas (*Parliamentary Secretary to the Ministry of Labour*). – '. . . in the industry of professional football there are no effective arrangements for airing grievances and discussing outstanding problems. Because of that, neither the players nor the clubs had an opportunity of an exhaustive examination, face to face, of the points of difference between them until they met under the auspices of the Ministry. As my Hon. Friend has said, we then found and identified 22 points of difference.

'. . . I hope that the parties will see the advantages of establishing within the industry appropriate and permanent machinery for negotiation and consultation.'

The 'new deal' finally signed soon changed the face of English football. Looking back at the end of its first season, Jimmy Hill was aware that not everything his initiative had achieved would be for the benefit of the game.

New Deal Gets off to a Fair Start

To pass an opinion on the effect of the no-maximum wage principle has had on soccer at the end of the first season is like trying to decide the winner of a mile race on his performance to the first bend.

Certain trends have become apparent. In the days of the pay pause when unions discuss three per cent or five per cent rises the country's leading professionals have attained an astronomical increase of 200 to 300 per cent.

Frankly I have been astonished how quickly the star salaries have soared. Way down in the Third and Fourth Divisions players have had to face the fact that the money is not there and unless directors, players and Football

League legislators soon get to grips with the problems confronting their clubs and the League, the clubs also may not be there.

Another disturbing feature is that in the original home of sportsmen the British public will now only attend soccer matches when their team is winning; the cry is for better football but only winning football can bring spectators in.

The two may be linked in some cases yet only a dozen out of 92 clubs per season can be winners whereas in theory any number could be playing attractive football. The passive interest remains in every town but the public does not show the inclination to watch unless it can be sure of going home with a win.

The standard of soccer has certainly not fallen, nor has it risen in proportion to the wage increases. Only a fool would expect so much so soon. The seeds of change have been sown and slowly but surely the standard of play will improve. There will still be appalling matches, the game is that difficult, but as the years pass our stars will increasingly be able to hold their heads high alongside the Puskas's and Di Stefano's of this world.

5 May 1962   *Jimmy Hill*

Bill Slater added some interesting views on the conflict of requirement of players and spectators when discussing the 'Price of Perfection' with Hugh McIlvanney in 1963.

The Price of Perfection

Few men of his generation have been more deeply involved with sport in theory and practice than W. J. Slater. As a footballer he has won 20 England Amateur Caps and 12 Full England Caps, represented Great Britain at the 1952 Olympics and England in the World Cup in 1958. During the past 11 years with Wolverhampton Wanderers he has won three League Championship medals and an FA Cup winners' medal – and before that he had taken an FA Cup runners-up medal as an

amateur with Blackpool. Now he is a lecturer in the physical education department of Birmingham University.

I have been thinking a great deal recently about the fundamental implications of the blend of skill and chance in the best competitive games. It is natural, of course, when you are sitting in a university instead of running around as a performer, that you do perhaps tend to intellectualise overmuch. But the recent stir about the need for brighter cricket, brighter football and so on has convinced me that others may have been experiencing the same sort of impressions and doubts as I have.

What I feel, for a start, is that too many people have a ludicrously simple idea of how our principal games should be brightened up. I mean, they seem to think all you have to do is tell the captain to be positive and aggressive and you've guaranteed yourself wonderful sport. Most of the violent criticisms of that Fifth Test in Australia were based on demands that would have falsified the game completely. Possibly England did score too slowly on the first day – but Australia's aim was first and foremost to retain the Ashes and she was sensible to use whatever tactics seemed appropriate and fair. If she had not done so she would have falsified the whole Test series.

The use of all legitimate means to secure victory is the only true foundation of competitive games and it's disastrous nonsense to suggest that men should abandon it. And the securing of victory starts with the avoiding of defeat. If players attacked to open up their game in order to entertain spectators and without regard for winning then this would threaten and ultimately destroy the competitive basis of their play – and produce an exhibitionism even less palatable to those watching.

The conflict of interest between games players and their audience is an extremely serious one in the sense that there is no obvious way of resolving it. It's my feeling that a defensive trend shows to a greater or lesser extent in all games and that it's the inevitable result – you might say the expression – of improvement in performance. As standards rise, so it becomes more difficult to retrieve an error and therefore more vital that you should not make one.

My most urgent feeling about competitive games at the present time is that we must acknowledge that the element of chance is not something to be despised, to be taken out of them. I think it's the thing that keeps the best games linked with life, stops them from being mere synthetic exercises in technique.

In basketball, for example, where natural hazards have been reduced to something like the minimum – they have a round ball, an ideally smooth floor surface, no bodily contact, uninhibited handling of the ball, etc. – in that game there is such perfection that it is almost utterly predictable. In many cases the factors are so foreseeable that experts can not only forecast winners, but percentage results and probably actual scores to within a few points. I am told that in chess it's possible, in theory, to produce a machine which plays perfectly, never makes a false move. If two such machines play against each other it just isn't a game any more.

All this prompts me to agree with suggestions that Test wickets should not be covered. The increase in natural hazards would achieve liveliness in a much healthier way than by trying to persuade players to adopt false attitudes. In the same line of thinking, I believe that some of the people who are advocating summer football might not get the sort of game they imagine they would.

They might find that the better weather and ground conditions simply produced a greater degree of defensive competence and therefore less of what they look upon as brighter play. That happens to a great extent in places like Italy and South America. The hazards produced by our winter conditions make the risk of attacking worthwhile. There is always the chance of a slip or mistake of some kind and you say: Let's have the slips in front of their goal – and you try to get the ball up there.

It is something of a paradox in games that players must strive for perfection and yet, in doing that, must in a way destroy the games. As the players become more skilled so they must – as far as external conditions will permit – eliminate chance. And I feel it's part of the concept of sport that chance should have a place. I suppose those people who argue that fox-hunting is a sport are doing so on the grounds that the fox has a chance of getting away. A biological sport is, I seem to remember, a chance mutation.

But that's not the end of the story. As performers in all kinds of sport strive for perfection and push up standards, there are other prices to be paid. At the top you find increasingly there is scope only for the complete-ness of what can be called the professional approach. Sport in the past in this country has served many ends – it's been recreational, health giving, socially enriching, educational in all sorts of ways. But now it seems to be turning in on itself.

With high standards I think the tendency to cheat and foul increases. There is so much more at stake. I don't just mean foul practices on the field – I also mean things like taking drugs. Nobody takes drugs to play for the Extra 'B' fifteen or to run at the works club sports meeting.

And there are other problems as standards rise. Simply because there is further to go to the top, young performers must start out earlier. It's reported that in Australia there are regional swimming championships for seven-year-olds. What's the next step? Do we start to breed athletes and swimmers?

Of course, there is something immensely exciting and compelling about pushing up standards and breaking records. And currently I think the prices are worth paying. But only just. They could very easily become excessive.

5 November 1967   *Hugh McIlvanney*

With the heading 'Fuzz Friendly', Alan Hubbard wrote about the largest soccer tournament in the world, which also has an important social purpose aiming to use sport in the best of all ways.

Fuzz Friendly

No one kicked a copper in the groin, spat obscenities or attempted to inflict G B H on the players or one another. It hardly seemed like a football night at Wembley.

Mind you, there was, as they say, a considerable police presence – at least a couple of thousand Bobbies and cadets on and off duty at an occasion that barely merited a passing paragraph in the nationals. After all, it was only the largest soccer tournament in the world.

Doubtless the finals on Thursday of the Metropolitan Police Youth Five-a-Side competition ranked well down the League table behind McFarland's defection and Tottenham's missing £52,000. And they were considered small beer compared to the Daily Express's National Championships won by Arsenal on the same floor the night before.

But as a social exercise the kick-about between 14 teams of assorted shapes, size and sex, under the surveillance of avuncular Old Bill had a significance extending well beyond the confines of Wembley Arena.

From almost 60,000 boys and girls in the Greater London area, the finalists emerged to contest a now annual event designed to turn the friendly face of the fuzz to cockney youngsters. Organised by the Met and sponsored by the Midland Bank, we have a new policemen's ball game to prove that soccer can still be fun to play and safe to watch.

The police themselves turned up to cheer by the posse, not in their Pandas, but T-reg Cortinas, mainly in plain clothes and with the wife and kids.

Some have formed a fan-like attachment to teams they have helped nurture in the line of community liaison duty, like Linda, a pert, pocket-sized WPC who has adopted Tottenham Ladies. Cheering her under-14-year-olds to victory obviously made a welcome change from helping chuck out the hoolies from White Hart Lane every other Saturday.

Even if a couple of lads did get their collars felt when things got a bit overheated during the Boys'-under-15 Final there wasn't much misbehaviour on the pitch to spoil the good nature of the night.

Originally the brainchild of former Commissioner, Sir David McNee, and Trevor Brooking, the police fives has blossomed in three years from an East End diversion into a London-wide knock-out affair featuring this year 5,772 teams from schools and youth clubs in the Met's 24 police districts.

'The bottom line is crime prevention, of course,' says Chief Inspector Mike Hedges, who runs New Scotland Yard's youth programme. 'You have to accept that a lot of young people get into trouble and many of our clients are under 17.

'The whole idea of this competition is to bring together youngsters, their parents and the police to forge a better understanding with football as the common denominator. It is a sport which cuts across all ethnic and social barriers.'

The Yard also promotes angling, darts, and disco-dancing competitions among London's youth and is currently talking with Lord's about an indoor cricket tournament similar to Wembley's mini-soccer show.

The onlooking police brass at Wembley as well as FA chairman, Bert Millichip, are aware that this softly-softly approach offers no immediate solution to the stricken terraces of professional football, but it might ensure that the game has a more decent future.

There is also the chance that it could throw up some useful talent, although the player with the most potential on Thursday looked to be a 10-year-old lass from Barnehurst. Tara Proctor, 4ft nothing, scored exactly half the 36 goals amassed by Millwall Lionesses en route to their under-11 final against a team of Surbiton fourth-formers. The couple she added brought her winner's medal and an approving glance from Bobby Robson.

Tara finished top of a mixed coaching class organised by Don Howe and has beaten 48 boys to earn further FA tuition at Bisham Abbey. If nothing else her Greaves-like goal instinct shows that the women's soccer need not be all hit-and-Ms.

28 November 1983   *Alan Hubbard*

A Sporting Print by E. Blyth looked at the gentlemanly gamesmanship between prep school headmasters.

Prepschoolmanship

It is being argued that modern Association football is controlled from the touch-line; and that the issue is really fought by the rival managers long before the game is ever started.

Such tactics may seem strange, and yet they have been known and practised in the sphere of preparatory school football for many years. In this case it is the rival headmasters who are engaged in the preliminary struggle.

The opening round usually takes place on neutral ground at the beginning of term. The headmaster of school A happens, by chance, to meet his ancient rival, the headmaster of B, in – say – the local sports shop, where both are buying footballs. The exchanges will be outwardly friendly, and will follow the accepted pattern for such occasions. 'We've a poor side this year,' says one of them jovially, 'I doubt if we shall give you a game!' His opponent, who was on the point of saying this himself, must now change his tactics. 'We *had* a good side, but Smith major has mumps and Brown has cut his hand while carpentering. We shan't stand a chance without them!' Both will then retire to their respective fortresses and will report to the Common Room that the opposition appear to have a hot side and are clearly confident of winning.

The next few weeks will be spent in careful study of what is known, in racing circles, as 'collateral form'. This may prove extremely complicated, and can take on the appearance of an advanced question in a Common Entrance maths paper. 'If School A loses 3–0 to C (on their ground, with a referee who doesn't know the off-side rule) and C then beats B by 2–1 (obviously a fluke) what is the probable outcome (i) When A plays B at home, (ii) When A plays B away (on their potty little ground)?'

These problems having been finally thrashed out, the great day of the match dawns either bright and clear ('our fellows are no good when it's dry') or dull and wet ('my boys are hopeless in the mud'). Such alibis are essential to the face-saving so important to schoolmasters.

A, let us suppose, are playing away, on B's ground. For years this was held to be a disadvantage, but the modern view, based on dietary research, maintains that the advantage really lies with A's team, who will at least have been given a period for digesting their lunch while travelling to the game, whereas B's eleven may have been eating within a few minutes of the start. This is a greater handicap than is at first apparent, for all small boys gobble their food when excited, and all kitchen staffs serve boiled beef and dumplings, followed by suet pudding and treacle, on the day of a match.

The two headmasters meet for a few seconds before the game, but tradition wisely lays down that they watch it from opposite corners of the ground.

Tradition also demands that neither headmaster shall actually invade the playing pitch during the game; but apart from this they are entitled to do almost anything which they believe may add the necessary impetus to their respective teams. The methods used will vary from a friendly exhortation by nickname (always popular with any parents that may be on the touch-line) to remarkable exhibitions of frustration and near-apoplexy. At the turn of the century the headmaster of a Sussex school used to pace the touch-line shouting: 'The cane for you to-night – and you!' whenever his forwards missed chances in front of goal.

When the game is ended, both headmasters have tea in the study. This may be the most difficult moment of all, for while the winner must be suitably magnanimous, the loser must contrive to suggest that, despite the excellence of the game, he is still in some slight doubt as to whether the best side really won. But the tea itself is always elaborate and the influence of crumpets, toast and layer cake will produce the unanimous opinion that 'it was a pretty near thing', even though the winning margin was in the region of eight or ten goals.

The tea-party finally breaks up in much good-fellowship. 'We'll have a poor side next year' is the final gambit; 'I doubt if we'll give you a game.'

12 December 1958   *H. E. Blyth*

Bob Houston revelled in a nostalgic BBC programme.

Play it Again, Football . . .

Is it really 20 years? Two decades of Saturday night Indian takeaways, feet up and 'Match of the Day' . . . that's a lot of chicken dhansak and a lot of football.

The BBC's inspired decision to mark the programme's twentieth anniversary with 'Action Replay' and an opportunity to wallow in the soothing mud of nostalgia was particularly welcome in the week in which I went into training for another season of British Rail coffee and sandwiches (when available) in the ceaseless search for the football reporter's Holy Grail.

We have just seen the past, and it worked. The Beatles as soundtrack was a bit obvious, but the cheerful innocence of Kenneth Wolstenholme's commentary, a real leather ball that all but became indistinguishable on a muddy pitch, and a crowd which managed to support its heroes without obscenities reminded us of where we've been.

It was a pity that Greavsie wasn't called in to talk us through that marvellous goal against Manchester United at White Hart Lane, but then he's tied up by the opposition.

When the rose-tinted spectacles are put firmly back in the case, what are we to make of it all? Did those glimpses of a bygone era prove anything? For me, they certainly did.

For instance, how do you convince your kids that the likes of Greaves, Charlton and Law really were a different breed and class? No amount of parental droning could compete with that glorious moment when Greaves, against Manchester United, stumbled into midfield possession, looked up and decided that the odds were good enough to go for goal. After all, there could only have been four defenders to take on.

And all my Jock chuntering which my offspring have had to put up with became obsolete with the feline speed Denis Law displayed as he pounced on that parried save. And what about Paddy Crerand's through ball that set up the chance? And yes, the sight of Bobby Charlton meeting the ball on the half-volley does rank with that lingering shot of Marilyn Monroe walking away from the camera in 'Niagara' as one of the definitive memories for my generation.

Now even the kids had to admit that all my mutterings about coaches might contain more than a grain of truth. Significantly, the Sixties matches between Liverpool–Arsenal and Spurs–Manchester United were from that Arcadian time before England won the World Cup and a generation of managers – including the redoubtable Sir Alf himself – drew the wrong conclusions.

Those games confirmed my fervently held view that the coach, in his Sixties manifestation, was not the malevolent influence he has since become. And the average player then – Arsenal's Geoff Strong will do as an example – seems an outrageous individualist when stood against his eighties equivalent.

Only the most spectacularly gifted of the current generation seem able to crawl out from under the totalitarian mantle of modern coaching philo-sophy, whose only contribution seems to have been to organise better the negative aspects of football.

The Seventies arrived with Leeds United's sadist demolition of a hapless Southampton, with a brief, fearful glance at the crowd trouble at The Hawthorns after that notorious refereeing decision that ripped the mask from Revie's children.

The times had changed and Leeds United were the principal sowers of the harvest we are still reaping . . . except that most of them could play a bit.

26 August 1984   *Bob Houston*

Run-of-the-mill matches in Ireland are not great crowd pullers as viewed by Eamonn Dunphy, another Irish soccer player with a way with words as well as a football.

A Game With Its Heart Elsewhere

To lose one manager may be regarded as a misfortune, to lose both looks like carelessness. Apologies to Oscar Wilde but in the light of recent events Irish football men could be forgiven such sardonic humour.

Having barely recovered from the shock of John Giles's abdication, the Irish game received more alarming news last week when his successor as international team manager, Alan Kelly, stepped down in response to pressure from the Preston North End board. The resulting confusion is only partly relieved by the temporary appointment of ex-Portsmouth veteran Eoin Hand for this week's game against world champions Argentina.

Still, given the amount of irony and contradiction already built into our game, a little confusion should not disturb us unduly. Irish soccer is alive and well but its hearbeat is located somewhere between Manchester and Liverpool. Throughout the country there is widespread and growing devotion to the 'foreign' game, but this interest is focused almost exclusively on the English league, and Irish domestic soccer in the shape of the League of Ireland has profited little from it.

The typical Irish soccer fan enjoys his football courtesy of Jimmy Hill and 'Match of the Day' or the English newspapers. If he's in an expansive mood he joins the weekly exodus to places of pilgrimage like Liverpool, London or Manchester.

In the short term the fact that the passion exists is encouraging. The long-term problem is how to exploit what in football terms represents a great natural resource. For if the oil that Mr Haughey suggestively hints lies off the west coast is our best hope of material wealth then the growing passion that the nation's youngsters have for soccer is its sporting equivalent.

One has only to see the spread of football fever through the rural heartland of Ireland to appreciate this. Thanks to television Liam Brady, John Giles, David O'Leary, Kenny Dalgleish, even, God help us, Tommy Docherty are the new folk heroes of rural Irish life.

In renowned Gaelic strongholds like Kilkenny, Carlow and astonishingly, Kerry, soccer is challenging the traditional games for the hearts and minds of youngsters. The defection to Manchester United of the country's best Gaelic footballer, Kevin Moran, merely confirms the trend. More kids than ever before are playing soccer and the odds are that in the next 10 years an ever-increasing number of talented young players will emerge. Good news for the English clubs who have traditionally reaped this particular harvest, but because of their haphazard scouting system English clubs often miss a high proportion of the best players who are then left to contemplate a future in the League of Ireland.

Historically this rather unattractive option has meant that a good young footballer will, rather than submit his talents to the whimsical nature of most League of Ireland clubs, turn away from soccer to the socially more acceptable games of rugby, or Gaelic football. Two of our great contemporary sportsmen, Kevin Moran and Tony Ward, did precisely this. How many more players of that calibre have been lost due to the inadequacies of the domestic game we can only guess.

A more pressing question is whether we will continue to waste such potential. Apart from international games and the occasional important league fixture, soccer in Ireland is not a spectator sport. Although there are exceptions – Dundalk, Shamrock Rovers and current champions Limerick United – League of Ireland gates have remained depressed throughout the boom years.

Only half a dozen of the league's 16 clubs offer the kind of facilities likely to seduce the spectator from his Sunday afternoon armchair from where he can watch 'The Big Match' with Brian Moore.

11 May 1980   *Eamonn Dunphy*

The vast bulk of Observer *soccer writing has been in reporting run-of-the-mill every week matches. Selection from these is impossible, except for a token couple. John Arlott's first match in 1959 was anything but ordinary, as was one in the following year:*

Harmer's Day and Everton's Ruin

Tottenham Hotspur 10   Everton 4

Since Stoke City beat West Bromwich Albion 10–3 in 1937 no club's score had reached double figures in a First Division match – until yesterday.

Then Tottenham Hotspur outwitted, outpaced and outclassed a sluggish and undistinguished Everton team, and beat them 10–4 at White Hart Lane.

The score, and its handsome manner, should convince the Tottenham management – old and new – and the White Hart Lane crowd, once and for all that five straight runners do not make an attack.

Once more – and it would appear, as grudgingly as ever – Harmer was brought back into the Hotspur forward line; and, as so often before, he gave its dash informed direction. He created five fine goals and himself scored a spectacular sixth with a raking drive amazingly powerful in one so slight.

Out of the Tottenham half-back line, Blanchflower and Iley drove forward, confidently, fiery and acquisitive and, as the Everton inside-forwards and wing half-backs gave way before them, created the setting for Harmer.

Harmer, in turn, discovered for himself cool islands of space and time, whence he chipped, flicked and stroked the ball through subtle lines and arcs to send his four lively and ranging outsiders racing in on the Everton goal. Like some cockney waif, fraily poised on twiglike legs, he seemed to challenge his opponents even to discover his whereabouts, while he proved himself the most delicate and accurate user of a football the game has known.

The fact that he doesn't risk his frail physique in vain tackles on men big enough to brush him aside must, surely, be a reasonable price to pay for his constructive services.

Collins, Everton's costly inside-forward, lacked Harmer's ability to slip his marking defender, and – hard as Hickson and J. Harris chased – his fellow forwards were less intelligent in taking-up position than Harmer's.

In defence, Baker and Hopkins were more adroit in covering Ryden's mistakes than Bramwell and Sanders had time to be about those of Jones. Fourteen goals are not scored in a match without the aid of defenders' errors. On the other hand, forwards finishing rarely punishes those errors with such precise severity as on this day.

The Tottenham scorers were, before half-time, Stokes, Smith, Robb, Smith, Stokes, Medwin; and after it, Smith, Harmer, Smith, Ryden.

For Everton, Harris levelled the scores at 1–1 and completed a hat-trick with two goals in the second half before Collins, at length moving up from his deep position, placed a strong shot from 20 yards well wide of Hollowbread.

Mr Nicholson, Tottenham's new manager, inherits some fine and entertaining footballing talent. Mr Carey, however, when he takes over the Everton team, will need to give its defence greater pace and method, and sounder ideas of covering.

If he does not do so, Harmer may well again send his cavalry in to pierce its shallow line of static and uncoordinated defence.

5 October 1959   *John Arlott*

Patterns of Glory
– and Goals

Tottenham Hotspur   4   Burnley   4

It is honour to a footballer to have played at White Hart Lane on 3 December, 1960 – and delight to 58,000 people to have watched them. There and then, the reigning Champions of the Football League and their heirs-apparent showed that title to be illustrious indeed. The shape of the scoring – Burnley losing 4–0 and yet recovering to draw the game – was enough to make it a memorable occasion. Yet the true greatness of the day lay in the standard of play. On a pitch so slimy as to place precise ball control beyond the hope of ordinary mortals, these two sides produced the arts, skills, rigours and drama of football in glorious profusion.

As soon as the ball was rolling, Burnley moved into attack, McIlroy fencing with MacKay to send Connelly and Pilkington clear on the wings.

Before Tottenham had settled to their game Burnley had three corner kicks and a free kick on the left within a couple of minutes, and made scoring chances which Robson, Connelly and McIlroy could not quite take.

To their credit, Tottenham refused to be hustled: although the foothold was so treacherous that once a defender committed himself he had no hope of recovery, Norman and his backs strove still to make every clearance a pass.

Gradually, too, MacKay began to storm up and down the midfield and Blanchflower to direct the long ball like a probing lance into the Burnley defence. Ahead of them White, icily delicate, controlled the pace of attack, building it towards a characteristic Tottenham peak.

First, a corner-kick which passed high over to the left and was returned by MacKay to Norman – brought up out of defence to head in precisely such a pass: he did so.

Then MacKay sent a long throw-in up to the goal line where Smith headed it on to Jones whose quick hook shot went in off the underside of the crossbar.

Next, Smith began a movement which White and Allen continued down the left: as the defence moved to cover Smith Jones shot into an open goal.

Three goals had been scored in three minutes! And the game was still not a quarter done. It seemed, however, to be decided when White pulled a corner kick back to MacKay, whose long range shot bounced off Black-law's chest for Tottenham's fourth goal.

Certainly few sides in England could hope to make good a four-goal deficit against this Tottenham team. But, like Spurs earlier on, Burnley continued to play their normal measured game, and a few moments before half-time Connelly finished just such a neat scoring move as had failed before.

Tottenham began the second half as Burnley had the first; now it was for them that the ball would not go into the net. Blacklaw saved handsomely from the head and foot of Jones, Allen struck the goalpost with an angled shot.

But Burnley scored. Pilkington drove a low centre across the Tottenham goal; Henry, jabbing out his foot, could only partially stop the ball and, as he fell over, Robson kicked it into goal.

Again Tottenham replied with attack and, as Allen seemed on the verge of scoring, Cummings swept the ball away, down to the Tottenham goal where Norman only partly cleared, and the faithful Pointer, seizing on the loose ball, ran in and scored with an angled shot.

Blanchflower struck the inside of the Burnley goalpost with a lob; Smith at one end, and Miller at the other, had long shots spectacularly saved. Then Norman essayed yet another short pass out of defence: it stuck in the mud, Connelly raced on to it and in a quick exchange of passes with Robson, cut out for himself the position to shoot the fourth Burnley goal.

4 December 1960   *John Arlott*

Not all the writing dealt with the serious side of soccer, as the next small selection indicates. The Observer *ran a competition for the 'Sports Nut' of the year. Inevitably soccer had a number of candidates, but it was three years before they produced the nuttiest character of the year in 1983 as judged by David Randall.*

Anyone who queues for his pension with his football gear under his arm is definitely a sports nut. When he is still playing in the local Sunday league at the age of 74 it is time to do something about it. We have. Jack Wattam is unquestionably *The Observer* Sports Nut for 1983.

Jack was playing football before Stanley Matthews was even born. Last month just days before he went into hospital for a colostomy he was nipping down the right wing for Weelsby Rovers in the Grimsby Sunday League.

They lost 10–0 that day, but when you have been a parks footballer for as long as Jack has having your nose rubbed in the municipal dirt is just part of the game. In 5,000-odd matches he has dealt it out as well as taken it. Hard, but fair.

It was hard in the beginning too, selling newspapers and hot cakes around the houses to put a few more pennies down on his first pair of boots. 'A pair of Mansfield Hotspurs with great steel toe-caps. Nineteen shillings they were.'

Within a year they were his. 'The thing I remember from those days is the ball. When it was wet the leather got so heavy that it would knock you down and the lace would make a mark across your forehead. And the shirts were all wool and if it rained you were carrying about 3 lbs. of water on your back.' He was the park player in his element, whether for Burtons Park Thursday, Grimsby Hotspur, or Weelsby Rovers, his club for the past 20 years. When he joined them they were in the First Division of the Sunday League, a side to be reckoned with on the parks of Grimsby. Now, with a forward line with an average age of 50, they are bottom of the tenth, though good enough to beat Grimsby Transport Police 2–1.

Weelsby Rovers play football for the love of it, smiling, even through seasons like last when they conceded 224 goals and scored but 25 . . . Jack Wattam the footballer kept going. Thursday League and Sunday League until he was 69 and then just Sunday League. Never a booking, never a sending-off, always a handshake at the end of the game. He is the very model of the park footballer. 'I've had a few knocks,' he says, 'but I found that if you kept going then it soon wears off.' On and off the field that's Jack's motto for all seasons.

15 January 1984   *David Randall*

Geoffrey Nicholson found some interesting soccer teams in his 'Name Game' entries.

Virgin and the Bastard

'At last,' wrote David Pyatt of Enfield, introducing his entry to our Name Game, 'I have found a use for the somewhat esoteric knowledge that a real Bastard refereed the FA Cup final (1888), and that the 1914 Liverpool Cup final team contained the most exquisitely named footballer of all time: Fairfoul.'

We invited competitors to select a team – cricket, football, Rugby League or Union – not on merit but according to the aptness of their surnames. They had to be genuine past or present players of some standing, but could be played out of position; Dusty Hare, after all, sounds more like an overworked wing than a full-back.

The response was astonishing, not only in numbers – some 300 teams were submitted – but in enthusiasm. Roy Williams of Wimborne said: 'I haven't enjoyed anything quite so much since schooldays when I used to play "Owzat", an imaginary cricket match, and picked teams and made scoreboards for such selections as the Mass Murderers XI versus Great British Sea Captains.'

280

Others got so carried away that they made things more difficult for themselves by composing specialist teams like David Pyatt's Festival of Light soccer XI: Priest, Paul, Saul, Daniel, Gabriel, Pray, Bishop, Cross, Christian (capt), St John, Isaac. 'There is, of course,' he added, 'no vice-captain.' (If you don't remember Pray, he played for Bury in 1900, while Christian was an Old Etonian of 1879).

A. C. Toole of Bracknell and A. Mitchell of Binfield launched a High Fliers football team of Swift, Nightingale, Bird, Sparrow, Crowe, Heron, Robins, Starling, Woodcock, Partridge and Peacock. And from P. Marriott of Cambridge came a wet-weather team of Poole, (Paddy) Rice, Nelson, Webb, Waters, Mariner, Coates, Brolly, Marsh, Waddle and Drake.

To play football against the Metropolitan Police: Hood, Kopa, Robb, Steel, Sweeney, Law, Crooks, Coppell, Laidlaw, McNab and Dibble (from Andrew Browell, Newcastle-upon-Tyne).

4 May 1980   *Geoffrey Nicholson*

In his judgment the following week Geoffrey Nicholson awarded the prize to a rugby selection, but soccer provided the runner-up.

Our man on the football terraces is D. H. Holdstock (no doubt a club director) of St Leonards-on-Sea, who writes: 'Starting with the goalie, names like Armstrong, Divers, Palmer and Twist came to mind, but I finally decided on Denial (Oxford United, '62). Full-backs present numerous possibilities – Craggs, Burley, Lynch, Block – but for effectiveness I've settled for Fowler and Rough.

'The mind boggles at a half-back line where you've managed to squeeze your way past Boyle and Whitehead only to find your passage blocked by Pyle. But perhaps these are a little too painful, so we'll have Clinging, Clamp and, if you're past them, Carver. A snappy forward line of Quigley and Swift on the wings, strikers Flack and Pythian, with what better captain than Leadbetter. A possible substitute for games against Italian or Argentinian opposition would be Dick Le Flem.'

Mr Holdstock also nominates a no-hopers XI to play against: Leek,

Pratt, Fell, Hasty, Pyle, Ricketts, Hampton, Willey, Dick, Trollope, Slack. Substitutes: Nimmo, Askey.

11 May 1980   *Geoffrey Nicholson*

At the end of 1982 The Observer *published a sample of the clever, trite and terrible things people in sport had said. Football figured prominently in these quotes of the year.*

Quotes of the Year

'Half a million for Remi Moses? You could get the original Moses and the tablets for that price!' – *Tommy Docherty.*

'You're the best supporters in the country and we're the most attack-minded team.' – *Allan Clarke to Leeds crowd.*

'The people who've kicked us when we were down – we'll kick them twice as hard on the way back up.' – *Martin Wilkinson, Clarke's assistant, after relegation.*

'It's a pity your hooligans aren't coming. We like your hooligans. We think you have the best hooligans in Europe.' – *Greek taxi driver when informed that many English fans were visiting Salonika.*

'I've played recently with Rossi and Boniek and the rest of them and I know I'm just as good as they are.' – *Kevin Keegan.*

'To call Keegan a susperstar is stretching a point. Skill-wise, there are a lot of better players around. He's not fit to lace my boots as a player.' – *George Best (Keegan claimed that Best had contributed to the game's declining popularity).*

'I'm finished with England. I'll never kick a ball for my country again. After ten years and 60 caps, I deserve better than to have to learn of my omission indirectly through the media.' – *Kevin Keegan when left out of Bobby Robson's first England squad.*

'When you've been thrown out of clubs like Barrow and Southport, you learn to live with disappointment.' – *Peter Withe, on his omission from Robson's squad.*

'We're getting Port Vale into the First Division. One at a time!' – *Ritchie Barker, Stoke City manager on signing the third player in as many months from his Fourth Division neighbours.*

'We are pulling out because F A D S is an upright and clean company – that is something which can no longer be said about soccer. Football is a sick sport. We would rather sponsor netball.' – *Malcolm Stanley, managing director of F A D S.*

'When I said even my Missus could save Derby from relegation, I was exaggerating.' – *Peter Taylor.*

'I understand that Fashanu took his own masseur to the ground, and that is something I cannot condone.' – *PFA secretary, Gordon Taylor.*

'Clough talks in riddles. He says things like "If you were half as flamboyant on the pitch as you are off it, you'd be a world-beater." What good is that?' – *Justin Fashanu.*

'Imagine Franz Beckenbauer trying to play for Watford. He'd just be in the way.' – *Frank McLintock.*

'Watford are setting English football back 10 years.' – *Terry Venables.*

'How obtuse. If Watford could put the game back 10 years, it would be in a better state than it is now. There would be no £1 million players and wages to suit, there would be less debts, and more fans would be watching.' – *Danny Blanchflower.*

'We want football to tell us exactly what they would like in the ideal world and then, I'd assume, we will tell them what they can have.' – *John Bromley, Head of I T V Sport.*

'Well, that't the magic of television, isn't it? You hype the sound up a bit, point the cameras where the crowd is thickest, cut out all the boring rubbish, and you've got a Big Match.' – *Ted Ayling, LWT 'Big Match' director.*

'For the players he left behind at Manchester United, there will be one lasting memory of Gary Birtles. His weird, way-out gear . . . the fancy bow-ties, winged collars and spectacular suits that nobody else would wear without the courage of four bottles of wine.' – *Steve Coppell.*

'He's fast, strong, sharp and skilful but otherwise he's useless.' – *Norwich manager, Ken Brown, on Tony Woodcock.*

'The chairman (Mark Hulyer) has assured me that my job is safe.' – *Ken Craggs, Charlton manager, the day before he was fired.*

'What chance have you got when the League president is chairman of Notts County? They average 8,000 a match. He wants more football for his club, not less. Second-rate clubs will keep soccer in a second-rate situation.' – *Keith Burkinshaw, Spurs manager.*

'The Super League idea has as much chance of getting through as there is of Arthur Scargill admitting he needs a wig.' – *Fulham chairman Ernie Clay.*

'The contract Manchester United offered me was really excellent. What City offered was far in excess of that. I couldn't believe it. It was much too high.' – *Trevor Francis recounting how he'd joined City.*

'This is your club now. I love you all. I am going to come amongst you this afternoon.' – *Derek Douglas addressing the crowd before Wolves' first game after escaping from liquidation.*

'When I was a director of Sheffield United for six months, the chairman told me normal business standards didn't apply in football. It was the most stupid advice I ever had.' – *Mike Watterson, new Derby County chairman.*

'You ask what constitutes a crisis here. Well, if we ran out of white wine in the boardroom.' – *Patrick Cobbold, Ipswich chairman.*

Robert Chesshyre found much to intrigue him as he rounded up the start of the 1973 season.

We shall not, we shall not be moved

After the bombast, the bomb hoaxes. The pre-season hullaballoo about hooligans gave way to the game itself, and the floggers and birchers stepped aside for the anonymous telephone callers.

At Villa Park they played bravely on in defiance of a bomb warning, and not a man stirred when given the chance to leave the crowd: at Doncaster, the epic clash with Stockport was interrupted while the main stand was cleared and searched.

Play resumed after six minutes, which says something for the size of the crowd. The experience proved too harrowing for one Stockport player, who had himself sent off – presumably to make a quick getaway from the war zone.

But the mighty Derek Dougan achieved more disruption than the hoaxers. As the Norwich keeper dived in vain to prevent a second Doog goal, he collided with a post and did himself a mischief. It was 16 minutes before play resumed with a patched goal and a patched goalie.

'The bookies have made us favourties and they don't give much away,' remarked Liverpool manager Bill Shankly in peculiarly garrulous mood yesterday. His team justified the odds – just winning 1–0 against the Watney Cup holders, Stoke.

The other big boys made the first Saturday a congenial workout. Derby beat Chelsea; Arsenal handed Manchester United the kind of thrashing they appeared to enjoy so much last season; Leeds, with Bremner scoring early, destroyed Everton, under the new management of Billy Bingham; Wolves taught Norwich that it takes more than a summer's tan to cure footballing inadequacies.

But the best performance must have been that of newly promoted Burnley, who beat Sheffield United 2–0 away. They lost one player carried off and another was booked – about par for a good clean game of football. QPR achieved a creditable draw with Southampton.

Denis Law said something about manager Tommy Docherty's acumen in giving him a free transfer from Manchester United by scoring two goals – one with an overhead bicycle kick – on his return to Manchester City.

The two Nottingham clubs – together again in the Second Division – sent supporters scrabbling for the record books by collecting eight goals between them. Bonfires were lit on the banks of the Trent.

County's four were at Crystal Palace, where Big Mal – fresh from his tour of South Africa with a Bunny Girl – has been employing a psychologist. A drop in division obviously won't blunt the Palace penchant for healthy entertainment – on and off the field.

Out of the side was John Jackson, the goalkeeper who stood alone for many a season between Palace and relegation: the psychology of that Allison decision must baffle the odd remaining fan.

Mixed – and predictable – fortune for the Charlton brothers in their first ventures into management: Jack's Middlesborough won against a Portsmouth side that's been spending money as if it's going out of circulation; Bobby's Preston lost in the Villa bomb arena.

Gates were down 40,000 on the first Saturday of last season. Those who stayed away missed two dismissals and 39 bookings and an assortment of fan thuggery.

Perhaps stimulated by the performance of his supporters, who had 80 of their number locked up last week for putting the Royal Mail in peril and wrecking a train, Hugh Curran, of Oxford, was sent off. He is a man not unfamiliar with the processes of football justice.

The Watford–Huddersfield contest at the quaintly – and not so aptly named – Vicarage Road collected four bookings, including one on a Watford man for 'throwing his boot at the ball'. Hold on . . . isn't that the object of the game?

A few fans – determined not to relinquish the hard-won spotlight – kept up the enthusiasm of their pre-season training.

Manchester United supporters smashed windows at Euston, and a couple were stabbed. Those who survived this battle invaded the Arsenal pitch 20 minutes before the game. A handful were back on the streets in quick time, escorted by the police.

At Derby, 10 assorted fans were arrested and will be in court tomorrow.

Birmingham police made a pre-emptive strike, collecting bottles and cans from supporters before they boarded their football specials, and pulled 'known troublemakers' from the queues. Not terribly sporting, one might think: like sending a player off before the match on the strength of his record.

On second thoughts, that might be an idea. . . .

Meanwhile, in darkest Africa Mr Shariff Abubakar Omar will be scanning the results anxiously. He is the Kenyan witchdoctor who offered his services to Sir Alf – or any club willing to supplement circuit training with black magic.

Perhaps after the Arsenal drubbing of Manchester United, a quick telegram to Tommy Docherty will land him a retainer.

26 August 1973   *Robert Chesshyre*

Julie Welch gazed into a crystal ball and found a humorous, if slightly distorted, vision of the 1984/85 season about to start. This was her presentation of 'That Was the Season that Might Be'.

SEPTEMBER: Tommy Docherty resigns as manager of Wolves. Derek Dougan cites 'personality differences'. Bert Millichip issues new FA guidelines for celebrating goals; players not allowed to close their eyes when they kiss. Robert Maxwell's uncle buys Nottingham Forest. Glenn Hoddle sprains his wrist while signing a new contract and will be out of the game for three weeks.

Fulham Rugby League Club move from Crystal Palace to Brentford. England warm-up for their World Cup campaign by losing 1–0 to the Isle of Wight after losing seven first-choice and four second-choice players. Three Birmingham players are sent off in a midweek charity match. Jack Charlton starts a hare-coursing club in the Newcastle car park.

OCTOBER: FA School of Excellence closes due to truancy. Bobby Robson names his England team to play Finland. Glenn Hoddle suffers a groin strain while answering Bobby Robson's phone call and will be out for a further three weeks. Wimbledon go top of the Second Division with record gates of 300. Bobby Robson re-names his England team to play Finland after six more players pull out. Terry Neill becomes new Wolves manager.

Birmingham have four players sent off during 5-a-side training. Fulham Rugby League Club move from Brentford to West Molesey. As seven more players pull out of the England squad to play Finland, Bobby Robson awards first caps to Rochdale's Terry Pillock and Hartlepool's Winston Froggett. Jack Charlton accidentally shoots spectator. England lose 18–0 to Finland. Bobby Robson blames the press.

NOVEMBER: Terry Neill resigns as manager of Wolves, citing 'communication problems – neither of us could stop talking'. Robert Maxwell's

287

90-year-old grandmother takes over the chairmanship of Luton. Bert Millichip issues a fresh FA directive that congratulatory slaps on the back must be placed not less than six inches above the waistband.

Birmingham have two players sent off during the pre-match team-talk. As Wimbledon maintain their place at the top of the Second Division, the club are forced to hire 60 folding chairs from the local Conservative Association to accommodate the extra crowd. After losing his entire first choice squad for the match against Turkey, Bobby Robson recalls Kevin Keegan at a fee of £500,000. Gordon Lee takes over as Wolves manager. Fulham Rugby League Club move to a hangar at Heathrow Airport.

DECEMBER: Bad weather conditions cancel out a full programme on the first Saturday. Two Birmingham players are sent off in Tesco and Glenn Hoddle pulls a ligament switching on the weather report. Luther Blissett appears before a League disciplinary committee for bringing the game into disrepute after shaking hands with John Barnes following his five-minute hat-trick.

Gordon Lee resigns as manager of Wolves. Derek Dougan cites 'a difference of opinion – he said I was a megalomaniac and I said I wasn't'. Robert Maxwell's 12-year-old nephew buys Liverpool. Fulham Rugby League Club move to a packing depot in Rotherhithe after the entire team is nearly wiped out by a jumbo jet.

JANUARY: Plymouth Argyle beat Manchester United 3–0 in the third round of the FA Cup despite being bottom of Division Three. Ron Atkinson offers £1 million for their centre-forward, £200,000 down and the rest in cuff-links. Don Revie takes over as Wolves manager. At the top of the Second Division, Portsmouth overtake Wimbledon to lead by a point.

Wimbledon's gates slump to 40. Manager Dave Bassett comments, 'You can't blame the crowd, they have become conditioned to success.' Glenn Hoddle turns up to play against West Ham but breaks his toe in the tunnel tripping over a leftover sack of Trevor Brooking's fanmail. Jack Charlton applies for planning permission to turn St James's Park into a trout farm. Bert Millichip issues a new FA directive ordering all players to take a cold shower before kick-off. Crewe ask permission to postpone their match against Rochdale because all their first-team players have one of their headaches. In the fourth round of the FA Cup, Plymouth beat Watford 4–2 despite having lost 8–0 to Port Vale in midweek.

FEBRUARY: Robert Maxwell's second cousin offers £10 million for

Manchester United – £1 million for the club and the rest for Ron Atkinson's cuff-links. Bobby Robson names his England squad to play Northern Ireland. Ian Botham pulls out in order to make a career in cricket. A crowd of 30,000 turns up to watch Glenn Hoddle make his first team comeback against Newcastle, but the match is cancelled after Jack Charlton's foxhounds accidentally kill a linesman. In the fifth round of the FA Cup, Plymouth are given a walkover against Everton after they turn up at Goodison to find Fulham Rugby League Club using the pitch.

Ron Saunders fines six Birmingham players for not trying after none are sent off in their 8–0 Cup win over Wimbledon. So many Wimbledon fans make the pilgrimage to St Andrews for the game that they have to share a Mini. Don Revie leaves Wolves to take up a £6 million contract establishing an international squad for Papua New Guinea.

MARCH: Derek Dougan awards the manager's job at Wolves to a block of wood. In the sixth round of the FA Cup, the eight Birmingham players not currently serving suspensions win at St James's Park after the Newcastle goalie is eaten by ferrets. Plymouth Argyle beat Luton 8–7. The Milk Cup trophy has to undergo extensive repairs after Bruce Grobbelaar drops it while raising it aloft to celebrate Liverpool's victory. Bell's announce a new award – the Bell's Wolves manager of the month. Bert Millichip issues a new FA directive ordering all outfield players to wear yashmaks.

APRIL: The block of wood resigns as Wolves manager, Derek Dougan cites 'personality differences'. Brian Clough signs Glenn Hoddle for Nottingham Forest, saying, 'He will bring a welcome touch of class to the physiotherapy room.'

Ron Atkinson arranges to be carried to the dugout in a rickshaw after the extra weight of cuff-links makes it impossible for him to walk. Robert Maxwell announces a new million-pound League for clubs owned by members of the Maxwell family. Fulham Rugby League Club moves to the Orkneys.

MAY: Bobby Robson becomes manager of Wolves saying, 'After all my ups and downs with England it will be nice to be in a steady job again.' In the FA Cup Final Plymouth Argyle are given a walk-over due to the fact that the entire Birmingham team are under suspension. Portsmouth are promoted to Division One and in the ensuing excitement Alan Ball's voice breaks. Worried about his personal safety, Ron Atkinson has himself melted down into ingots and stored in a bank in Threadneedle Street. Alan Ball demands a pay rise now he won't be able to travel half-fare on buses any more. *The Observer* finally publishes a correct set of League tables.

26 August 1984   *Julie Welch*

The last rites are always sad as a club faces certain relegation. Julie watched Stoke City suffer at the serious end to the season to which she had given such a light-hearted introduction.

. . . Meanwhile, Far Away

It has got to be bad when the sponsor of the match ball prefers to remain anonymous. And as Stoke, long since relegated and written off, approached their last 90 minutes in the big time for a while to come, there were other signs of their melancholy decline. The terraces and stands, enviably clean and spacious, were too big for the handful of hard-core Potters that nobly tried to fill them on Friday night.

Even the discoloured notice in an empty looking house opposite the Victoria Ground seemed to contribute to the aura of past glories; it was still advertising the Supporters' Club Christmas Disco at the Golden Goblet Suite, Ritzy, Newcastle (members £1).

The old man placing the cushions on the seats of the directors' box was asking his companion if Stoke would be in the *Guinness Book of Records*. He had the following grisly statistics in mind: if Stoke were to win that night against Coventry, their season's total (which would then have been 20 points) would still be worse proportionately than the 18 mustered by Leeds United in 1947, and by Queen's Park Rangers in 1959 under the old two points for a win system. If they lost it would be the all-time worst, full stop.

The present manager, Tony Lacy, had taken the team to one draw and nine defeats. Their previous manager, Bill Asprey, had a nervous breakdown. There were two fans near me who said Painter was Stoke's top goalscorer. 'Can't remember when he scored it, though.'

290

Earlier, driving up the M6 towards the Potteries, there had been a distinct feeling of swimming against a strong tide – a few cars beribboned with flapping Sky Blue scarves heading one way, while in the opposite direction streamed an endless exodus from Manchester and Liverpool towards Wembley.

Coventry buffs, of course, had something to go for – if they won that night against Stoke, plus their two remaining fixtures against Everton and Luton, they would manage to avoid the drop. But, all hope gone, Stoke fans had no reason to buy tickets at all, so hooray for them, the few thousand who did turn up to cheer on their team in the fading evening sun.

As play got underway, supporters in a nearby block turned their conversation to next season's away trips. 'They say Carlisle's nice in mid-winter.' 'Oh, booger off.' The match itself probably encapsulated the story of Stoke's season. They took the game to Coventry spiritedly, defended stoutly when they had to, then in the second half went one down when Bould handled the ball as he took on Regis, and Pearce scored from the penalty.

There were three minutes left on the clock when Stoke themselves were awarded a penalty. Tony Waddington, who used to manage Stoke in the good old days, half rose from his seat near the directors' box with his hands clasped as though in prayer. Every single Stoke supporter stood up, arms aloft. Painter placed the ball on the spot, measured his run-up, and jutted his jaw. And then sent the ball against the crossbar.

Afterwards I fell to reminiscing about times gone by with the World's Greatest Living Expert on Stoke. There was that epic series of League Cup Semi-finals against West Ham in '71 to '72, when in the fourth match Bobby Ferguson was injured Clyde Best refused to go in goal though he was the nominated replacement. Bobby Moore took over from him between the sticks and they went on to win 3–2 before beating Chelsea in the final.

That was the team which contained Banks, Pejic, Conroy, Greenhof, Eastham . . . and a year before lost in the FA Cup Semi-Final against Arsenal when, on a murky night at Goodison, a linesman mistook a man selling peanuts for a Stoke player and kept his flag down as the off-side Charlie George scored what was near enough the winner.

'It's awfully sad,' said the World's Greatest Living Expert. 'That club ran on Tony Waddington's vision. They didn't win many trophies, but they brought class and style and glamour to a poor area. Once Waddington went they lost that vision and became scratchy and ordinary.' But at their best? 'They were the Royal Doulton of football.'

No doubt that still implied second best in a Wedgwood stronghold like

Stoke, but their class had been unmistakable, the descent to the common-place a sad let down.

19 May 1985   *Julie Welch*

In his football round up of 20 March 1988 Bob Houston looked ahead to a televised Sunday game in which Liverpool seemed set to shatter more records.

Anfield Tear-jerker

If Liverpool shatter Leeds United's undefeated record of 29 matches from the start of the season when they meet Everton in the 138th Merseyside derby, the Goodison Park faithful will not be the only disappointed men around 4.30 this afternoon.

It's difficult, of course, but spare a thought for the nation's bookmakers who have already taken to leaking tear-stained statements of how much they stand to lose if the Red Army takes another step on its long march rewriting the Football League record books.

Between sobs, it's possible to gather the information that the bookies stand to pay out a £1 million if Liverpool do complete the League programme unbeaten.

A Ladbroke's spokesman said yesterday: 'The odds are down to 6–4 now from 100–1 when we started laying this bet six months ago. We have taken big bets at 33–1 and 12–1. There must be a million riding on this one and bookmakers across the country will be hoping Everton crack it. They are our best chance of avoiding a big pay-out.'

20 March 1988   *Bob Houston*

To the bookmakers' relief Liverpool lost at last. But they have had more than their share of those glory days which footballers and supporters dream.

The Jekyll and Hyde nature of British football in the eighties was encapsulated by Liverpool. The ugly aspect was to the fore at the Heysel as their fans caused tragedy and disgrace. The endearing face of the game was projected by Merseyside's response to the Hillsborough disaster and by the dignified reaction of the players, manager and officials of the Liverpool club. If their subsequent triumph on the field was inevitably shadowed by that terrible event they still restored some glory to the game with their majestic play.

In the League it was a titanic performance to overhaul Arsenal after earlier being 19 points adrift and despite the final congestion of fixtures. By Cup Final day they looked certain of being League champions again and, as Hugh McIlvanney recorded, theirs was a memorable perform-ance on an emotional Wembley occasion.

The Lasting Quality of Mersey

Talk of turning the Cup Final into a Hillsborough memorial was always foolish.

It is enough for such an occasion to produce a competitive, entertaining football match. This one, at least in its extra-time climax, offered some-thing historic.

Through most of the regular hour-and-a-half the lead Liverpool had claimed from their first semblance of coherence after four minutes seemed to be allowing them to come home with the cheeky authority of Steve Cauthen riding a waiting race in front.

But all of their composure and relaxed skill counted for nothing when, in the 89th minute, Everton at last found the penetration they had lacked so conspicuously before and forced in an equaliser through McCall.

The pace of the match had always been remarkable, considering the draining heat that had built up on this summery afternoon and as the extra half hour began it was inevitable that tired legs should leave gaps where previously there had been blocking tackles.

So goals were to be expected, especially as one of the freshest men on the field was Rush, once the most-feared finisher in Europe but now brought on belatedly by Liverpool to substitute for Aldridge in the 72nd minute.

293

Sure enough, Rush did score but even by the elevated standards of his prime the goal was an astonishingly contrived blow. Spinning with deadly economy on an angled pass from Nicol on the left, the great forward smashed the ball with his right foot high beyond Southall.

And that was only the first flourish in a flood of excitement. Soon Everton had equalised once again as McCall took the ball on his chest outside Liverpool's penalty area and looped a splendid volley inside Grobbelaar's left-hand post.

Still, Liverpool would not be thwarted and a clever header by the rampant Rush put them ahead once more. Now they were determined to hold on and their manager Kenny Dalglish remained on course for the most extraordinary accumulation of triumphs English football has known.

Dalglish took the Double of League championship and FA Cup in his initial managerial season of 1985–86, then only a freakish Cup Final defeat by Wimbledon last year prevented him from doing the Double again. Now the same magnificent achievement is at his mercy again as Liverpool stride confidently towards a First Division title for which only Arsenal have even an outsider's chance of competing.

Even more significant than Dalglish's accomplishments in the football contest has been the unforgettable dignity this normally laconic and sometimes publicly awkward young man has brought to the aftermath of the Hillsborough catastrophe. He will be deeply glad that on a day when many of his club's supporters sweltered in T-shirts or bare torsos, he was able to give them the more lasting warmth of the success to which they have become accustomed.

21 May 1989   *Hugh McIlvanney*

This salute to Liverpool was a salute to the best of British football over the past twenty years. An inspired Arsenal deprived Liverpool of the double with almost the last kick of the season, but they remained the team of the year and of the decade.